lonely planet

SWITZERLAND

AF216034

Caroline Bishop, Marc Di Duca, Anthony Haywood,
Simon Richmond, Kerry Walker, Nicola Williams

Meet our writers

Caroline Bishop
@carolinebishopauthor

Based in Lausanne, Caroline is a travel writer, copywriter and the author of several novels.

Marc Di Duca
@marcdiduca

Marc has been a travel guide author for over two decades, covering destinations as diverse as Siberia and the Caribbean for Lonely Planet.

Anthony Haywood
anthonyjhaywood.com

Anthony is based on th border of France, Germany and Switzerland, and loves skipping across these lines to explore the best of the region. One of his favourite pasttimes is drifting down the Rhine.

Simon Richmond

Simon is a travel writer and photographer with more than 25 years' experience of researching and writing travel guidebooks, other non-fiction books, features and news.

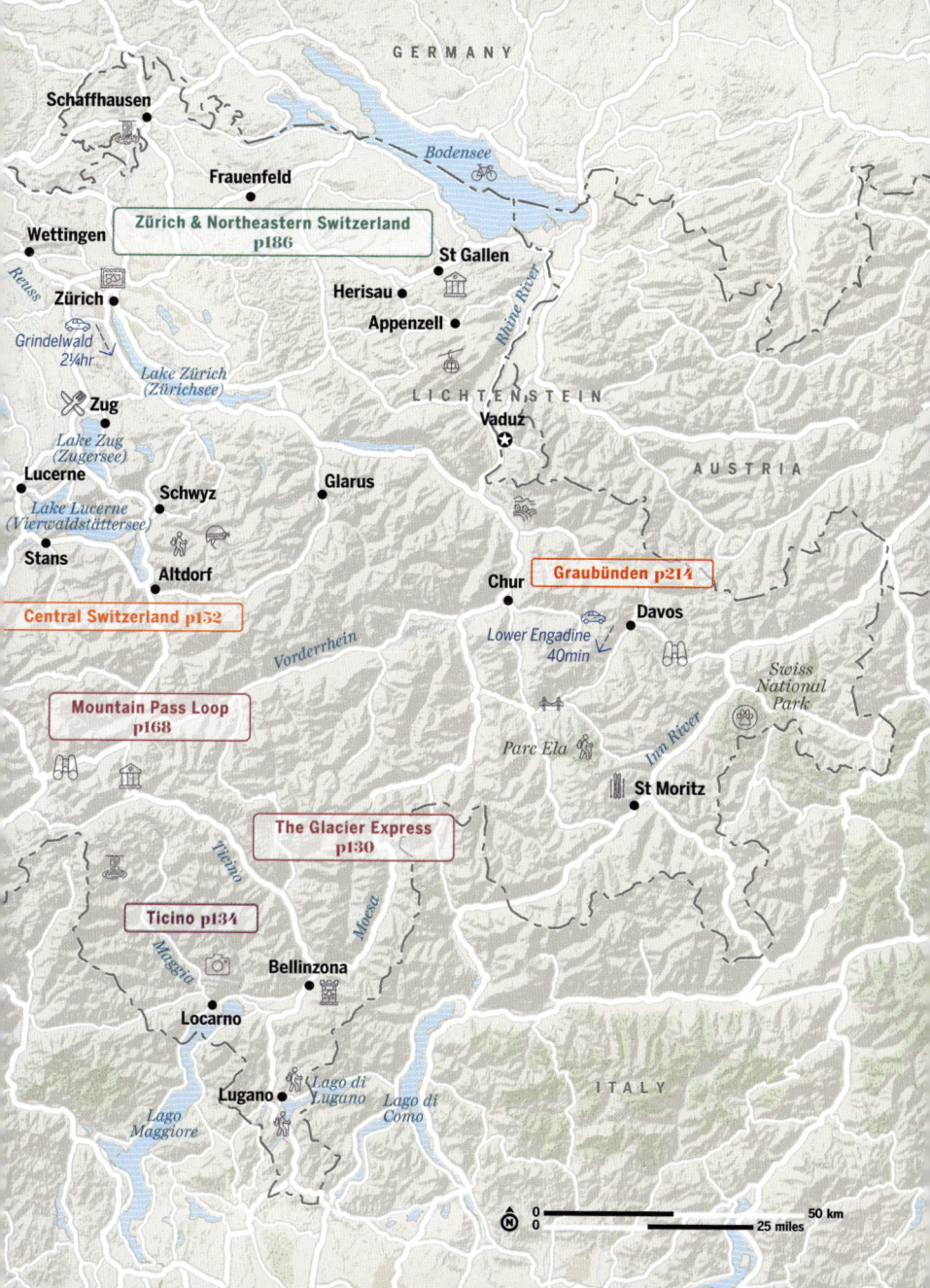

GERMANY

Schaffhausen

Frauenfeld

Bodensee

Zürich & Northeastern Switzerland
p186

St Gallen

Wettingen

Herisau

Appenzell

Reuss

Zürich

Rhine River

Grindelwald
2¼hr

Lake Zürich
(Zürichsee)

LICHTENSTEIN

Vaduz

AUSTRIA

Zug

Lake Zug
(Zugersee)

Lucerne

Schwyz

Glarus

Lake Lucerne
(Vierwaldstättersee)

Chur

Graubünden p214

Davos

Stans

Altdorf

Lower Engadine
40min

Swiss
National
Park

Central Switzerland p152

Vorderrhein

Mountain Pass Loop
p168

Parc Ela

Inn River

St Moritz

The Glacier Express
p130

Ticino

Ticino p134

Maggia

Moesa

Bellinzona

Locarno

ITALY

Lago di
Lugano

Lugano

Lago di
Como

Lago
Maggiore

0   50 km
0   25 miles

Tuck into culinary adventure. Seek out art that's as wild as it is beautifully rich. Feel the adrenaline rush as you hit another crazy, outdoor extreme. Hike to heaven. Soul dance among mountains of myth and crashing waterfalls. Embrace railroad romance on a glamorous Grand Tour. Lizard-lounge on a summer beach and dip in winter's glittering ice-frosted lakes. Helter-skelter up hairpins and dizzying mountain passes, past glaciers and gorges and green pastures sprinkled with flowers and cows and alpine tradition in spades. Sigh.

This is Switzerland.

TURN THE PAGE AND START PLANNING YOUR NEXT BEST TRIP →

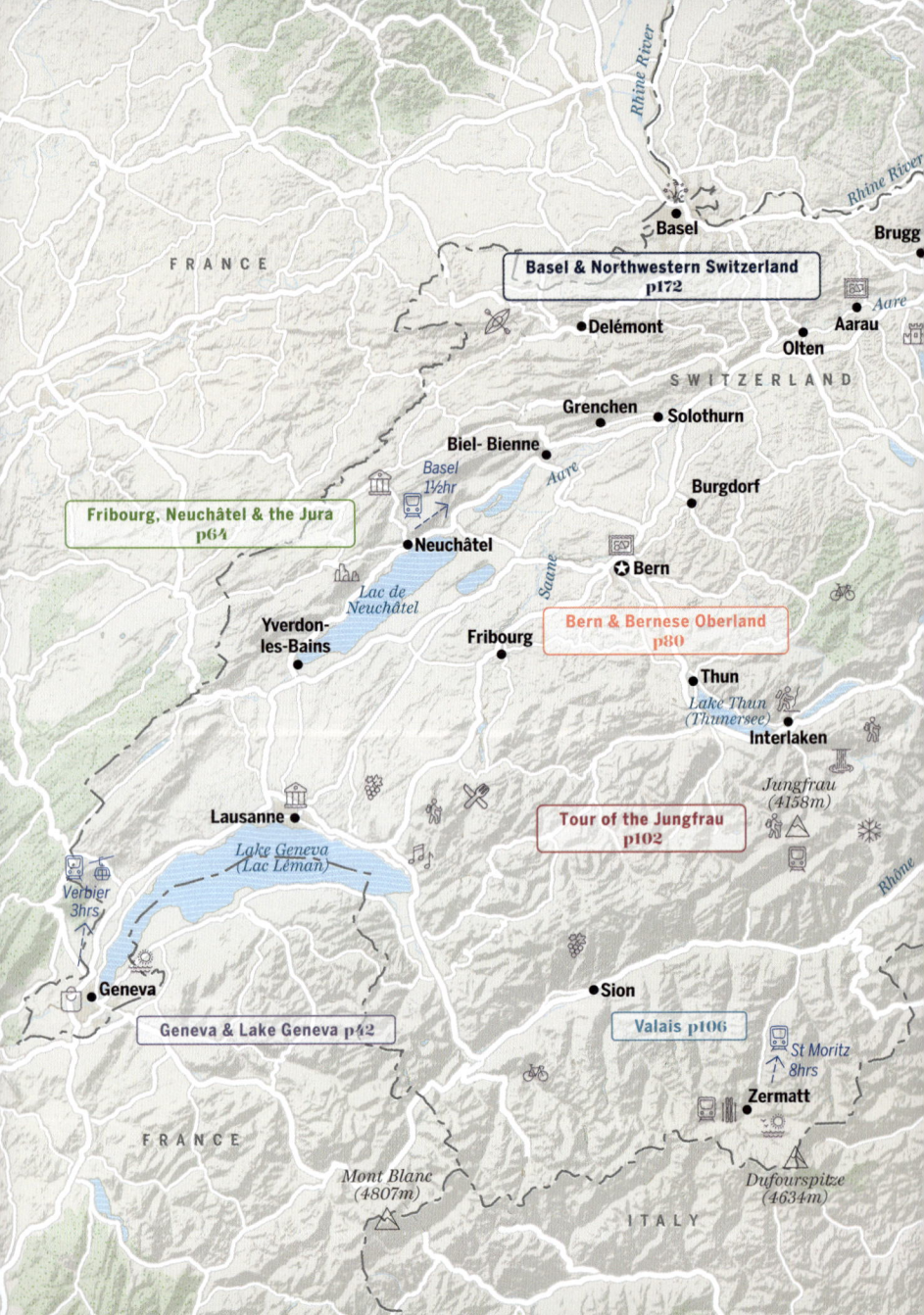

FRANCE

Rhine River

Basel

Brugg

Basel & Northwestern Switzerland
p172

Aare

Aarau

Delémont

Olten

SWITZERLAND

Grenchen

Solothurn

Biel- Bienne

Aare

Burgdorf

Basel
1½hr

Fribourg, Neuchâtel & the Jura
p64

Neuchâtel

Saane

★ Bern

Lac de
Neuchâtel

Yverdon-
les-Bains

Fribourg

Bern & Bernese Oberland
p80

Thun

Lake Thun
(Thunersee)

Interlaken

Lausanne

Jungfrau
(4158m)

Lake Geneva
(Lac Léman)

Tour of the Jungfrau
p102

Verbier
3hrs

Rhône

Geneva

Sion

Geneva & Lake Geneva p42

Valais p106

St Moritz
8hrs

Zermatt

FRANCE

Mont Blanc
(4807m)

ITALY

Dufourspitze
(4634m)

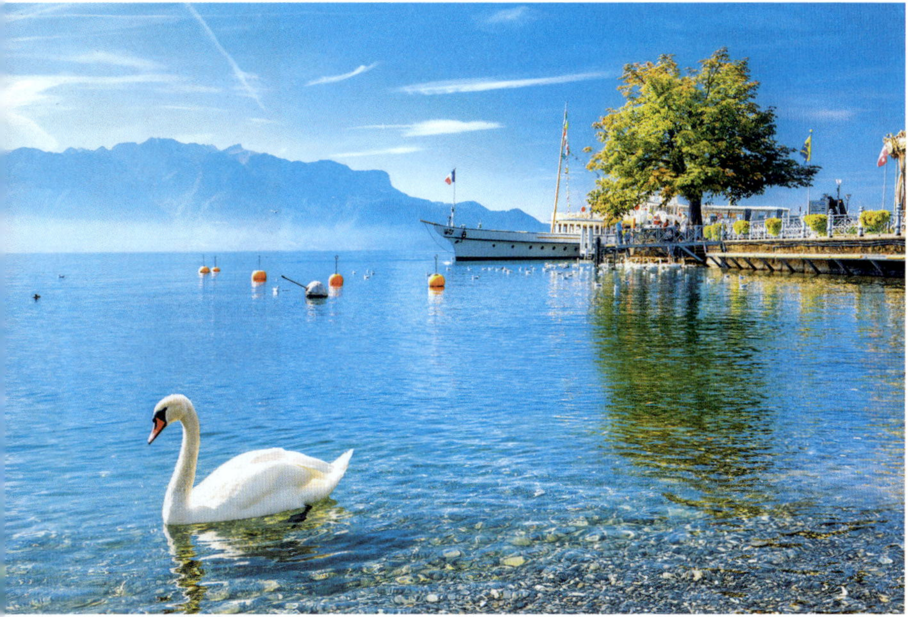

Vevey (p50), Lake Geneva (p42)

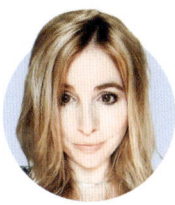

Kerry Walker

@kerryawalker

Kerry is a lifelong fan of the Swiss Alps, an avid hiker and the author of multiple Lonely Planet guidebooks.

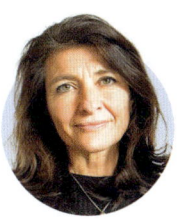

Nicola Williams

Nicola Williams lives on Lake Geneva. She is a travel writer and editor, specialising in France, Italy and Switzerland for Lonely Planet, *The Telegraph* et al.

Previous spread Harder Kulm (p100)
HAIDAMAC/SHUTTERSTOCK

Contents

KIT LEONG/SHUTTERSTOCK

Travelling by train, Pilatusbahn (p166)

Restaurants typically offer bottled mineral water, still or sparkling.

In German-speaking Switzerland, 6pm dinner is the norm; in French- and Italian-speaking parts, it's more like 7.30pm.

In summer seek out cheese crafted by shepherds: *fromage d'alpage/ Hobelkäse/ formaggio d'Alpe.*

RÖSTI, CHEESE
& CHOCOLATE

It's inevitable that a land of four languages and cultures cooks up an unprecedented mashup of culinary adventure. The best Swiss dining is as much about experience as cuisine extraordinaire: fondue in a forest, fish lakeside, a fiery shot of *génépi* at 3500m. If alpine tradition gives Swiss cuisine its earthy soul, geography gives it edge and richness, all washed down with free-flowing craft beers and fine wines impossible to find outside Switzerland.

→ RACLETTE GOLD

Vie for a prized scraping of *la religieuse* – the salty, crispy crust that forms on the side of the half-moon cheese as it sizzles on the upright table grill.

Left DuRhône Chocolatier (p49) **Right** Raclette. **Below** Meal at tibits

MENUS

Eating out becomes a whole lot cheaper with special lunch deals *(formules)* and evening *menus* (fixed-price multicourse meals).

↑ EAT GREEN

Plant-based buffets charged by weight are a thing: at the world's oldest veggie restaurant from 1888 (Zürich's Haus Hiltl) and new-gen vegetarian chain tibits *(tibits.ch)*.

Best Culinary Experiences

▶ **Watch traditional cheesemakers at work in Gruyères.** (p70)

▶ **Savour the gamut of silky-smooth Swiss chocolate on a Geneva chocolate crawl.** (p48)

▶ **Taste AOC Fendant with winemakers over a vineyard lunch on the wet 'n' wild banks of Sion's Bisse de Clavau.** (p113)

▶ **Pair Ticinese olive culture with lakeside romance on a hike along Lugano's Olive Trail.** (p140)

▶ **Celebrate ancient fruits of the land on a bike ride through Central Switzerland's rural Entlebuch valley.** (p156)

Swiss Travel Pass holders get free admission to 500+ museums countrywide.

▶ Watch for days when museums waive entrance fees; Zürich's **Kunsthaus** is free Wednesdays; museums around Lake Geneva (p63) and in Valais (p129), the first Sunday of the month.

Best Arty Experiences

▶ Take in Bern's **Zentrum Paul Klee** – the Swiss answer to the Guggenheim. (pictured; p100)

▶ Discover horological and mechanical art in the Jura. (p74)

▶ Unearth world-class art in Basel on a DIY tour. (p182)

▶ Curate your own modern-art exhibition at Aargauer Kunsthaus. (p181)

▶ Waltz through art history, from medieval sculpture to sassy Swiss design, in Zürich. (p194)

ARTISTIC
LICENCE

From the lively stained glass and swirls of Swiss abstract artist Augusto Giacometti to Zürich's rebellious Dadaists, Jurassien watchmakers and St Gallen's zany 'city lounge', which paints several streets a wild red, art in Switzerland is ever progressive. Track its rich and colourful course in a series of world-class museums.

ADRENALINE
RUSH

Intense excitement and spine-tingling thrills – those goosebump moments in life that make you want to dance for joy, throw your hat in the air, ring your bike bell – are abundant in Switzerland. Sparked by the unexpected, the soul-piercingly exquisite or the downright bonkers, adrenaline rushes here have their source in the extreme.

Best Extreme Experiences

▸ Hike to Switzerland's highest serviced mountain hut, Mönchsjochhütte. (p94)

▸ Check into Interlaken for skydiving, canyon swinging and whitewater sports. (p96)

▸ Be James Bond aboard the world's first rotating cable car, Rotair. (p166)

▸ Hurtle headfirst down the world's oldest bobsleigh run. (p235)

▸ Risk losing your head over the thundering waters of Rheinfall. (p202)

⬅ CRAZY CABLE CARS

Look to Switzerland's efficient network of cable cars for thrilling high-altitude ascents and gravity-defying 'firsts' – the world's steepest, the world's first roofless cabin, etc.

Above CabriO (p166), Stanserhorn
Left Olympic Bob Run (p235)

★ BE ORGANISED

Join an organised group activity (contact tourist offices) or hook up with a professional mountain guide: it unlocks experiences you can't always access alone.

HIKE TO HEAVEN

With colossal peaks and knife-edge valleys, glittering lakes and flower-strewn pastures at every turn, kicking back in Switzerland's phenomenal backyard is non-negotiable. To best unearth the natural treasures these sublime landscapes safeguard, stride out on your pick of 62,500km of footpaths. With stereotypical Swiss precision, trails are well signposted and maintained. The choice and range of hikes, walks and family rambles is phenomenal.

Tour of the Jungfrau
The big three
Big, bold views of the 'big three' – Eiger, Mönch and Jungfrau – steal the show on this iconic, multiday hike in the Bernese Alps. Bookend deliriously scenic days spent walking around lakes, peaks and waterfalls with star-topped nights in cosy mountain huts.

▢ *40min from St Moritz*

▶ p102

Lavaux
Bucolic vineyard rambles
From the shore of Lake Geneva, steeply terraced vineyards stagger sharply uphill to form the UNESCO-prized Lavaux vineyards (pictured). Dreamy day walks punctuated with wine tasting offer precious insight into viticultural tradition.

▢ *1hr from Geneva*

▶ p60

Zermatt
Matterhorn seduction
Switzerland's most iconic peak is your faithful companion on summer hikes above this legendary resort. Cable cars and a cogwheel railway whisk walkers up high, where trails of varying difficulty ribbon through wildflower meadows, across glacial rubble and around lakes.

▢ *1hr from Visp*

▶ p120

FRANCE

Doubs

Basel

Delémont

Biel-Bienne

Neuchâtel

Lac de Neuchâtel

Bern

Fribourg

Thun

Mönch (4107m)

Jungfrau (4158m)

40min Aletsch Glacier

Rhône

Zermatt 1h

Lausanne

Lake Geneva (Lac Léman)

Montreux

1h Lavaux

Geneva

Zermatt

Dufourspit (4634m)

Mont Blanc (4807m)

ITALY

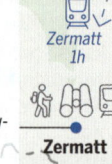

GERMANY

Schaffhausen

Koblenz

Lake Constance

Winterthur

Zürich

Lake Zürich

Zugersee

Lucerne

Lake Lucerne

SWITZERLAND

AUSTRIA

Rhein

Inn River

Parc Ela
Switzerland's largest nature park
Characterful villages, churches and an intoxicating mashup of Romanch, German and Italian cultures anchor this vast natural wilderness. Breathtakingly hairy mountain passes and the Landwasser Viaduct add manmade drama, but it's the 22km hiking trail that is the real showstopper.

🚗 *35min from Chur*

▶ p218

Swiss National Park
Nature gone wild
Untouched alpine beauty in Switzerland's only national park is off the charts. Tucked in a protected fold of the Lower Engadine Valley, this prized 172-sq-km wilderness shelters red deer, chamois, marmots and bearded vultures (pictured). Spot them on the high-level trails here.

🚆 *40min from St Moritz*

▶ p228

Parc Ela
35min

Parc Ela

Zernez

Swiss National Park

St Moritz 40min

Swiss National Park

Aletsch Glacier
Walking on ice
Nature's grandeur extends to the Alps' longest glacier (pictured), a 23km-long sea of white ice. Drink in its celestial beauty from hiking trails, from a suspension bridge, or – for aspiring explorers – on a roped expedition across the ice with crampons, harness and guide.

🚆 *40min from Brig*

▶ p94

Eiger (3970m)

40min
Tour of the Jungfrau

Bellinzona

Locarno

Lugano

Mendrisio

Chiasso

ITALY

N

0   50 km
0   25 miles

Zermatt's Matterhorn Alpine Crossing cable car to Italy is the world's highest alpine border crossing.

Verbier's daredevil zip line atop Mont Fort is the world's highest and the Alps' longest – it flies over the Tortin Glacier from 3300m.

MOUNTAIN
VISTAS

With the Alps rippling across much of the country, Switzerland pairs high altitude with euphoric panoramas. Peaks punch well above 4000m – mountains of myth where, for centuries, rock climbers have grappled for fame and a foothold in the realms of eternal ice. Fittingly, the weather gods control the ultimate requirement for venerating these celestial vistas: a clear blue sky. Should they not be game, save Switzerland's dizzying heights for another day.

→ EASY HIGHS

Cable cars provide seamless, relatively effortless, access to viewing platforms at altitude. Many summits sport a panoramic restaurant – revolving or celebrity-designed.

Left Mont 4 Zipline (p128), Verbier
Right Restaurant near the First Cliff Walk by Tissot (p93)
Below Mönchsjochhütte (p94)

GEAR UP

It's eternal winter above 3000m, July and August included. Come prepared for sun, snow and wind: trousers, boots, coat, gloves, hat, scarf and sunnies.

↑ SUNRISE VIEWS

Bookend your day with magical vistas, pink to fire-orange – overnight in a mountain hut *(refuge/Hütte/refugio)*. Bring your own sleeping-bag liner and comfy indoor shoes.

Best Mountaintop Experiences

▶ **Soak up peaks, glaciers and forests at a breathless 3454m at Jungfraujoch.**

▶ **Enjoy the ride of a lifetime in Zermatt to spot 29 peaks above 4000m.** (p120)

▶ **Eyeball Eiger up close on the gravity-defying First Cliff Walk by Tissot lookout platform above Grindelwald.** (p91)

▶ **Ride the funicular railway to Stoos and hike its peak-to-peak ridge trail.** (p164)

▶ **Bike up to Verbier's iconic Cabane du Mont Fort for a trompe l'oeil apricot and mountain panorama.** (p115)

Download the SBB app *(sbb.ch)* for train schedules and tickets. SBB offers numerous discount travel cards and fares.

With just a few journeys, an annual Half-Fare Travelcard *(Chf190)* is justified: half-fare on trains, lake boats and many cable cars.

RAILROAD
ROMANCE

▬▬▬ Swiss train travel is gold. No other country pairs slick, punctual trains and a kaleidoscope of spectacular views with such harmony and romance. Summer or winter, panoramic coach or commuter carriage, a Swiss slideshow of epic proportions has been seducing travellers since the glory days of the Grand Tour.

Best Railway Experiences

▶ **Bookend glitzy resorts with a bucket-list day on the Glacier Express.** (p130)

▶ **Find yourself in a magical snow globe aboard the Bernina Express.** (p266)

▶ **Chug through XXL alpine landscapes aboard the Centovalli Railway.** (pictured; p151)

▶ **Ride the world's steepest funicular to mountain hamlet Stoos.** (p164)

▶ **Join Lake Geneva and Interlaken on the luxurious GoldenPass Express.** (p243)

BEACH
VIBES

███ Switzerland's flush of alpine lakes and rivers provide ample opportunity to strip off, lizard-lounge on sand or rock, and – when it all gets too hot – dive in. This being hyperactive Switzerland, life by the water is as much about action afloat as sunset cocktails. Winter ushers in ice-cold dips and saunas.

★ LAKE AMENITIES

May to September, lake beaches have a hut renting SUP boards, kayaks, pedalos or windsurfers. December to March, mobile saunas dot pebble shores.

Best Beach Experiences

▶ Ride the Rhône's current on a menagerie of inflatable animals. (p55)

▶ Swim at a fortress-island in picture-book Rheinfelden. (p181)

▶ Enjoy a scenic lakeshore stroll and swim along the Sentier des Rives du Lac. (p57)

▶ Embrace beach life at altitude at Leisee in Zermatt. (p123)

▶ Pair a cycle along Bodensee's shore with a swim or beach relax. (p208)

← GET FISHY

In Basel, buy a *Wickelfisch* (a fish-shaped watertight bag to stow your clothes in and swim) from the tourist office to go with the flow in style.

Above Swimming in the Rhine River **Left** Leisee (p123)

HIT THE
ROAD

Scenic road trips are everywhere you look in this polished land of oversized mountains, thundering falls, glacier-carved gorges and glittering lake shores. The stuff of movies, this a blockbuster destination where sports-car enthusiasts and classic-car lovers come to motor at leisure. No need for the headscarf or vintage leather gloves, though convertible wheels are always nice. Pick your route right and you can join them.

GERMANY

Basel – – >
🚗 Aargau
1hr

● Delémont

Doubs

FRANCE

● Biel-
Bienne

● Neuchâtel

Lac de
Neuchâtel

✪ Bern

Fribourg Pre-Alps
Winter wonderland

When the helter-skelter of the mountains tires, take your foot off the pedal in Switzerland's gentler western corner. A patchwork of forests, pastures and lakes, this low-lying spot is easy to navigate in winter. Snowshoe in Les Paccots (pictured), dip into cheese fondue and sledge back to your car.
🚗 *30min from Fribourg*
▶ p76

Fribourg
●
↓ Fribourg Pre-Alps
🚗 30min

● Thun

Mönch
(4107m)

Jungfrau (4158m) △

Lausanne ●

🔭 🏔 ❄

Lake Geneva
(Lac Léman)

● Montreux

Rhône

● Geneva

Mont Blanc
(4807m)
△

Dufourspi
(4634m

ITALY

Appenzell
Swiss dairy country
In this deeply traditional region (pictured left), country lanes unravel like spools of thread around velvet-green meadows, steel-blue lakes and farming hamlets engulfed by glacier-licked peaks. Fields of cows and corn, fruit orchards, vineyards and Switzerland's most photogenic old town call for slow touring.

🚗 *75min from Zürich*

▶ p210

Aargau
Land of castles
Road-trip through a region straight out of legend. Storied villages and dozens of craggy castles (such as Schloss Wildegg, p181; pictured)– some moated, some museums, many ruined – pepper the countryside around medieval Aarau. The city, with a walled old town, was the ancestral home to the powerful Habsburgs who went on to rule the Austro-Hungarian Empire. Stick to valley backroads.

🚗 *1hr from Basel*

▶ p180

Furka Pass
King of alpine passes
Immortalised in a James Bond car chase, Valais' vertiginous **Furka Pass** is Swiss alpine-pass king. Since 1867 it has chicaned around a jaw-dropping 21km of white-knuckle hairpins from the tiny village of Gletsch to Andermatt. Stretching your legs on the cinematic Rhône glacier is the icing on the cake.

🚗 *30min from Andermatt*

▶ p169

Ticino Alps
Dolce vita
The Alps in the south are as magnificent as elsewhere, but tempered with Italian *dolce vita*. The drive from the north, across St Gotthard Pass (pictured left) and past Bellinzona, is a prelude to the road trip around lakeside Locarno.

🚗 *90min from Andermatt*

▶ p148

Graubünden
Switzerland's least populated canton
The country's largest canton is a natural marvel. Be it navigating heart-pumping hairpins on the Flüela, Julier or Albula passes, joining the dots between Romansch hamlets in the remote Engadine, or motoring off-grid in the national park, Graubünden is road-trip nirvana.

🚗 *1½hr from Zürich Airport*

▶ p214

GERMANY

Koblenz
Schaffhausen
Winterthur
Zürich
1½hr
Lake Zürich
Graubünden
Appenzell 75min
Appenzell

Lucerne
Lake Lucerne
Zugersee

AUSTRIA

Rhein
Inn River

Eiger (3970m)

urka Pass 30min
cino Alps 90min
Furka Pass

SWITZERLAND

Zernez
Swiss National Park
Parc Ela
St Moritz

Mesolcina
Ticino
Bellinzona
Locarno
Lugano
Mendrisio
Chiasso

ITALY

N
0 ——— 50 km
0 ——— 25 miles

July and August are hot and sunblazed. Cable cars whisk hikers and bikers up to dizzying heights in the Alps. Urban beaches buzz.

→ Cherry Festival

Watch ladder-laden cherry runners scamper through the old town and toast the harvest at Zug's cherry fest in June.

📍 Zug
▶ zug-tourismus.ch

Swiss National Day

Fireworks light up lakes, mountains, towns and cities countrywide on 1 August, a national holiday celebrating Switzerland's creation.

Lucerne Festival

Chamber orchestras and soloists from all corners of the globe perform at Lucerne's summer classical music fest; five weeks.

📍 Lucerne
▶ lucernefestival.ch

JUNE

Average daytime max: 21.5°C
Days of rainfall: 12

JULY

Switzerland in
SUMMER

→ Zürich Street Parade

It's dubbed the world's biggest techno music parade, in August, and is most definitely a street party to remember.

📍 Zürich

▶ streetparade.com

Verbier Bike Festival

Pair e-biking with gourmet snacking and music during Verbier's four-day biking fest in mid-August.

📍 Verbier

▶ verbierbikefestival.com

Montreux Jazz Festival

A fortnight of jazz, pop and rock in early July is reason enough to slot Riviera queen Montreux into your itinerary.

📍 Montreux

▶ montreuxjazzfestival.com

SWITZERLAND PLAN BY SEASON

Average daytime max: 23.1°C
Days of rainfall: 12

AUGUST

Average daytime max: 22.8°C
Days of rainfall: 11

→ Tavolata

In food-obsessed Valais in August, locals gather in vineyards around long shared tables for wine-fuelled banquets alfresco.

📍 Valais

▶ tavolata-valais.ch

🧳 Packing Notes

Sunscreen and sunglasses, particularly for high altitudes. Swimmers and towel to dip in rivers and lakes.

September's golden days and grape harvests pair perfectly with alpine rambles – there is no finer month for hiking in the Alps.

Autumn is the season for leaf peeping in golden larch forests, wildlife spotting in the Swiss National Park and harvest festivals galore.

→ **Sheep Shearing Fest**

In the village of Savognin in the peaceful, off-the-map Parc Ela, locals turn out in force for October's sheep shearing.

◈ Savognin

Genevans enjoy a day off work on Jeûne Genevois, the first Thursday after the first Sunday in September. Traditionally, it was a day of fasting.

SEPTEMBER

Average daytime max: 18.7°C
Days of rainfall: 10

OCTOBER

Switzerland in
AUTUMN

↘ La Désalpe de Charmey

Cows in Charmey descend from their summer grazing pastures in spectacular folksy style; last Saturday in September.

📍 Charmey

Foire du Valais

Valais' 10-day regional fair showcases cuisine, viticulture, music, culture and traditional *combats des reines* (cow fights).

📍 Valais

▶ foireduvalais.ch

Glacier Skiing

South of St Moritz at Dia-volezza, October skiers glide up by cable car to 2978m to fly down glacial slopes.

📍 Diavolezza

▶ corvatsch-diavolezza.ch

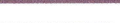

NOVEMBER

Average daytime max: 14.6°C
Days of rainfall: 9

Average daytime max: 8.6°C
Days of rainfall: 10

→ Castagnatas

As farmers limber up to harvest olives and sweet chest-nuts ripen, sun-soaked Ticino shines. Chestnut festivals punctuate October.

📍 Ticino

🧳 Packing Notes

Layers to cope with four-seasons-in-a-day weather, sunscreen and hat, a light waterproof jacket or windbreaker.

Days are short and it's cold everywhere in December. But there are Christmas markets and festive celebrations around the corner.

↙ L'Escalade

Torch-lit processions, fires, a running race and chocolate cauldrons make Geneva's biggest festival on 11 December bags of fun.

📍 Geneva

▶ escalade.ch

Ski Season

December ushers in winter skiing on snowy, downhill and cross-country slopes in mountainous regions.

Snow Polo World Cup

A frozen lake in St Moritz is the chic venue for this four-day event attracting world-class polo players.

📍 St Moritz

▶ snowpolo-stmoritz.com

DECEMBER

**Average daytime max: 4.9°C
Days of rainfall: 11**

JANUARY

Switzerland in
WINTER

↘ Harder Potschete

What a devilish day it is on 2 January in Interlaken when warty, ogre-like *Potschen* run around town causing folkloric mischief and fiendish merrymaking.

📍 Interlaken

▶ harderpotschete.ch

Carnival

Pre-Lenten parades, music and stark-raving bonkers fun sweeps through Catholic cantons during Fasnacht (Carnival). Catch the party in Basel and Lucerne.

Demand for accommodation peaks in ski resorts during school holidays in February. View tours and overnight adventures in advance at lonelyplanet. com.

SWITZERLAND PLAN BY SEASON

Average daytime max: 4.2°C
Days of rainfall: 10

FEBRUARY

Average daytime max: 5.3°C
Days of rainfall: 9

Cold-water swimmers: January is the month to dip in Lake Geneva's icy waters and sweat in a sauna. Hit Geneva or Hermance.

🧳 Packing Notes

Warm layers countrywide. Thermal underwear, hat, gloves, snood and wool socks are alpine essentials.

Spring Skiing

The tail end of the ski season stays busy thanks to warmer temperatures, sun-sure days and – some years – Easter holidays.

→ Engadine Ski Marathons

Watching 11,000 cross-country skiers warming up to *Chariots of Fire* for this iconic 42km skate in March is unforgettable.

📍 Engadine Valley

▶ engadin-skimarathon.ch

Snow Pride

Before ski lifts close in April, Verbier hosts a snowy Pride with drag shows, DJs, après ski parties and abundant LGBTQI+ glitter.

📍 Verbier

Zermatt Unplugged

Dance in ski boots to live music on the slopes. Zermatt's five-day music festival stages 130-odd concerts on several outdoor stages.

📍 Zermatt

▶ zermatt-unplugged.ch

MARCH

Average daytime max: 9.8°C
Days of rainfall: 11

APRIL

Switzerland in
SPRING

→ Sechseläuten

Zürich celebrates winter's end with costumed street parades and the burning of the firework-filled 'snowman' Böögg; third Monday in April.

📍 Zürich

Fête de la Tulipe

Revel in a sea of tulips in bloom at April's Fête de la Tulipe in the lakeside town of Morges. Lake Geneva views are sublime.

📍 Morges

Easter ushers in a switch in seasonal schedule for paddle steamers on lakes, with cruises now joining year-round commuter boats.

SWITZERLAND PLAN BY SEASON

MAY

Average daytime max: **14°C**
Days of rainfall: **11**

Average daytime max: **17.6°C**
Days of rainfall: **12**

Spectacular flowers in manicured lakeside towns burst in bloom. In rural Switzerland, flower farms open their 'pick-your-own' fields.

 Packing Notes

Layers for changeable weather; an umbrella and rain jacket for April showers; cap/sunhat and sunscreen

SWISS ALPS
Trip Builder

TAKE YOUR PICK OF MUST-SEES AND HIDDEN GEMS

▬▬▬ A natural barrier of soul-soaring beauty, the Alps have always been a blessing and a burden when it comes to journeying around Switzerland. Mountain scenery is XXL in the country's 16 Alpine cantons (out of 26), but you'll need to navigate up, over, around or through to soak it up.

🗺 Trip Notes

Hub towns Chur, Interlaken, Lugano.

How long Allow two weeks.

Getting around Train or car – both are good. Chur is the starting station for the panoramic Bernina Express via 55 tunnels and 196 bridges to Tirano in Italy. The Glacier Express departs from St Moritz.

Tips Train aficionados swear winter's snow scenes are unmatched. Motorists, check if mountain passes are open (typically late May to October) on alpen-paesse.ch. July and August is classic car season.

FRANCE

Saône

Doubs

Doubs

Biel- Bienne

Lauterbrunnen
Wax lyrical like Goethe and Lord Byron over the ethereal beauty of this postcard-perfect village (pictured), nestled deep in a valley of 72 waterfalls. Star diva is the wispy Staubbachfall.
🚆 *20min from Interlaken*

Neuchâtel

Lac de Neuchâtel

Fribourg

Lausanne

Lake Geneva (Lac Léman)

Montreux

Geneva

Rhône

Verbier

FRANCE

Verbier
Ski, bike, hike, revel in the small-town vibe in this ritzy diamond of the Valaisian Alps (pictured): small, stratospherically expensive and cut at all the right angles to make it sparkle in the eyes of accomplished skiers and piste-bashing stars.
🚆 *2½hr from Geneva Airport*

Isère

Grindelwald
Hit one of Switzerland's oldest resorts for a dizzying dose of film-set Eiger views, alpine hikes, hair-raising descents and – in winter – epic sledge runs. Count a day for Jungfraujoch.

🚆 *30min from Interlaken*

Maienfeld
Little wonder the alpine landscape here (pictured) inspired Heidi's 19th-century creator: meadows sprinkled with wild flowers, timber chalets and bell-clanging cows in this Graubünden village are the stuff of Swiss dreams.

🚆 *70min from Zürich*

St Moritz
White-knuckle ski and sledge runs, snowy yoga, a hearty bowl of *Gerstensuppe* (barley soup) in a mountain hut and heart-pounding views: meet the world's oldest ski resort (pictured) from 1864.

🚆 *3hr from Zürich*

Fiesch
Catch a cable car in this picture-postcard riverside village in Valais to be mind-blown by the 23km-long Aletsch Glacier. Explore it by on a roped hike (summer) or skins (winter).

🚆 *3hr from Verbier*

Andermatt
Enjoy low-key village charm, big-wilderness hiking and historical military secrets in this old staging post on the north–south St Gotthard route. Four alpine passes loom large nearby.

🚆 *2hr from Zürich*

Lago di Lugano
Add a pinch of Italianate sass to your alpine holiday with this sparkling blue lake in southern Ticino. Summit Monte Brè for views deep into the Alps.

🚆 *2hr from Zürich*

Map labels

GERMANY

Schaffhausen
Basel
Koblenz
Delémont
Winterthur
Zürich
Lake Zürich
Lake Constance
Bern
Lucerne
Lake Lucerne
Maienfeld
Chur
Thun
Interlaken
Lake Thun
Lauterbrunnen
Grindelwald
SWITZERLAND
Rhein
Fiesch
Andermatt
Zernez
Swiss National Park
St Moritz
Ticino
Adda
Zermatt
ITALY
Locarno
Bellinzona
Lago Maggiore
Lugano
Lago di Lugano
Mendrisio
Chiasso
ITALY

0 — 50 km
0 — 25 miles

WINE TRAILS
Trip Builder

TAKE YOUR PICK OF MUST-SEES AND HIDDEN GEMS

▬▬ Savouring reds, whites and rosés in Switzerland is a rare joy in this globalised world – few are exported and many are natural, biodynamic or organic. Even better, wine tasting translates as vineyard bike rides, encounters with third-generation winegrowers, long lunches between vines and unlimited merrymaking at folksy wine festivals.

🗺 Trip Notes

Hub towns Geneva, Sion, Neuchâtel, Lugano.

How long Allow one week.

Getting around Trains link Geneva, Sion and Lausanne. Trains stop at Lutry, but arriving by boat is more fun; walk or cycle in situ. Zürich to Schaffhausen is 50 minutes by train. A car gives you unrestricted access to rural wineries in Ticino, Drei-Seen-Land and the Jura.

Tips April to September is best for vineyard walks and bike rides; October ushers in harvest celebrations.

Neuchâtel

This medieval waterfront town is the urban hub for tasting Œil-de-Perdrix wine from surrounding vineyards. Fruity rosés fuel the Route du Vignoble vineyard trail between Neuchâtel and Biel lakes.

🚗 *45min from Bern*

FRANCE

Saône

Doubs

Lavaux

Discover top-drawer whites crafted by independent producers in UNESCO World Heritage vineyards rising high above Lake Geneva's brilliant-blue shores. Wine villages Lutry and Cully are as pretty as a picture.

🚆 *1hr from Geneva*

Doubs

Biel-Bienne

Neuchâtel

Lac de Neuchâtel

Fribourg

Lausanne ● 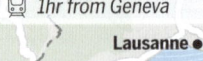 ● Lavaux

Lake Geneva (Lac Léman)

● Montreux

Geneva

Geneva

Cycle through vines to Hermance and return to Geneva (pictured) for drinks in a bar in this cosmopolitan city on Lake Geneva's southern tip. One-third of Swiss wines come from the eponymous canton.

🚆 *7min from Geneva Airport*

Rhône

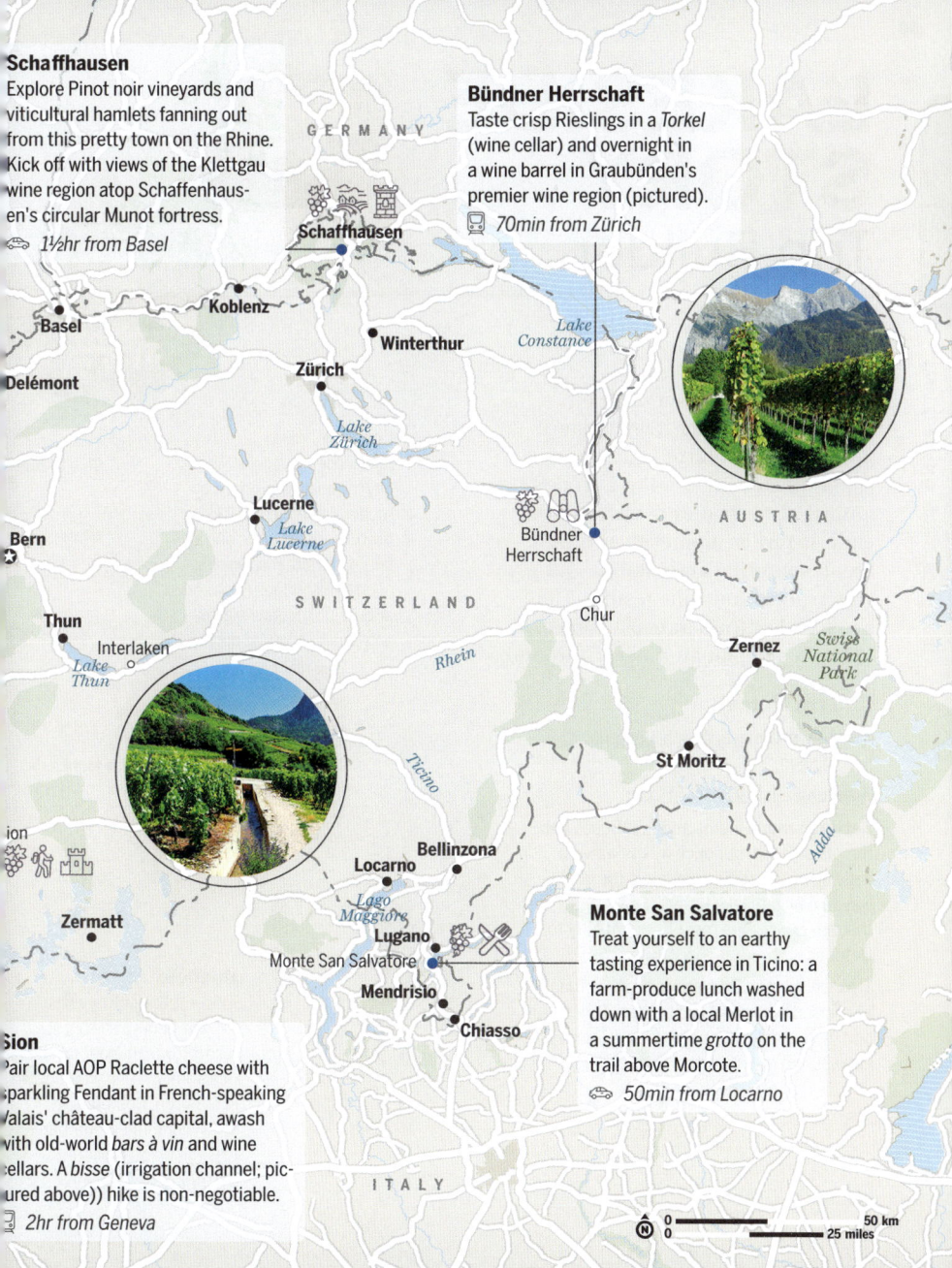

Schaffhausen

Explore Pinot noir vineyards and viticultural hamlets fanning out from this pretty town on the Rhine. Kick off with views of the Klettgau wine region atop Schaffhausen's circular Munot fortress.

🚗 *1½hr from Basel*

Bündner Herrschaft

Taste crisp Rieslings in a *Torkel* (wine cellar) and overnight in a wine barrel in Graubünden's premier wine region (pictured).

🚆 *70min from Zürich*

GERMANY

Schaffhausen

Koblenz

Basel

Winterthur

Lake Constance

Zürich

Delémont

Lake Zürich

AUSTRIA

Bern

Lucerne

Lake Lucerne

Bündner Herrschaft

SWITZERLAND

Chur

Thun

Interlaken

Lake Thun

Zernez

Swiss National Park

Rhein

ion

Zermatt

Rhein

St Moritz

Ticino

Adda

Bellinzona

Locarno

Lago Maggiore

Lugano

Monte San Salvatore

Mendrisio

Chiasso

Monte San Salvatore

Treat yourself to an earthy tasting experience in Ticino: a farm-produce lunch washed down with a local Merlot in a summertime *grotto* on the trail above Morcote.

🚗 *50min from Locarno*

Sion

Pair local AOP Raclette cheese with sparkling Fendant in French-speaking Valais' château-clad capital, awash with old-world *bars à vin* and wine cellars. A *bisse* (irrigation channel; picured above)) hike is non-negotiable.

🚆 *2hr from Geneva*

ITALY

N

0   50 km
0   25 miles

LAKESIDE STORY
Trip Builder

**TAKE YOUR PICK OF MUST-SEES
AND HIDDEN GEMS**

▬ Ticking off every hue of grey, green and blue, Switzerland's glittering portfolio of lakes is superlative. Gem-sized to Europe's largest, these bodies of water unveil endless thrills: alpine adventure, scenic motoring and hiking, watersports and wine tasting. Here are six lakes from a treasure chest of 1500-plus to plot an itinerary around.

🗺 Trip Notes

Hub towns Geneva, Zürich, Lucerne, Kreuzlingen.

How long Allow 10 days at least.

Getting around Trains and PostBuses link the major lakes, but once by the water, a belle époque paddle steamer is the cool way to navigate lake waters. Boats and themed cruises are most frequent May to October.

Tips On the ground, use local rather than anglicised names, so Lac Léman, Zürichsee and Vierwaldstättersee (not Lake Geneva, Lake Zürich or Lake Lucerne).

FROM LEFT: JOACAF/SHUTTERSTOCK, SERGII FIGURNYI/SHUTTERSTOCK, MALEO PHOTOGRAPHY/SHUTTERSTOCK

FRANCE

Lucerne
Recipe for a gorgeous Swiss city: a cobalt lake ringed by mountains, a medieval old town, beautiful music and a fairy-godmother sprinkling of covered bridges (pictured above right), sunny plazas and candy-coloured houses.
🚆 *50min from Zürich*

Doubs

Biel- Bienne

Neuchâtel

Lac de Neuchâtel

Fribourg

Lausanne

Lake Geneva (Lac Léman)

Montreux

Geneva

Rhône

Montreux
Follow 19th-century artists to Lake Geneva's jazziest resort town, magnet for the rich, famous and everyone in between. Don't miss a stroll along the flower path to Château de Chillon.
⛴ *1hr from Lausanne*

FRANCE

Isère

Zürich
The urban lake experience: feast on world-class art and design in a smorgasbord of museums (such as the Kunsthaus, p197; pictured far left), then make a pilgrimage to the 'writing room Europe' in St Gallen's UNESCO-listed abbey.

🚆 *50min from Basel*

Bodensee
Cycle along Lake Constance's southern shore from Kreuzlingen, past emblematic apple orchards, flowery parks, picturesque old towns and bijou beaches. There's buckets of watersports on the cross-border lake.

🚗 *1½hr from Zürich*

Zug
Lap up lakeside life in Switzerland's wealthiest canton on the glittering Zugersee. With chestnut trees-shaded beach, cobbled medieval old town and a spectacular cherry culture, Zug town is supermodel gorgeous.

🚆 *20min from Zürich*

Lake Uri
Fly with the wind: windsurf, foil or sailboat in central Switzerland. Pick up a trail encircling the lake in the meadow where Switzerland's founding oath was signed.

🚗 *1½hr from Zürich*

Zermatt
Nowhere does alpine lakes better than Valais' glitziest mountain hangout. Bag five lakes in a day – and a perfect shot of the Matterhorn reflected in Stellisee – on the 5-Seeweg hike.

🚆 *70min from Brig*

Walensee
Shake things up with a cruise on the northeast's unsung wild card. Sandwiched between the jagged Churfirsten range and Flumserberg, this fjord-esque lake (pictured) is spectacular. Swim in summer.

🚗 *45min from Zürich*

GERMANY

Schaffhausen
Koblenz
Kreuzlingen
Bodensee
Basel
Winterthur
Delémont
Zürich
Lake Zürich
Zug
Lucerne
Lake Lucerne
Lake Uri
Walensee
Bern
Thun
Interlaken
Lake Thun
Chur
Rhein
Zernez
Swiss National Park
St Moritz
SWITZERLAND
Zermatt
ITALY
Locarno
Bellinzona
Lugano
Lago Maggiore
Mendrisio
Chiasso
ITALY

0   50 km
0   25 miles

NORTHERN TREASURES
Trip Builder

TAKE YOUR PICK OF MUST-SEES AND HIDDEN GEMS

Switzerland reserves a secret stash of riveting villages and wilderness for those who go the extra mile north. From soaking up ancestral savoir-faire in cheese dairies and wineries, to floating down the Rhine or retreating to a log cabin overnight, here are some ideas for a bucolic spin through pastoral gold in the country's oft-overlooked north.

Trip Notes

Hub towns Basel, Aarau, St Gallen.

How long Allow one week.

Getting around Trains connect towns, but you'll need a car to properly explore the Val-de-Travers and other rural folds of the Jura. Basel has two train stations; Aarau and St Ursanne rail services use the Swiss Basel SBB. Bus it to the Aargau castles.

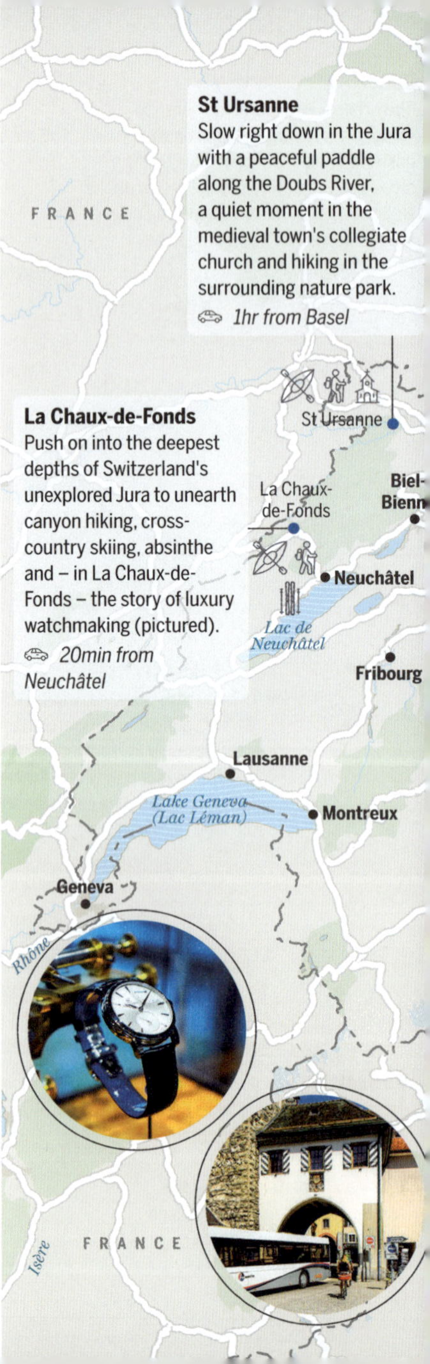

St Ursanne
Slow right down in the Jura with a peaceful paddle along the Doubs River, a quiet moment in the medieval town's collegiate church and hiking in the surrounding nature park.
1hr from Basel
La Chaux-de-Fonds
Push on into the deepest depths of Switzerland's unexplored Jura to unearth canyon hiking, cross-country skiing, absinthe and – in La Chaux-de-Fonds – the story of luxury watchmaking (pictured).
20min from Neuchâtel
FRANCE
St Ursanne
La Chaux-de-Fonds
Biel-Bienne
Neuchâtel
Lac de Neuchâtel
Fribourg
Lausanne
Lake Geneva (Lac Léman)
Montreux
Geneva
Rhône
Isère
FRANCE

FROM LEFT: RAY-HSIN CHANG/FLICKR/CC BY-SA 2.0 ©, JUDITH LININE/SHUTTERSTOCK, PATRYCJA GROBELNY/SHUTTERSTOCK, SINA ETTMER PHOTOGRAPHY/SHUTTERSTOCK

Basel
Throw yourself into city life – world-class art, culture, a gorgeous cobbled Altstadt, riverside alfresco dining and swimming – in Switzerland's third-largest city. Carnival season is crazy here.

🚄 *1hr from Zürich*

GERMANY

Koblenz

Schaffhausen

Bodensee

Winterthur

Basel

Aarau

Zürich

St Gallen

Delémont

Lake Zürich

Appenzell

Lucerne

Lake Lucerne

St Gallen
Bookend this cultured town's trophy site – the UNESCO World Heritage–listed Abbey, with cathedral and sublime rococo abbey library. Spot a camel, griffin, Hercules, all sorts.

🚗 *1hr from Zürich*

Appenzell
Feel rural Switzerland's folksy heartbeat pulsate in frescoed lanes and gabled houses in the fairy-tale Altstadt (old town). Gen up on rural tradition in the Museum Appenzell (pictured below). Taste the country's tangiest cheese.

🚗 *1hr from Zürich*

Schaffhausen
Use riverside Schaffhausen (pictured below) as a base for Rheinfall, Europe's biggest plain waterfall. Make time for a river cruise to gingerbread-cute Stein am Rhein.

🚗 *40min from Zürich*

Bern

Thun

Interlaken

Lake Thun

Chur

Rhein

Zernez

Swiss National Park

SWITZERLAND

St Moritz

Locarno

Bellinzona

Zermatt

Lugano

Lago Maggiore

Mendrisio

Chiasso

Aarau
Explore the original homeland of the Habsburg dynasty, a tranquil, photogenic town (pictured left) with a well-preserved old town, fabulous art gallery and proximity to three beautiful castles.

🚗 *40min from Zürich*

ITALY

N
0   50 km
0   25 miles

URBAN BEAUTIES
Trip Builder

TAKE YOUR PICK OF MUST-SEES AND HIDDEN GEMS

■■■■ The perfect foil for Switzerland's natural rural beauty is its urban edge. Travelling by train from city to city unveils avant-garde art museums, architectural curiosities and cultural happenings. It also shines light on the country's mixed bag of cultures, eloquently expressed in four languages and a bonanza of varied travel experiences.

🔯 Trip Notes

Hub towns Geneva, Zürich, Basel, Lugano.

How long Allow 10 days.

Getting around No need for your own wheels on this city-hopper trip, which champions urban walking. CGN *(cgn. ch)* boats service Lake Geneva towns year-round; Lake Zürich cruise boats are seasonal. SBB trains service all towns, plus Geneva and Zürich international airports.

Tips Rest your legs with a shared bike or free-floating e-scooter. Tourist offices have maps and run guided city tours.

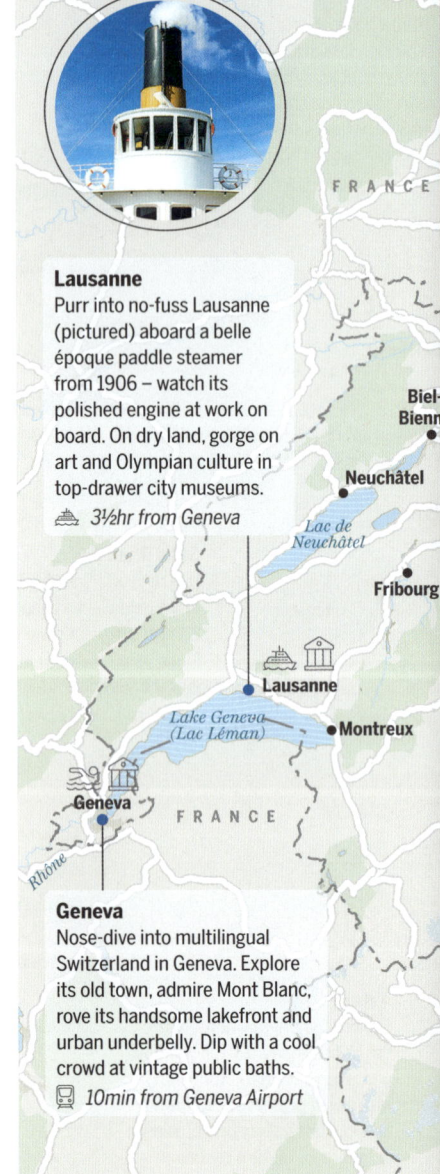

F R A N C E

Lausanne

Purr into no-fuss Lausanne (pictured) aboard a belle époque paddle steamer from 1906 – watch its polished engine at work on board. On dry land, gorge on art and Olympian culture in top-drawer city museums.

🚢 *3½hr from Geneva*

Biel-Bienne •

Neuchâtel •

Lac de Neuchâtel

Fribourg •

🚢 🏛

• Lausanne

Lake Geneva (Lac Léman)

• Montreux

🏊 🏛

Geneva

F R A N C E

Rhône

Geneva

Nose-dive into multilingual Switzerland in Geneva. Explore its old town, admire Mont Blanc, rove its handsome lakefront and urban underbelly. Dip with a cool crowd at vintage public baths.

🚆 *10min from Geneva Airport*

Basel
Drink in the unique French-German-Swiss cocktail in this sassy riverside border town with a string of top-billing art museums, colourful carnival (pictured right), cellars and pop-up summer bars.

🚆 *75min from Bern*

GERMANY

Schaffhausen

Koblenz

Winterthur

Basel

Delémont

Zürich

Bodensee

Zürich
Marvel at just how 'big city' Switzerland gets in its leading metropolis. Tour the old town (pictured), marvel at Chagall stained glass, zip between river banks and watch sunset make its splash from a lakeshore lido.

🚆 *75min from Basel*

Lake Zürich

Lucerne

Lake Lucerne

Bern

Chur

Rhein

SWITZERLAND

Thun

Interlaken

Lake Thun

Zernez

Swiss National Park

St Moritz

Bern
Ditch your best French for German, and allow the Swiss capital (pictured) with a big medieval heart to win you over with its cobbled Altstadt and world-class galleries. In summer sightsee afloat the Aare River.

🚆 *75min from Lausanne*

Zermatt

Locarno

Bellinzona

Bellinzona
Guess how many have never heard of Ticino's head-turning tiny capital? Explore forts with top-of-the-beanstalk views of the old town's cafe-rimmed piazzas, Renaissance churches and the snowcapped Alps beyond.

🚆 *20min from Lugano*

Lugano
Load Italian in your translation app for arrival in Switzerland's hot south. Soak up Lugano's palm-fringed lake, views atop its old-fashioned Monte Brè funicular and *grotto* dining culture.

🚆 *2hr from Zürich*

Lago Maggiore

Lugano

Mendrisio

Chiasso

ITALY

0 — 50 km
0 — 25 miles

Ⓝ N

GRAND TOUR
Trip Builder

TAKE YOUR PICK OF MUST-SEES AND HIDDEN GEMS

██████ Geneva and Montreux were ports of call for English aristocrats touring Europe to complete their education in the 17th century. Thomas Cook included the Gemmi Pass in its first escorted tour to Switzerland in 1863, and the rest is history. Here are eight classic stops to include in your trip.

🗺 Trip Notes

Hub towns Montreux, Interlaken.

How long Allow two weeks.

Getting around Purists claim car is best (avoiding motorways), but a combo of trains (panoramic, steam, cogwheel), cable car and PostBus allows you to safely admire the mesmerising scenery. Aim for April to September if motoring, December to March for snowy scapes by rail.

Tips Switzerland Tourism (*myswitzerland. com*) maps out a modern Grand Tour with hundreds of stops. Download its Grand Tour app.

Gruyères

Snap a Grand Tour selfie with bewitching turrets at Château de Gruyères (pictured), former residence of 19 Gruyères counts and an emblem of the medieval village famed for its eponymous cheese.

🚌 *40min from Montreux*

Biel-Bienne

Neuchâtel

Lac de Neuchâtel

FRANCE

Fribourg

Lausanne

Gruyères

Montreux

Château d Chillon

Lake Geneva (*Lac Léman*)

Geneva

Rhône

Château de Chillon

Admire the timeless beauty and romance of the Swiss Riviera fortress, on the swanky shore of Lake Geneva, where Lord Byron penned a poem in 1816.

🚶 *40min from Montreux*

FRANCE

Interlaken
Swoon like Victorian ladies did over uplifting views in this fabled mountain town, or ditch the chandelier-glamour vibe for heart-racing action: this is the country's extreme-sports hub.
🚆 *50min from Bern*

Davos
The jagged Silvretta Alps star on the iconic drive across the Flüela Pass (pictured) from the Lower Engadine to this historic mountain resort. Go slow to savour every second.
🚆 *25min from Filisur*

The Faulhornweg
Chug deliciously slowly back in time aboard a romantic cogwheel train (pictured) that has climbed up to Schynige Platte in the mythic Bernese Alps since 1893. The killer alpine views up top have not changed.
🚆 *2hr from Interlaken*

Furka Pass
Channel your inner James Bond for the drive across this vertiginous mountain pass in northeast Valais – a Grand Tour must since the 1860s. Pair it with three more passes for the ultimate road trip.
🚗 *30min from Andermatt*

Landwasser Viaduct
Every Glacier Express passenger is desperate to spot this 1901 engineering marvel flash by. Enjoy more luxurious views of the six-arch viaduct on a short hike from Filisur.
🚆 *1hr from Chur*

Matterhorn
Ski, hike, hang out in chic bars with the Zermatt jet set: whatever you do in this glitzy, car-free resort, it's this hypnotically beautiful, unfathomable monolith that you won't be able to stop looking at.
🚆 *35min from Visp*

GERMANY

Schaffhausen

Koblenz

Bodensee

Basel

Winterthur

Delémont

Zürich

SWITZERLAND

Lake Zürich

Lucerne

⚲ Bern

AUSTRIA

Thun

○ Chur

Davos

Interlaken

Faulhornweg

Landwasser Viaduct

Swiss National Parke

Zernez

△ *Furka Pass*

St Moritz

Bellinzona

Locarno

atterhorn

△ Zermatt

Lago Maggiore

Lugano

Mendrisio

Chiasso

ITALY

| 0 | | 50 km |
| 0 | | 25 miles |

7 Things to Know About
SWITZERLAND

INSIDER TIPS TO HIT THE GROUND RUNNING

1 Weather Check

In a country where storms suddenly sweep in at altitude and big blue skies can be crucial to a day's activity, consulting the local weather forecast on MetéoSchweiz/Suisse is a national pastime. Download the app *(meteoswiss.admin.ch)* and search by 'postcode, mountain or city'. The Climate Monitor, with comparative rain and sunshine stats, is also an interesting read.

2 Raising the Alarm

Do not be alarmed if you suddenly hear the terrifying wail of sirens in the distance. Assuming it is 1.30pm on the first Wednesday in February, no need to panic: it is just the annual drill. Once a year, the country's 7200 sirens are activated to ensure that the population can be appropriately warned in the case of a real emergency.

3 Ordering Wine

In restaurants and wine bars, wine is measured in decilitres and priced on menus per dl. So don't order a glass of wine – rather, ask for multiples of déci. Two déci is roughly one glass.

4 Swiss Softs

Blend in with the local crowd at waterfront snack bars *(buvettes/Buvetten)*: order a Rivella, Sinalco (like Orangina) or a herbal blue Zyt.

5 Ski Hack

Beat queues and save money by purchasing ski passes and ski hire online. For skiing more than one week, the Magic Pass *(magicpass. ch)* – covering unlimited access to lifts in 100 resorts – saves the day. It's valid one year, bagging lift access to summer hiking and biking trails too.

6 Local Lingo

Switzerland has three official federal languages: German (about 64% of the population), French (20%) and Italian (7%). Romansch (1%) is mainly spoken in Graubünden.

German-speaking visitors might understand little: the Swiss write in *Hochdeutsch* (High German) but speak Swiss German, a different language. Greeting a fellow walker or shopkeeper with *Grüezi* (Hello) goes a long way. *Merci* is thank you in Swiss German; only some cantons use the German *Danke*.

Forget the school French you learnt for breakfast, lunch and dinner. In Switzerland it's *déjeuner*, *dîner* and *souper*, respectively. Then there's the (so much easier) Swiss words for 70 *(septante)*, 80 *(huitante)* and 90 *(nonante)*.

Some 200 Swiss-Italian words are not in the regular Italian dictionary, but Italian speakers still get around Ticino with ease. To reserve a restaurant table, say *Posso riservare un tavolo?* Ticinese don't use the Italian *verb prenotare* (to reserve).

7 Cheese Machines

Forget junk food. Vending machines here give out refrigerated half-rounds of tangy AOP cheese, ready-grated fondue kits, farm eggs, artisanal honey, air-dried beef and jam. Around Lake Geneva, Tout Cru vending machines feed meat lovers with hand-cut steak tartare 24/7; track them at toutcru.ch.the day.

Read, Listen, Watch & Follow

 READ

Hotel du Lac (Anita Brookner; 1984) Travel to Lake Geneva with a romantic novelist.

The Alp (Arno Camenisch; 2014) Romansch novel: a summer in the Alps with a dairy farmer, farmhand, cowherd and swineherd.

Slow Train to Switzerland (Diccon Bewes; 2013) London to Lucerne by train, bus and boat.

Seinetwegen (For His Sake; Zora del Buono, 2024) The 2024 winner of Switzerland's prize for German-language literature.

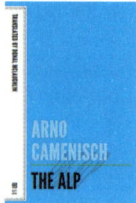

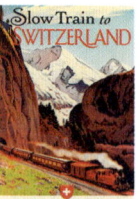

 LISTEN

A Tramp Abroad (Mark Twain; 1880) Swiss road trip essential: the audiobook of Twain's highly entertaining account of his 1878 hike through the Alps.

Women (Pilar Vega; 2021) Ticino-born, Zürich-based and of Caribbean origin, Pilar Vega (pictured) is a rising star on Switzerland's new-wave R&B soul scene.

Dancing Alone Again (Benjamin Amaru; 2025) Lose yourself in the melancholic soundscapes of singer-songwriter Benjamin Amaru.

Stereo Crush (Gotthard; 2025) All 16 albums of Switzerland's best-known hard rock band have reached number one in the Swiss album charts.

ELENA TERNOVAJA, CC BY-SA 3.0, VIA WIKIMEDIA COMMONS ®

SWI

(swissinfo.ch/eng/podcasts) Indispensable source of Swiss news and current affairs, with regular in-depth podcasts. Or download SWI's app.

WATCH

Struggle for the Matterhorn (1928) Silent B&W film about the race to conquer the Matterhorn.

The Divine Order (pictured above right; 2017) Swiss women's fight to vote underpins this story of a village housewife turned activist.

Journey of Hope (pictured below right; 1990) Oscar-winning tale of a Kurdish family seeking a better life in Switzerland.

Je Suis Noires (2022) Documentary about a Swiss-Congolese's identity quest as a black Swiss woman.

Mike Casa Comedy (@mikecasacomedy) Funny, insightful TikTok vignettes on Swiss life, culture and more.

DANIEL AMMANN/ZODIAC/KOBAL/SHUTTERSTOCK

CINEMATIC COLLECTION/CHANNEL FOUR/ALAMY

FOLLOW

Switzerland
(*myswitzerland.com*)
Switzerland tourism

ch.ch
(*ch.ch*) Practical tips on daily Swiss life

Swiss Family Fun
(*swissfamilyfun.com*)
Just that, by Tanya in Zürich.

World Radio Switzerland
(*worldradio.ch*)
Geneva-based, English-language radio station.

Swiss Info
(*swissinfo.ch*) News, culture and fresh perspectives.

↖ Sate your Switzerland dreaming with a virtual vacation at lonelyplanet.com/switzerland

GENEVA &
LAKE GENEVA

CULTURE | FISH & WINE | BEACHES
RESEARCHED BY NICOLA WILLIAMS

GENEVA & LAKE GENEVA

▬ Trip Builder

GENEVA & LAKE GENEVA BUILD YOUR TRIP

Western Europe's largest lake is as chic, glossy and naturally good-looking as the eponymous city encrusting its southern tip. Scratch the surface to reveal edgy art, great music and some of Switzerland's finest wines.

Catch 140,000-odd tulips in bloom in lakeside **Morges** (p52)
⛴ *3hr from Geneva*

Morge

Admire Mont Blanc from a belle époque steamer or **Château de Nyon** (pictured, p51)
⛴ *75min from Geneva*

○Nyon

Thonon-les-Bains

Listen to classical music at dawn at Geneva's retro baths, **Bains des Pâquis** (p55)
🚶 *15min from Gare de Cornavin*

Hermance

Dip into a winter-cold lake and cheese fondue in **Hermance** (p57)
🚌 *30min from Geneva*

Paddle across the line where the Rhône and Arve rivers mix at **Pointe de la Jonction** (p63)
🚌 *20min from Gare de Cornavin*

Celebrate local history and chocolate tradition in **Geneva** (p48)
🚶 *15min from Gare de Cornavin*

Geneva

SWITZERLAND

Lac de Joux

FRANCE

Learn about Olympic history and heritage in **Lausanne** (pictured below, p53)
🚆 *40min from Geneva*

Cycle through UNESCO-listed vineyards in **Lavaux** (pictured bottom, p60)
🚆 *25min from Lausanne*

Enjoy a slow scenic train along the lake to flower-filled **Montreux** (pictured, p52)
🚆 *1hr from Geneva*

Explore the mighty **Château de Chillon** (pictured; p53) fortress where Lord Byron penned a poem in 1816
🚶 *40min from Montreux*

Moudon ●

Bulle

S W I T Z E R L A N D

Lausanne

Cully

Gruyère Pays-d'Enhaut Regional Nature Park

Vevey ○

Montreux ●

Lake Geneva (Lac Léman)

Ⓝ
0   10 km
0   5 miles

Practicalities

FRAMALICIOUS/SHUTTERSTOCK

ARRIVING

Geneva Airport Gateway to Lake Geneva, in Cointrin, 4km northwest of the centre. Trains (11 minutes) and bus 10 (*tpg.ch;* 25 minutes) link the airport with the town centre.

Gare de Cornavin Regular rail connections link Geneva's downtown train station with dozens of Swiss towns. Hop on bus 8 or 25 to main street Rue du Rhône (10 minutes).

HOW MUCH FOR A

Public transport ticket Chf3

1dl glass of Lavaux wine Chf5–8

Cheese fondue Chf30

GETTING AROUND

Boat With shimmering Lake Geneva rarely out of sight, the journey here often becomes the destination. Yellow *mouette* (seagull) boats take Genevans between lake shores and CGN (*cgn.ch*) steamers service towns around the lake.

Public transport Buses, trams and trolleybuses make light work of getting around Geneva. Download the TPG+ app to buy public-transport tickets or purchase at dispensers at stops. Locate and grab a bike by app in Geneva and Lausanne with Donkey Republic (*donkey.bike*).

Train Regular SBB trains (*sbb.ch*) trundle along the northern shore of Lake Geneva. Montreux is a hub for scenic journeys aboard panoramic trains, cogwheel railways and funiculars operated by MOB (*mob.ch*).

WHEN TO DO

JAN-MAR
Cold winter days can be cloudy lakeside, but there's blue skies up high in ski resorts.

APR-JUN
Sunny days see flowers bloom and cafe pavement terraces spring into action.

JUL-SEP
Beaches and bar terraces buzz. Now's the time to swim in Lake Geneva.

OCT-DEC
Grapes ripen in Lavaux vineyards. September celebrates the harvest.

EATING & DRINKING

Cosmopolitan Geneva is so international that old-school Swiss cuisine is the exception to the rule: urban streets burst with upmarket bistros, brasseries and restaurants cooking up every cuisine under the sun. Away from the city, traditional *filets de perche meunière* (perch fillets pan-fried in butter and parsley), *féra* (whitefish) and *caquelons* (large ceramic bowls) of cheese fondue (pictured) kick in. Eat fish during the local perch-fishing season, June to December, when you can be sure of enjoying the morning's catch.

Best perch fillets
Café de la Poste

Must-try winter fondue
Bains des Pâquis (pictured; p55)

CONNECT & FIND YOUR WAY

Wi-fi Find free hotspots all over town, including at Geneva airport; log in and receive a code by SMS to connect. Many cafes, bars and restaurants offer free wi-fi.

Navigation Local tourist offices distribute city maps, marked with cycling lanes and routes. In stormy weather or during high winds, lake boats don't run.

WHERE TO STAY

Geneva is pricey; many hotels are cheaper at weekends when business travellers head out of town. As a student city, Lausanne offers more competitive rates. Both have hostels.

City, Town & Village	Pro/Con
Geneva	Transit hub. Accommodation, dining and nightlife for all budgets.
Nyon	Enchanting small-town vibe. Midrange to upmarket hotels.
Lausanne	Best budget option. Buzzing cafe/bar scene and nightlife.
Lutry	Vineyard accommodation at a price.
Vevey	Peaceful, lakeside village vibe.
Montreux	Convenient for eastern end of Lake Geneva. Tourist-packed in summer.

CITY PASSES

Cut costs with a Geneva or Lausanne City Pass (Chf30/40/50 for 24/48/72 hours), covering free public transport and admission to dozens of museums and monuments.

MONEY

Hotel guests in Geneva *(geneve.ch)*, Lausanne *(lausanne-tourisme.ch)* and Montreux *(montreux riviera.com)* receive a free Transport Card covering unlimited public transport during their stay. It also yields discounts on some local sights and activities.

01

Geneva Chocolate
CRAWL

SHOPPING | CAFE LIFE | FOOD

The country that gave the world melt-in-your-mouth chocolate – Rodolphe Lindt invented conching in Bern in 1879 – is predictably famed for its silky confectionery. Deep-dive into the sweet treat's rich Genevan heritage on a tasting stroll around a chocolate-box assortment of *haute chocolatiers.*

EVANNOVOSTRO/SHUTTERSTOCK

🍨 Sweet Tip

My favourite dessert at **La Bonbonnière** is 'Le Piemont', a cake made with chocolate-hazelnut brownie, a mucilage confit (a floral, slightly tart pulp with lychee notes, naturally present in cocoa pods), milk *gianduja*, and a creamy Madagascar chocolate mousse. Not only is this cake delicious, it is also 100% vegan and gluten-free.

■ *Recommended by* **Cyril Burgnard**, *Genevan chocolate maker*

🗺 Trip Notes

Getting around From the **Geneva tourist office** at Gare de Cornavin, walk 15 minutes or take bus 8 or 25 to boutique-lined Rue du Rhône.

When to go Cooler months are best: March or April for Versoix' two-day Festichoc chocolate festival, December for Geneva's chocolate-cauldron-fuelled Fête de l'Escalade (pictured).

Give back Buy a 24-hour Choco Pass (Chf30) at the tourist office covering nine chocolate-shop tastings; Chf1 goes to MyClimate 'Cause We Care', championing sustainable tourism.

Lake
Geneva

Q du Mont-Blanc

03 Explore the Rue du Rive boutique of **Favarger** (*favarger.com*) – its 1826 factory brought chocolate-making to Geneva. Buy hazelnut Avelines, heritage chocolate bars styled like it's 1826 or a chocolate fondue set.

05 Winston Churchill and Grace Kelly loved **DuRhône** (*durhone chocolatier.ch*), an 1875 *haute chocolaterie*. Noble du Rhône bars are rippled like water and specked with gold – indulge over the city's best hot chocolate in the cosy cafe.

Pont du Mont-Blanc

Île Rousseau

Pont des Bergues

Pont de la Machine

Rhône

Promenade du Lac

R du Rhône   Q du Général-Guisan

Pl de la Fusterie

R du Rhône

Jardin Anglais

Pl du Port

01 Sink your teeth into a *pain au chocolat* (chocolate pastry) oozing velvety artisanal chocolate by inventive chocolatier-pastry chef **Guillaume Bichet** (pictured above; *guillaume-bichet.ch*). His fruit ganaches are also heavenly.

Pl du Molard   R Neuve du Molard

Pl Longemalle

Q du Général-Guisan

R du Rhône

R Pierre-Fatio

R de Rive

R de Rive

R du Prince

R de la Madeleine

R Verdaine

Bd Helvétique

02 Follow Genevans to **Auer** (pictured left; *chocolat-auer.ch*) to splash out on a *marmite de l'Escalade* – a chocolate cauldron emblazoned with the city's coat of arms. Back home, smash it and scoff it.

04 Push through the crowds at cafe-shop **La Bonbonnière** (*labonbonniere.ch*), a 1921 vintage with a chocolate school, and enrol for an on-the-spot discovery workshop – personalise your own chocolate bar in 30 minutes.

Parc des Bastions

OLD TOWN

Bd Jaques Dalcroze

N

0   200 m
0   0.1 miles

02 Belle Époque
ROMANCE

DAY TRIP | HISTORY | CRUISING

Lake Geneva's fleet of vintage paddle steamers is the world's most beautiful. Cruising on the exquisitely restored *Montreux* from 1906, or perhaps the *Vevey* with original chestnut marquetry and smoking room, casts a new spin on sightseeing. Set sail from steamer hubs Geneva or Lausanne.

How To

Getting here & around
Geneva and Lausanne
are hubs for CGN *(cgn.
ch)* steamers, cruises
and commuter boats on
Lake Geneva. Mix and
match.

When to go Summer
assures frequent sail-
ings under blue skies:
soak up 360-degree
lake views from the
open-air top deck.
Sunset is extra magic.

Cent saver Compare
fares. Depending on
how many boats you're
taking, CGN's *carte
journalière* covering a
day's unlimited boat
travel can be cheaper
than a return.

Deep Dive into Le Lac

Known as Lac Léman or simply *'le lac'* locally,
there is no finer lakeside address to learn
about this lake's biodiversity, climate, natural
heritage and glamorous past as a stop on the
historic Grand Tour than the **Musée du Léman**
(museeduleman.ch) in **Nyon**. The best view
of the fairy-tale turrets encrusting this small
lakeside town's photogenic hilltop ch â teau is
from the water – count 75 minutes by steamer
from Geneva, 25km south. Once you disembark,
the 180-degree panorama of Lake Geneva and
France across the water (spot medieval **Yvoire**,
from where French workers arrive each morning
by commuter boat) that unfolds from **Château
de Nyon**'s lake-facing terrace is unmatched.

Continue the deep dive into local lake culture
at Nyon's **Village des Pêcheurs**, a three-
minute walk south along Quai Louis Bonnard.

⛵ Cruise Control

Lunch and dinner cruises
afloat a 19th-century
steamer up the romance
tenfold. The ultimate cruise?
During Europe's largest
inland regatta, the **Bol d'Or
du Léman** in June, when a
CGN steamer cruises right
between the 500-odd yachts
taking part in the return race
from Geneva to Bouveret on
the lake's eastern tip.

Far left Steamboat, *Vevey*, **Left** Musée
du Léman **Above** Village des Pêcheurs

Picture-postcard fishermen's cabins and traditional boats line the quayside where Nyon's last professional fishers head out to cast nets for the lake's signature perch and *féra* (whitefish).

Flower Trails

What with its 13th-century **château** (*chateau-morges.ch*) on the lakefront and the majestic Mont Blanc puffing out its snow-white chest on the horizon, seduction stakes in **Morges** are high. Late March to mid-May, lose yourself in a sea of tulips at April's Fête de la Tulipe when 140,000-odd tulips – 300 varieties – transform the quays and Parc de l'Indépendence into an ocean of colour. July to October, dahlias bloom. Count 1¾ hours by CGN steamer from Nyon.

Continue the flower fest in **Montreux**, another 15 minutes by boat, along the serene **Chemin Fleuri** (Flower Path). Expect Disney movie stuff the length of this lakeside footpath. Spellbinding floral displays are tropical in colour, variety and abundance, and views of alpine mountain peaks across the water in France are soul-soaring.

⚠ Mont Blanc View

Split between Switzerland and France, Lake Geneva is a vast body of water covering 580 sq km and is 310m deep in parts. Beyond 32 fish species, aquatic garter snakes and pesky duck fleas – not fleas at all, but larvae that try (and fail) to attach themselves to humans on hot summer days causing harmless but itchy skin for unsuspecting lake swimmers – no known monsters occupy the lake's famously cool, crystalline waters. On bluebird days, admire the snow-white peak of Mont Blanc (4808m) from a steamer's top deck. A chunk of western Europe's highest peak is Swiss, but its summit belongs to France.

Left Château de Chillon
Below Olympic Museum

Follow the path for 2.5km (40 minutes) along the shore from the fashionable town's lakefront to Switzerland's best-preserved medieval fortress.

A Flush of Castles

With its medieval arrow-slit turrets and witch-capped towers, there is no more enticing or emblematic chateau on Lake Geneva's castle-encrusted shores than **Château de Chillon** (chillon.ch). This ace of an oval-shaped castle was largely built in the 13th century by the House of Savoy; observe how its landward side is heavily fortified. Inside, courtyards, towers and halls safeguard period arms, furniture and artwork, medieval-frescoed chapels and grizzly Gothic dungeons – subsequently immortalised by a flush for writers and painters, Lord Byron, William Turner and Gustave Courbet included.

Olympian Drama

It was during the belle époque in the 1860s that Lausanne's neighbourhood of Ouchy morphed from fishing village to thriving port and 'the place to be'. Aristocracy flocked to balls at the **Beau Rivage Palace** hotel. In 1877 a funicular was built, linking the glittering lake with medieval **Lausanne** up top. Docking in Ouchy, promenade east along the waterfront to the outstanding **Olympic Museum** (olympics. com/museum) to soak up Olympian drama, exhibits and historic footage. Drinks, brunch or lunch and the lake view in its restaurant is a spectacular affair.

03 Urban
ADVENTURE

ART AND CULTURE | DRINKING | NIGHTLIFE

▬▬ Like the swans that glide gracefully across its eponymous lake, cosmopolitan Geneva is a rare bird. Look beyond its luxurious palace hotels, haute-couture jewellers and glittering pencil fountain to unearth a grittier, rough-cut diamond. This is the counterculture that makes the other Geneva tick.

Contemporary Art

A space to watch is **L'Appartement Gallery** (lappartement-geneve.com). Its balconies overlook Lac Léman and Jardin Anglais. The gallery has been conceived with extraordinary attention to volume, light, acoustics and design. Its first exhibitions presented a serious yet diverse edit, which went beyond certain rigid aspects of the art world.

🗺 Trip Notes

Getting around Walk. Buses, trams and boats save tired legs. Buy tickets (three-stop single/hour/day Chf2/3/10) on the TPG+ app (tpg.ch).

When to go Spring for drinking alfresco; June to early September for urban beaches, outdoors concerts, cinema and music festivals; winter for snow-capped peaks and glacial cold-water dips.

Urban art tour Glean the stories behind graffiti and street art in the industrially edgy La Jonction 'hood on a half-day bike tour (welo.swiss).

■ **Recommended by Angela Hertault,** Geneva Art Consultant @angela_hertault

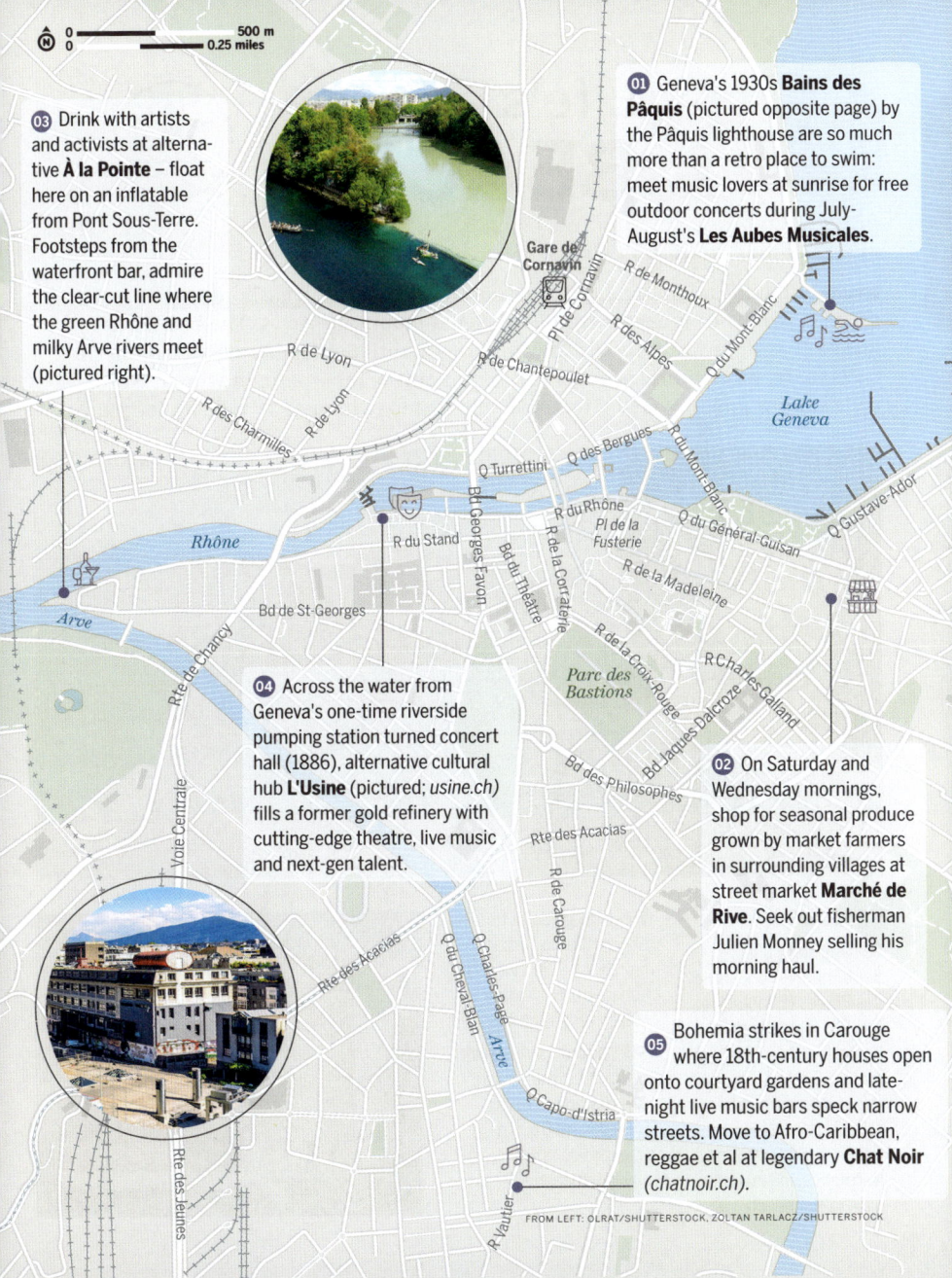

03 Drink with artists and activists at alternative **À la Pointe** – float here on an inflatable from Pont Sous-Terre. Footsteps from the waterfront bar, admire the clear-cut line where the green Rhône and milky Arve rivers meet (pictured right).

01 Geneva's 1930s **Bains des Pâquis** (pictured opposite page) by the Pâquis lighthouse are so much more than a retro place to swim: meet music lovers at sunrise for free outdoor concerts during July-August's **Les Aubes Musicales**.

04 Across the water from Geneva's one-time riverside pumping station turned concert hall (1886), alternative cultural hub **L'Usine** (pictured; *usine.ch*) fills a former gold refinery with cutting-edge theatre, live music and next-gen talent.

02 On Saturday and Wednesday mornings, shop for seasonal produce grown by market farmers in surrounding villages at street market **Marché de Rive**. Seek out fisherman Julien Monney selling his morning haul.

05 Bohemia strikes in Carouge where 18th-century houses open onto courtyard gardens and late-night live music bars speck narrow streets. Move to Afro-Caribbean, reggae et al at legendary **Chat Noir** (*chatnoir.ch*).

04

Life's a
BEACH

SUMMER FUN | DRINKING | WATER SPORTS

Inland it might be, but Lake Geneva sports a smorgasbord of *plages,* – shingle, pebble or grass – with phenomenal mountain views. The beach party kicks off as days warm in late May and rages until September when summer cafes, bars, watersports schools and rental outfits hibernate. In winter, Nordic-style saunas pop up, daring intrepid cold-water swimmers to take an icy plunge.

🗺️ How To

Getting here May to September, TPG's Ligne des Plages (Beach Line; bus 29) joins the dots between urban beaches around Geneva. City buses serve suburban beaches in Corsier, Vésenaz, Collonge-Bellerive and Hermance. In Lausanne, walk to the beach.

When to go June to September for urban beaches in Geneva and Lausanne. November to March for sauna life.

SUP, pedalo and kayak rental At Marti Marine (*martimarine.ch*) in Geneva and Cousin (*bateaux-location-ouchy. ch*) in Lausanne.

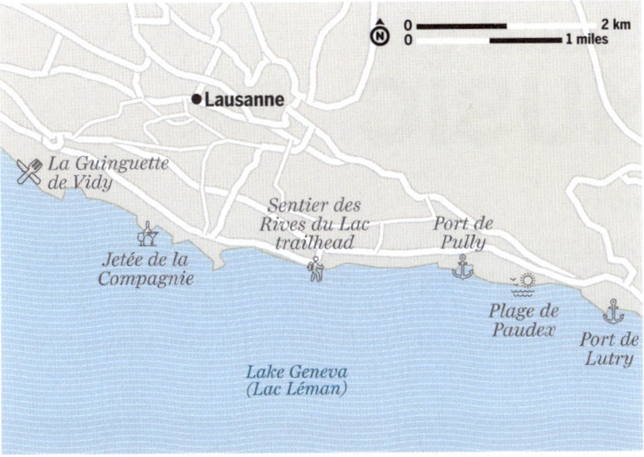
0
0
2 km
1 miles
Lausanne
La Guinguette de Vidy
Sentier des Rives du Lac trailhead
Port de Pully
Jetée de la Compagnie
Plage de Paudex
Port de Lutry
Lake Geneva (Lac Léman)

Top left Port de Lutry
Bottom left Hermance

Scenic Trips to the Shore

Bike ride to the beach Dust off urban cobwebs in Geneva with a bucolic ride by bicycle – traditional or electric – past vineyards, wineries and fields of sunflowers to quaint **Hermance**, northeast of Geneva on the French–Swiss border. Plane trees shade the medieval village's lakefront and families adore its grassy beach. Remains of a 13th-century castle flank the tiny port where fisherman Julien Monney sells his expertly filleted perch and ready-to-eat *féra marinée* (marinated whitefish) at his artisanal fishery. Count on an hour (less with an e-bike) to cover the 14.5km ride starting in Geneva on Quai Gustave Ador's bike lane. Brown signs indicate bike route 46 to Hermance. Find a sauna here in winter.

Lakeshore beach walk In student-filled Lausanne, the peaceful **Sentier des Rives du Lac** is a perfect crowd escaper. The footpath ribbons along the lakeshore from Tour Haldimand on Quai d'Ouchy to Lutry, 4.7km east. Bar a few local runners, it's just swanky lake cottages and under-the-radar beaches backed by fig or willow trees for company. In **Port de Pully**, 2km into the walk, boats bob in the bijou pleasure port and the all-wood children's playground is unparalleled. Ten minutes further on **Plage de Paudex**, spiky Dent d'Oche (2222m) and other French alpine peaks across the water dominate the pretty patch of grassy, diving board–clad beach. Vineyard and mountain views crescendo in medieval **Port de Lutry**, with a pebble beach backed by lawns.

Best Beach Bars

Restaurant de la Plage

Drink in five-star views of Geneva's main urban beach and Jet d'Eau pencil fountain from this trendy restaurant-bar in Eaux-Vives.

Au Près de l'Eau

Pair countryside vibe with beach cool (and superb empanadas) at Hermance's favourite alfresco bar, in a flower garden above the water. In winter try fondue in a chicken coop turned romantic cabin.

Jetée de la Compagnie

Yoga, DJ sets and sunrise concerts unfold at Lausanne's hippest lakeside 'beach', with bar in an industrial container, waterside tables and sundecks for bronzing.

La Guinguette de Vidy

Graze on tasty charcuterie and cheese platters at this waterfront *guinguette* (open-air cafe) by Lausanne's Plage de Vidy.

05 Sound of **MUSIC**

FESTIVALS | CULTURE | NIGHTLIFE

There's far more to Swiss music than cowbells, yodelling and alpenhorns. A rich portfolio of music festivals celebrating all sounds spangles Lake Geneva's cultural calendar, which peaks in July and August with scores of top-drawer concerts to choose from. As compelling as the music is the choice of venue: stages pop up in parks, on beaches, rooftops, even afloat.

Paléo Festival Nyon

CYRIL ZINGARO/EPA/SHUTTERSTOCK

📍 How To

Getting here Use public transport to access the big-name festivals. Extra SBB night trains run to/ from Geneva and Lausanne during the Montreux Jazz Festival.

When to go July and August for summer festivals. The autumnal grape harvest in September ushers in atmospheric concerts in wine cellars and châteaux.

Tickets Buy online in March for Paléo; April for Montreux. Download the Paléo app for ticket resales; try your luck at the Montreux box office in situ during the festival.

MERCURY PHOENIX TRUST

Far left Paléo **Below left** Queen: The Studio Experience
Left Cully Jazz Festival

Summer Beats

Music at dawn Geneva raises the curtain on a rich repertoire of free outdoor concerts in July and August. Two stand out: sunrise concerts during **Les Aubes Musicales** at the **public baths;** and evening concerts in the park at **Parc de la Grange**.

Field rock Switzerland's headline summer festival **Paléo** (*yeah.paleo.ch*) fills fields in Nyon with rock, pop, seven outdoor stages and 230,000 festival-heads for six days of nonstop partying in July. Bob Dylan, Elton John, The Cure, Sting, Rosalía, Will Smith and David Guetta have all played here since 1976. Pitch up with a tent to camp.

Montreux myth Its name is a misnomer: all music genres star at the world-famous **Montreux Jazz Festival** (*montreux jazzfestival.com*). Pink Floyd, David Bowie, Elton John and Ella Fitzgerald have headlined here. For two weeks in July, 250,000 music lovers enjoy ticketed concerts, free jam sessions, dance classes, pool parties et al in the lakeside town. Pair the fest with a couple of hours at the captivating **Queen: The Studio Experience** museum, inside the band's preserved recording studio in the town's casino.

Jazz on the beach What it says on the tin: live jazz hits the beach in Hermance at **Jazz sur la Plage** (*jazzsurlaplage.ch*), one weekend in early August. Its jazzy rival is April's week-long **Cully Jazz Festival** (*cullyjazz.ch*), filling vineyards and wine cellars in Cully with live jazz.

♫♪ Best Jazz Venues

La Jonquille

This is a really nice bar with an underground space with small stage, weekly concerts and jam sessions. It's quite alternative and creative.

Le Cormoran

This is a beautiful, ephemeral place on the lake, all wood, summer only, with DJ sets and live concerts on the stage with the lake behind. Lovely fish and chips. It's a good place for world music.

AMR

Just below Gare de Cornavin, this jazz club is well known among musicians. I learnt jazz improvisation here. It hosts concerts and jam sessions.

■ *Recommended by Louella Yearwood, Genevan jazz and surf-rock trumpeter and music teacher*

06 Handsome Vines & LUSH WINES

FOOD & DRINK | WALKING | FESTIVALS

▬▬▬ East of Lausanne, serried ranks of sun-blazed vineyards stagger up steeply terraced slopes above Lake Geneva to form the Lavaux wine region, a UNESCO World Heritage Site. Vineyard walking, *dégustation* (wine tasting), and gorging on ethereal lake and mountain views are big reasons to explore the gorgeous string of villages beading this world-acclaimed 40km stretch of vine and shore.

📍 **Getting here/ around** Train from Lausanne to Lutry (5 minutes) or from Montreux to Cully (20 minutes). Walk, cycle or hop aboard the tractor-pulled tourist train Lavaux Express *(lavauxexpress.ch)* in situ.

When to go April to September for vineyard walks; June for

exceptional-value tasting at Caves Ouvertes Vaudoises *(mescavesouvertes. ch);* October for flame-red foliage and harvest festivities.

Tasting Bring cash to buy wine at honesty fridges in vineyards. Taste and buy at the *caveaux des vignerons* (winegrowers' cellars) in villages.

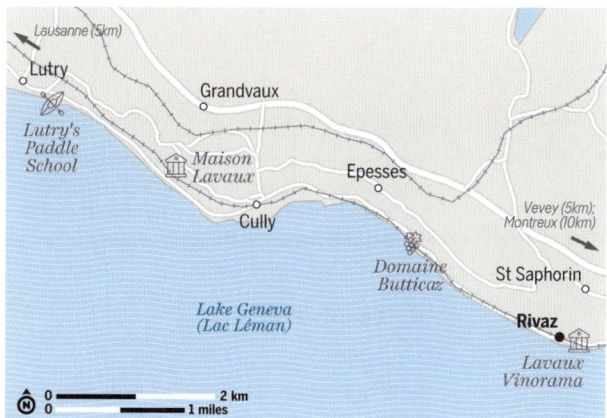

Walking & Cycling

Getting up close, on foot or by bike, is the best way to fully appreciate just how extraordinary these gravity-defying vineyards are. Pick up trail maps at the Lausanne or Montreux tourist offices or at the info point at Cully train station. From Lausanne, paths wind through the photogenic vineyards all the way to Château de Chillon. In medieval **Lutry**, 4km east of Lausanne, pick up the **Terrasses de Lavaux** (11.3km, 3¼ hours) trail to St-Saphorin. In Grandvaux, duck into **Maison Lavaux** (lavaux-unesco.ch), one-stop shop for wine-themed exhibitions and cultural events. Continue past the pretty wine-growing village of Riex to **Epesses**, fringed by unfathomably steep Dézaley vineyards. Right by the water, organic Grand Cru Dézaley wines crafted by seventh-generation winemakers at **Domaine Butticaz** are a personal favourite. **Lavaux Vinorama** (lavaux-vinorama.ch), 1.5km before your end point in St-Saphorin, is a modern tasting and discovery centre in a designer bunker. Watch a film and sample wine.

Paddling

Admiring the gorgeous sweep of vineyards from the middle of Lake Geneva is unforgettable. Rent a kayak or stand-up paddle, mid-March to October, from **Lutry's Paddle School** (lutry-paddle.ch) on pebble-grass beach Plage de Lutry in Lutry and paddle east. Views of the vineyards tangoing up the steep hillside are sublime. Book guided kayak excursions, including a family-friendly two-hour 'rando' from Port Rivaz to Lutry, in advance online.

Top left Terrasses de Lavaux
Bottom left Lavaux Vinorama

🍷 Tasting Notes

Appellations There are three: fruity AOC Lavaux wines made from Chasselas (whites) or Gamay, Pinot noir and Salvagnin (red) grapes; rare AOC Calamin Grand Cru wines, from fewer than 2% of Lavaux vineyards in Epesses; and prestigious AOC Dézaley wines.

Landscape 10,000 terraces, supported by 450km of retaining stone walls up to 6m high.

Viewpoints Medieval defence tower **Tour de Gourze**, a 3.4km (1½ hour) uphill hike uphill through vines from Riex; **Funiculaire du Mont Pélerin** in Vevey.

Lunch stop Pair a Lavaux white with Lake Geneva's finest *filets de perche meunière* (perch fillets pan-fried in butter) at lakefront **Café de la Poste** in picture-postcard Lutry.

Listings

BEST OF THE REST

Traditional Flavours

Bains des Pâquis   €

Meet Genevans at this self-service beach bar – rough and hip around the edges – at the vintage bath complex. Grab breakfast, a salad or dip into a *fondue au crémant* (sparkling-wine fondue).

Café Romand   €

In Lausanne, mussels, *malakoffs* (breaded, deep-fried cheese balls) and pork trotters are specialities at this old-world classic from 1951.

Bistrot des Halles   €€

Join locals at the zinc bar for *côte de boeuf* (steak), calf kidneys or other timeless classics at this bistro in Geneva's covered market.

Le Mazot   €€

Squirrelled away in the old town of lakeside Vevey, this family-run bistro is the spot to tuck into traditional fondue *moitié-moitié* (half Gruyère, half Vacherin Fribourgeois cheese) and steaks with a 'secret recipe' sauce.

More Châteaux

Château de Prangins

French-style gardens with ornamental beds and *potager* (vegetable garden) are a highlight of this 18th-century mansion with a history museum, 2km north of Nyon (*chateaude prangins.ch*).

Château de Coppet

In Coppet, midway between Geneva and Nyon, admire Louis XVI–style rooms where Paris society exile, Madame de Staël (1766–1817), entertained the great literary likes of Lord Byron (*chateaudecoppet.ch*).

Château de Rolle

Watch for art exhibitions celebrating regional and Swiss art talent in this hulk of a medieval fortress. It has held sentry over the lakefront village of Rolle since the 13th century (*chateauderolle.ch*).

Family Fun

Jet d'Eau

Getting soaked on the pier beneath Geneva's emblematic pencil fountain is a rite of passage – and a blessing on sweltering summer days. Water shoots up at 200km/h to create the 85m- to 140m-tall plume.

CERN

Rent a bike and embark on an imaginary mission to restart the particle accelerator at Geneva's European Organization for Nuclear Research. Tours and science shows in its visitors centre shine a light on its incredible work.

Plage des Eaux-Vives

Geneva's public single beach sports shallow waters, showers, accessible ramps and decent coffee to go. Tot-friendly Baby Plage,

Plateforme 10

with tyre swings roped in trees at its southern tip, is sandy.

Cathédrale St-Pierre

The 18th-century neoclassical portico at Geneva's cathedral is said to be inspired by Rome's Pantheon. Spiral up 150 steps in its twin towers for a lake panorama (magical at full moon – it stays open until 11.30pm).

Pointe de la Jonction

No TikTok prepares you for the psychedelic moment in Geneva when the Rhône meets the Arve River. Rent a kayak or stand-up paddleboard (*rafting-loisirs.ch*) to paddle across the line where the two mix.

Chaplin's World

Introduce the kids to the silent movies of Charlie Chaplin (1889–1977) at this highly entertaining house museum in Corsier-sur-Vevey, home to the London-born film star for the last quarter-century of his life.

24 Hours in Lausanne

Plateforme 10

Devour fine arts, photography, design and contemporary applied arts in a trio of museums alongside Lausanne train station. The daring architecture is a masterpiece in itself.

Le Barbare €€

Refuel on Lausanne's best hot chocolate, poured over vanilla ice cream in summer, plus superlative coffee, lunch and brunch year-round.

Cathédrale de Notre Dame

Head up high to Switzerland's finest Gothic cathedral crowning Lausanne's old town. Make a date with *le guet* (the watch) who still calls out the hour at night from the 79m-high belfry – the star-lit views of the city laid out at your feet are gold.

Chaplin's World

Great Escape

Party with the cool crowd at this veteran favourite, with grungy club-like interior and tree-shaded terrace above Place de Riponne.

MAD

Hit the re-imagined warehouse quarter of avant-garde Flon for live music, DJ sets and themed nights at this long-standing cafe-club on the central square, Esplanade du Flon.

Geneva Night Out

La Buvette du Bateau

Chink glasses aboard a retired 1896 paddle steamer by Geneva's Jet d'Eau. Dreamy views of the lake are unparalleled. The boat bar stays open until 2am Friday and Saturday nights.

Bongo Joe

This vinyl store 'n' cafe-bar in Geneva specialises in rare musical gems. Don headphones to listen to your own choice of tunes, or enjoy an occasional concert on the waterside terrace.

Le Baroque

Dress up to drink and dance until dawn with Geneva's glamorous set at the city's legendary nightclub, going strong since 1993. Doors open at 11.30pm Thursday to Saturday.

FRIBOURG, NEUCHÂTEL & THE JURA

CHEESE | WATCHES | NATURE

RESEARCHED BY CAROLINE BISHOP

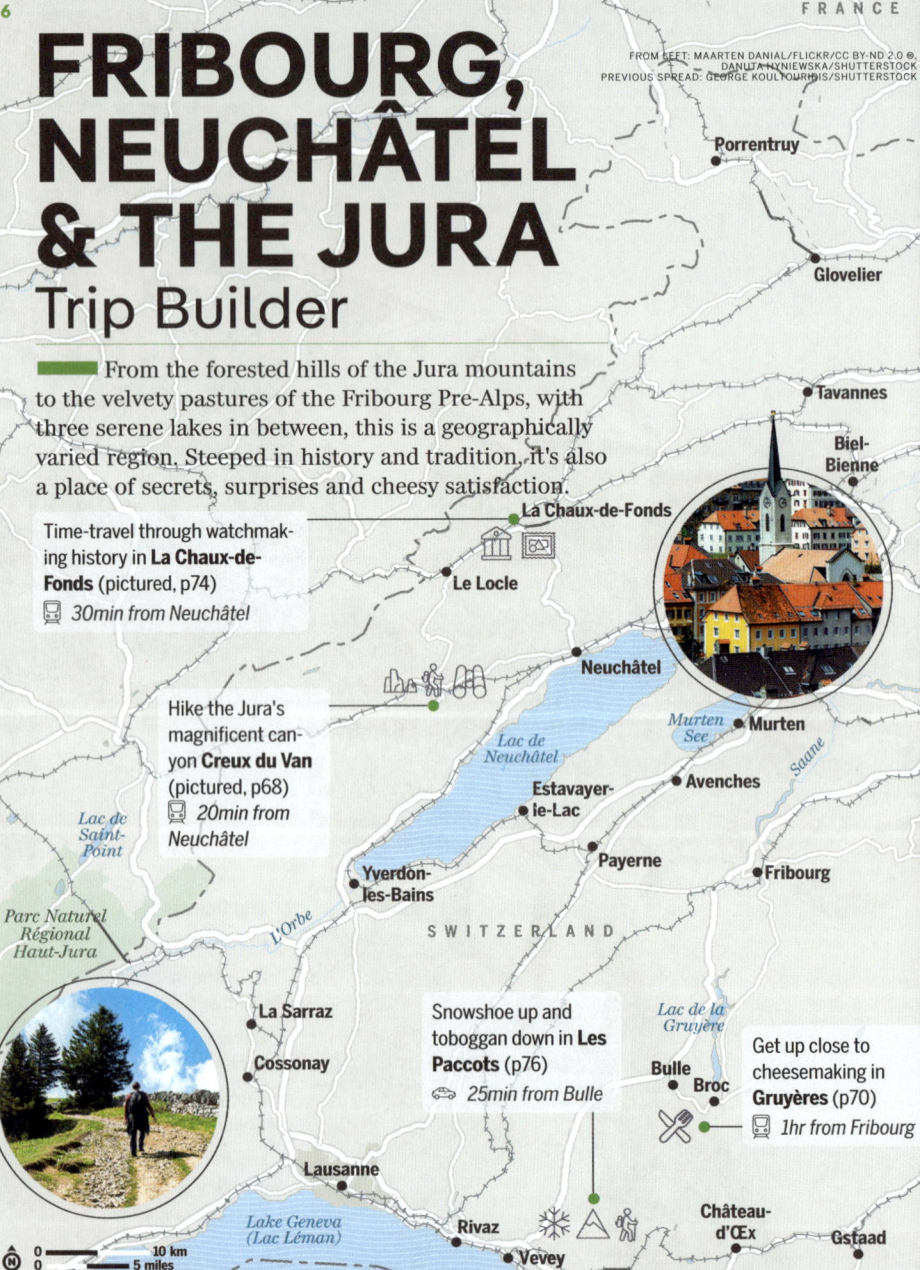

FRIBOURG, NEUCHÂTEL & THE JURA
Trip Builder

From the forested hills of the Jura mountains to the velvety pastures of the Fribourg Pre-Alps, with three serene lakes in between, this is a geographically varied region. Steeped in history and tradition, it's also a place of secrets, surprises and cheesy satisfaction.

Time-travel through watchmaking history in **La Chaux-de-Fonds** (pictured, p74)
🚋 *30min from Neuchâtel*

Hike the Jura's magnificent canyon **Creux du Van** (pictured, p68)
🚆 *20min from Neuchâtel*

Snowshoe up and toboggan down in **Les Paccots** (p76)
🚗 *25min from Bulle*

Get up close to cheesemaking in **Gruyères** (p70)
🚋 *1hr from Fribourg*

Porrentruy

Glovelier

Tavannes

Biel-Bienne

La Chaux-de-Fonds

Le Locle

Neuchâtel

Murten See • Murten

Lac de Neuchâtel

Avenches

Saane

Estavayer-le-Lac

Payerne

Fribourg

Yverdon-les-Bains

L'Orbe

S W I T Z E R L A N D

Lac de Saint-Point

Parc Naturel Régional Haut-Jura

La Sarraz

Cossonay

Lac de la Gruyère

Bulle
Broc

Lausanne

Lake Geneva (Lac Léman)

Rivaz

Vevey

Château-d'Œx

Gstaad

0   10 km
0   5 miles

Practicalities

ARRIVING

Geneva and Zürich airports Trains connect these international airports to Fribourg and Neuchâtel. Both cities are around 1½ to 2 hours from the airport; it takes a similar time by car.

MONEY

Overnight visitors automatically receive a Guest Card offering free or discounted entry to many museums plus free local transport.

FIND YOUR WAY

Tourist centres in Fribourg, Neuchâtel, Gruyères and La Chaux-de-Fonds provide details of self-guided hiking, cycling and themed walking tours.

WHERE TO STAY

Town/ Village	Pro/Con
Fribourg	Well located for day trips to the Pre-Alps. Limited selection of hotels.
Neuchâtel	Plenty of accommodation, from lakeside campsites to luxury hotels.
Gruyères	Gorgeous traditional Swiss appeal. Car-free. Only a few hotels; expensive and of varying quality.

EATING & DRINKING

Cheese is the cornerstone of this dairy-farming region and you're never far from a good fondue or a portion of meringues and Gruyère double cream (pictured). The popular Œil-de-Perdrix wine is produced in the vineyards around Neuchâtel, while Val de Travers is the birthplace of absinthe.

Best fondue Fromagerie d'Alpage de Moléson

Must-try bâtons à l'absinthe Jacot at the Maison de l'Absinthe (pictured)

GETTING AROUND

Train/Bus Hop by rail from Fribourg to Gruyères-gare and Bulle, and from Neuchâtel to Noiraigue, La Chaux-de-Fonds, Le Locle and Sainte Croix. Buses serve villages without train stations, including Les Paccots and Charmey, though they can be infrequent.

Car Offers more flexibility to reach the trailheads around Les Paccots, and avoids the steep climb up to Creux du Van.

JAN-MAR	**APR-JUN**	**JUL-SEP**	**OCT-DEC**
Skiing, snowshoeing and tobogganing on bluebird days	Spring flowers and tranquil early-season hiking	Holidays bring queues and crowds but lazy lakeshore days	Colourful hiking before the snow returns

06

A Cirque in
THE JURA

HIKING | WILDLIFE | ABSINTHE

Deep in the woods of Val de Travers lies the mighty **Creux du Van** (pictured). A steep ascent through dense forest leads to this magnificent amphitheatre of limestone cliffs, plunging 160m to the lush valley floor. Bring binoculars: ibex and chamois hang out here.

PATRICK HADORN/SHUTTERSTOCK

🗺 Trip Notes

Getting here Take the train to Noiraigue (20 minutes from Neuchâtel) or park at the station.

When to go May to October in good weather. Check conditions before you set out – if it's wet or icy the trail can be slippery.

What to spot Arrive in the early morning, when the trail is quiet, for the best chance of seeing Alpine ibex, chamois and – if you're extremely lucky – the shy lynx.

🍸 Absinthe Valley

Absinthe, that notorious, once-banned spirit, was first distilled here in Val de Travers. Visit one of the valley's distilleries, such as **Artemisia** in Couvet, to try and buy, and look out for absinthe-laced ice cream, soufflé and even dried sausage in shops and restaurants. The **Maison de l'Absinthe** in Môtiers has the backstory.

01 Prepare for a climb: from **Noiraigue** (pictured below), the 14km trail ascends through the trees, covering 730m elevation gain across 14 switchbacks.

Noiraigue

Areuse

800m

1000m

1000m

1200m

1200m

1300m

1400m

05 Alternatively, follow hiking trail 286 around the rim. Both paths eventually lead to **La Ferme Robert**, another refuelling pit stop with hearty food, a 45-minute walk from Noiraigue.

1200m

1400m

02 Linger at the top of the cirque, stroll around the rim and marvel at its sheer cliffs. There are no barriers, so watch your step!

04 Descend into the cirque's leafy bowl where you'll find the **Fontaine Froide**, a natural spring where the water is 4°C year-round, perfect for 'troubling' a glass of absinthe.

03 If you haven't packed a picnic, refuel at **Le Soliat** (pictured above), a farm and hotel-restaurant a 10-minute stroll from the hiking path. Non-hikers can arrive by car and park here, for a Chf9 fee.

N

0   500 m
0   0.25 miles

07

Cheese
COUNTRY

FOOD | FESTIVAL | TRADITIONS

Cows reign supreme in the Fribourg Pre-Alps, where alpine cheese has been produced since at least the 12th century. With its gorgeous cobbled streets and medieval castle, the hilltop village of Gruyères is an ideal base from which to explore the traditions of cheesemaking and taste the delicious result. The cows are fêted like queens in nearby Charmey each September.

KEITMA/SHUTTERSTOCK

🗺 **How To**

Getting around It's one hour from Fribourg to Gruyères by train. Charmey and Moléson are short hops from there by bus.

When to go Gruyères is at its geranium-strewn best in summer, but come in autumn for stunning fall colours and the *désalpe* celebrations.

Dietary advice The lactose-intolerant need not miss out: Le Gruyère AOP is actually lactose-free, since all lactose is metabolised into lactic acid during the production process. (If in doubt, seek advice.)

ETHAMPHOTO/ALAMY

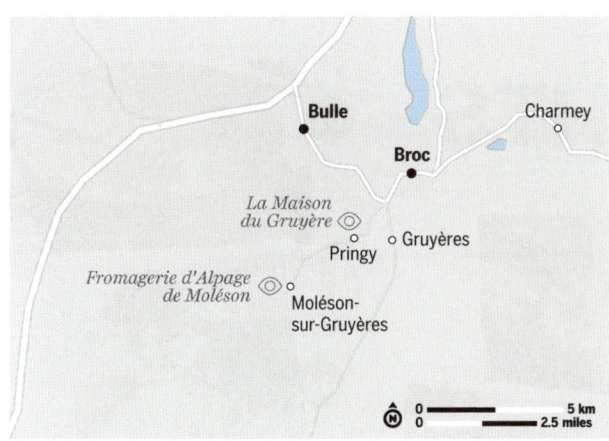

Alpine cheesemaking Wearing gumboots and a long apron, shirt sleeves rolled up, cheesemaker François tends the wood fire under a huge copper cauldron to heat the milk inside. When it's ready, he and his assistant haul the curds from the whey using a muslin and press it into moulds. Cheesemaking the traditional way is a hugely physical, demanding job requiring early starts (the milk arrives fresh from the cows at 7.30am) and François, cheesemaker-in-chief at the **Fromagerie d'Alpage de Moléson**, has been doing it for 40 years. Visit in the morning (book ahead) to watch him at work in the rustic wooden chalet that has stood at the foot of the Moléson mountain since the 17th century. The cheese he produces (Lutin du Moléson and Petit Moléson, both semi-hard cheeses similar to Gruyère) has the fragrant taste of Alpine herbs. Enjoy it in the on-site restaurant, which serves fondue, macaroni cheese and other Alpine dishes.

Gruyère at grand scale Next to Gruyères train station is the **Maison du Gruyère**, which produces Le Gruyère AOP, the region's most famous cheese. Every morning, 22 local farms supply their milk to the factory, where it's transformed into around 48 wheels of cheese – the maturing cellar can hold 7000. Come in the morning to witness the action from the viewing platform above the factory floor and see how the traditional process translates into cheesemaking at scale.

 Charmey's Désalpe

With cheese such a celebrated product in this area, it's only appropriate that the cows who provide the milk should be celebrated, too. In the village of Charmey, that's done with considerable pomp and ceremony on the last Saturday in September when the cows, having spent the summer grazing on the slopes, return home to the village farms.

Adorned with floral headdresses and decorative cowbells, these bovine beauties parade through Charmey accompanied by the farmers, also dressed in their Sunday best and carting the traditional cheesemaking equipment they've been using all summer. Thousands of spectators turn up to enjoy the day-long celebrations, and feast on cheese and wine.

Dairy
DELIGHTS

01 Fondue
Cheese melted in a *caquelon* (large pot) with white wine, garlic, lemon juice and a splash of kirsch, served with bread for dipping.

02 Raclette
A half-wheel of Raclette du Valais cheese is melted in portions on a special grill. Served with a potato and pickles.

03 Malakoff
Gruyère cheese, sometimes on a *rondel* of bread, battered and fried. Invented by Vaudois soldiers during the siege of Malakoff in the 1850s.

04 Meringues with Gruyère double cream
In addition to cheese, unctuously thick double cream is a speciality of the Gruyère region, typically served with locally made meringues.

05 Croûte au fromage / Käseschnitten
Cheese-on-toast, Swiss style. Bread is topped with ham and onions, smothered in cheese and baked in the oven.

06 Älplermagronen
This typical mountain food is a beefed-up

macaroni cheese with potato cubes and crispy onions, served with apple sauce.

07 Ramequin au fromage / Chäschüechli
Individual savoury tarts filled with a creamy cheese mix and baked until golden. Often sold at Swiss market stalls.

08 Salée au sucre
A sweet cream pie from the canton of Vaud. A regional variation, *gâteau du Vully*, is popular in neighbouring Fribourg.

09 Cholera
A traditional pie from Valais containing cheese, leeks, potatoes, apples, onions and sometimes bacon.

10 Tête de Moine
A cheese first made by monks in the Jura, hence the name 'monk's head'. Shaved into thin rosettes on a cheese curler called a *girolle*.

11 Cheese vending machines
Often seen in mountain villages, allowing on-demand access to packets of fondue mix and Raclette supplied by local farms.

08 Mechanical MARVELS

HISTORY | WATCHES | ART

▬▬▬ Granted UNESCO World Heritage status for their urban layout – designed in the 19th century to better serve the burgeoning watchmaking industry – the twin towns of La Chaux-de-Fonds and Le Locle still live to the rhythm of a ticking clock. The history of their craft is entwined with that of a third town in the Jura mountains, Sainte Croix, home to extraordinary mechanical art.

🗺 How To

Getting here Trains from Neuchâtel run to La Chaux-de-Fonds (30 minutes), Le Locle (40 minutes) and Sainte Croix (one hour).

When to go All year for the museums. Come in mid-June for guided tours and visits as part of Switzerland's World Heritage Days.

Where to stay Maison DuBois offers five themed rooms in a former watchmaker's home in Le Locle, with breakfast served on a watchmaker's workbench.

FRANCE
Tour Espacité
La Chaux-de-Fonds
Musée d'Horlogerie du Locle
Zenith Boutique Manufacture
Morteau
Le Locle
Espace de l'Urbanisme Horloger
Musée International d'Horlogerie
Montbenoît
Noiraigue
Areuse
SWITZERLAND
Buttes
Lac de Neuchâtel
Musée de la Mécanique d'Art et du Patrimoine de Sainte Croix
Estavayer-le-Lac
Sainte Croix
Yverdon-les-Bains
L'Orbe
0   5 km
0   2.5 miles

Cradle of watchmaking Considered the first watchmaking town in the Jura mountains, Le Locle is still home to the **Zenith Boutique Manufacture** factory, which opened here in 1865 and can be visited on a guided tour. Head to the **Musée d'Horlogerie du Locle** for elaborately decorated clocks and watches displayed in the former summer home of 18th-century master watchmaker Samuel DuBois.

Time travel In La Chaux-de-Fonds, the **Espace de l'Urbanisme Horloger** explains how the town was rebuilt with watchmaking firmly in mind after a devastating fire in 1794. View the resulting grid structure from the top floor of the **Tour Espacité** and pass numerous 19th-century watchmaking workshops and factories on a stroll about town. Save time for the **Musée International d'Horlogerie**, which journeys deep into the history of the craft.

🖼 Neuchâtel's Ancient Androids

Three very special automatons are on proud display at the **Musée d'Art et d'Histoire de Neuchâtel**. The Writer, the Musician and the Draughtsman are wind-up mechanical figures created by the Jaquet-Droz workshop in La Chaux-de-Fonds in the 18th century. Still in amazing condition, each contains hundreds of cams and levers forming an incredibly complex internal mechanism that allows it to act as its name suggests: the programmable Writer uses a quill and ink to write any text of 40 characters; the Musician can play five different melodies on the piano, and the Draughtsman can draw four different pictures. Catch a demonstration on the first Sunday of every month.

Mechanical art Watchmaking in the Jura developed alongside the related craft of mechanical art, and they are inscribed together on UNESCO's Intangible Cultural Heritage list. The sleepy village of Sainte Croix was once the centre of music box production, and the **Musée de la Mécanique d'Art et du Patrimoine de Sainte Croix** shows how this intricate craft boosted economic prosperity in the 19th century. The museum's most precious treasures are demonstrated on a guided tour: early mechanical jukeboxes; delicate singing birds; comical-but-creepy moving figurines; kitsch music-hall organs, and jaw-droppingly complex automatons created by contemporary Sainte Croix mechanical artist François Junod.

Top Musée International d'Horlogerie

09 Les Paccots
SNOW DAY

SNOW | NATURE | FONDUE

There's nothing like crunching through sun-speckled snow on a crisp, clear day – particularly when a warming fondue awaits. Pocket-sized paradise Les Paccots (pictured) delivers the perfect winter outing: peaceful snowshoe trails; glorious hilltop views; a cheesy lunch, and a thrilling toboggan descent.

© UFT/FTV

🗺 Trip Notes

Getting here Buses run infrequently from Châtel-St-Denis to Les Paccots (15 minutes). A car allows more flexibility and makes it easier to hire gear in Les Paccots village and then continue to the trail head.

When to go December to March. The area isn't particularly high (1100-1500m) so check snow conditions on fribourg.ch before you set out.

Challenging climb With an elevation gain of 500m, this trail is quite a workout but worth the effort.

❄ Snowshoeing Top Tips

Hire snowshoes with an integrated heel lift, which makes it easier to ascend.

Use walking poles to reduce knee pressure on both ascents and descents.

Bring plenty of water and wear wicking, breathable layers.

Carry a backpack with straps so you can tie your snowshoes on for the sledge down.

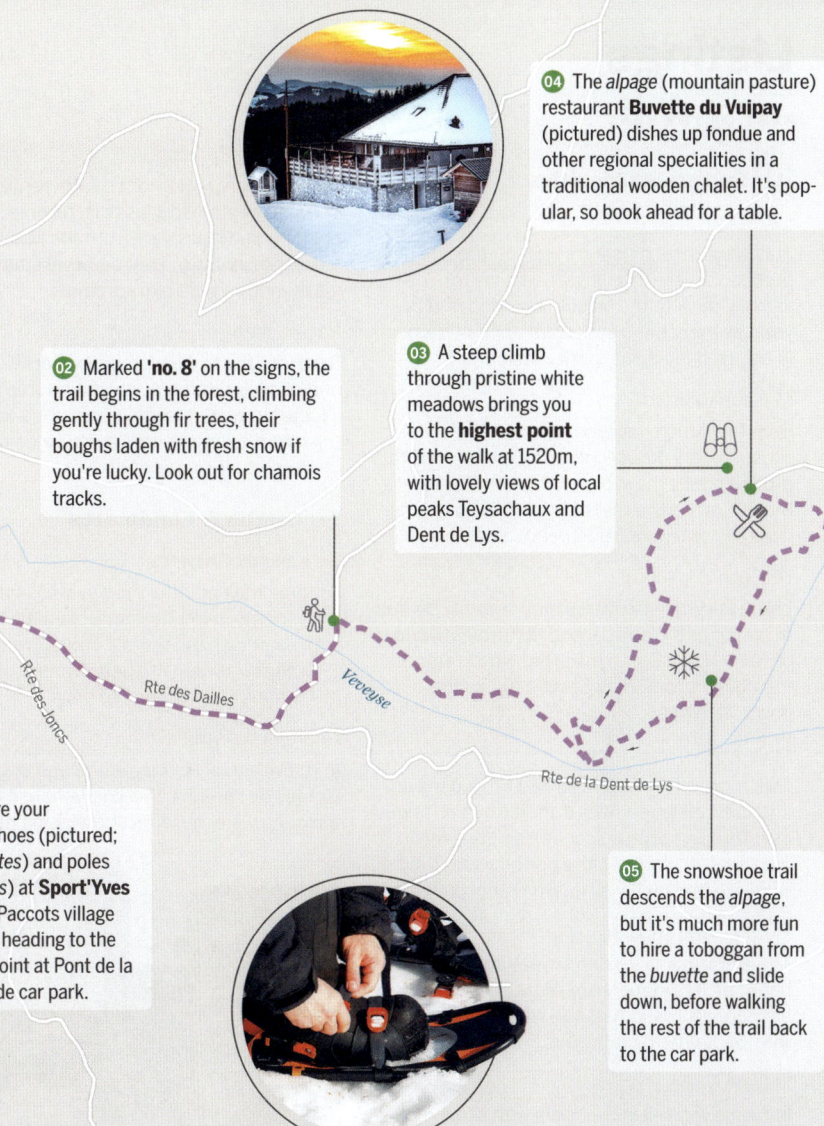

04 The *alpage* (mountain pasture) restaurant **Buvette du Vuipay** (pictured) dishes up fondue and other regional specialities in a traditional wooden chalet. It's popular, so book ahead for a table.

02 Marked **'no. 8'** on the signs, the trail begins in the forest, climbing gently through fir trees, their boughs laden with fresh snow if you're lucky. Look out for chamois tracks.

03 A steep climb through pristine white meadows brings you to the **highest point** of the walk at 1520m, with lovely views of local peaks Teysachaux and Dent de Lys.

Rte du Moléson

Paccots

Rte des Joncs

Rte des Dailles

Veveyse

Rte de la Dent de Lys

01 Hire your snowshoes (pictured; *raquettes*) and poles (*batons*) at **Sport'Yves** in Les Paccots village before heading to the start point at Pont de la Cascade car park.

05 The snowshoe trail descends the *alpage*, but it's much more fun to hire a toboggan from the *buvette* and slide down, before walking the rest of the trail back to the car park.

0   500 m
0   0.25 miles

Listings

BEST OF THE REST

 ## Cultural Curiosities

Laténium

This Neuchâtel museum, built on the site of prehistoric lake dwellings, takes visitors on a journey back to the Neolithic period and beyond, with reconstructions of ancient homes in the archaeological park outside.

Museum Murten

Beautiful Murten played a decisive role in Swiss history. Housed in an old water mill, this museum tells the story of the 1476 Battle of Murten, while the rest of the exhibition places it in the context of 6000 years of history.

HR Giger Museum

Leave fairy-tale Gruyères momentarily behind to step into the surreal and disturbing world of Hans Ruedi Giger, the artist who created the designs for Ridley Scott's 1979 sci-fi horror film *Alien*.

Musée des Grenouilles

This museum in Estavayer-le-Lac houses an unusual collection: 108 stuffed frogs arranged in anthropomorphic scenes depicting life in the mid-19th century, the period when they were created by Swiss guard François Perrier.

Espace Jean Tinguely-Niki de Saint Phalle

The extraordinary kinetic creations of Fribourg artist Tinguely are presented alongside the colourful, Gaudí-esque work of his second wife, de Saint Phalle, at this Fribourg museum.

Maison Cailler

Immerse yourself in chocolate with a tour of the Broc factory of Swiss brand Cailler, which makes some of the country's most popular chocolates. Tasting is, of course, part of the experience.

Vitromusée Romont

This museum in Romont's 13th-century castle showcases stained-glass art, reverse glass painting and glassware from the Middle Ages to the present day. The medieval stained-glass windows are extraordinary.

Papiliorama

Step into the tropics at this butterfly dome and zoo near Kerzers, which features a unique 'Nocturama' that re-creates night under a full moon, giving visitors the chance to get up close to nocturnal animals.

 ## Castles & Landmarks

Château de Gruyères

Topping the beautiful medieval village of the same name, this 13th-century castle is filled with paintings and murals dating from the 19th century when its then-owners would invite their artist friends to stay.

Château de Boudry

In the village of Boudry at the end of the Gorges de l'Areuse, this castle houses an interesting wine museum showcasing paintings,

Arènes d'Avenches

SARENAC77/SHUTTERSTOCK

winemaking equipment and documents related to wine culture in the surrounding area.

Arènes d'Avenches

Dating from the 2nd century AD, the amphitheatre of Avenches demonstrates the importance of this town in Roman times, when it was known as Aventicum. The attached tower houses a museum delving into this history.

Quirks of Nature

St Peter's Island

Catch a ferry to Île St Pierre/Sankt Petersinsel from Neuchâtel or Biel/Bienne and spend a few hours enjoying this peaceful nature reserve. The island's former monastery is now a hotel and restaurant.

La Brévine

This Jura village has the dubious honour of recording Switzerland's lowest ever temperature, of -41.8°C. Its expansive fields are perfect for cross-country skiing, and you can ice-skate on Taillères Lake if conditions allow.

Saut du Doubs

A pretty waterfall on the Doubs River sits on the border between Switzerland and France. Catch a boat from the riverside at Les Brenets, west of Le Locle, for the 20-minute cruise downstream.

La Grande Cariçaie

Clinging to the southern shore of Lac de Neuchâtel, this large nature reserve is home to a huge diversity of bird life, flora and fauna. Discover it on foot or by bike along 40km of designated paths.

Gorges de l'Areuse

On a hot day, step into this shady gorge created by the Areuse River. The 12km trail between Noiraigue and Boudry is peppered with pretty bridges, waterfalls and rock formations.

Café de l'Ange

Regional Flavours

Chesery   €€

Pick up some vintage tableware or bric-à-brac during your lunch at this cafe in Murten, which is also a *brocante* (thrift market). The savoury *gâteau du Vully* with salad is a winner.

Café de l'Ange   €€

Right by the Pont du Bern with a terrace overlooking the Sarine River, this traditional auberge is a great place to try fondue in Fribourg.

Le Chalet   €€

Tuck into *malakoffs* or fondue, followed by meringues with double cream, in this beautifully renovated chalet restaurant in Gruyères.

L'Enclume   €€

Cheese is the star of the show at this popular restaurant in Charmey, which serves three different types of fondue.

Brasserie Le Cardinal   €€

This traditional restaurant in Neuchâtel's old town is known for 'La Neuchâteloise', a potato galette topped with *tomme* cheese and slices of a local smoked pork sausage.

BERN & BERNESE OBERLAND

MOUNTAINS | ADVENTURE | FOLKLORE
RESEARCHED BY KERRY WALKER

BERN & BERNESE OBERLAND
Trip Builder

Beyond the medieval charm and modern art of Bern, dive into some of the most exhilarating landscapes in the Alps. Whether you're hiking, skiing or scaling a cliff ledge, this region bewitches with Eiger views, cloud-shredding peaks, glaciers, lakes and falls galore.

SWITZERLAND

Get cultural kicks in the medieval Altstadt and world-class galleries of **Bern** (pictured, p86)
🚆 *1hr from Zürich*

Embrace heart-pumping alpine sports in Victorian-era grand **Interlaken** (p96)
🚆 *50min from Bern*

Ramp up the downhill thrills at the peak of First in **Grindelwald** (p90)
🚆 *35min from Interlaken*

Gasp at waterfalls leaping over vertical cliff faces in **Lauterbrunnen** (p104)
🚆 *20min from Interlaken*

Stand at the top of Europe at 3454m **Jungfraujoch** (p93)
🚆 *55min from Grindelwald*

Wettingen

Aare

Reuss

Hallwilersee

Baldeggersee

Sempachersee

Lucerne

Bern

Thun

Saône

Aare

Lake Thun (Thunersee)

Interlaken

Brienzersee (Lake Brienz)

Aare

0 ____ 10 km
0 ____ 5 miles

ARTUR BOGACKI/SHUTTERSTOCK. PREVIOUS SPREAD: ROBIN MEIER/SHUTTERSTOCK

Practicalities

ARRIVING

Interlaken is the main hub for the Bernese Oberland, well connected by rail to the rest of Switzerland.

MONEY

Visit during shoulder seasons, book Supersaver train tickets in advance and invest in regional transport passes to save francs.

FIND YOUR WAY

The tourist information centre on Marktgasse in Interlaken is a one-stop shop for bookings, ski passes, hiking maps and more.

WHERE TO STAY

Town/Village	Pro/Con
Interlaken	Victorian-era glamour, uplifting mountain views, extreme sports and the widest array of accommodation.
Bern	Historic capital on the Aare River, with medieval arcades, Klee art and Einstein in the mix.
Lauterbrunnen	Waterfalls, alpine thrills, plus mountain trains and funiculars winging you up to giddy heights.

EATING & DRINKING

Refuel at mountain huts with *Älplermagronen* (pictured; a creamy take on macaroni cheese) or a *Berner Platte*, a hearty platter of cured meat, pork knuckle, potatoes and sauerkraut. Nibble on *Zibelechueche*, onion tart studded with bacon and caraway seeds, at Bern's folksy November Zibelemärit.

Best tasting menu with Eiger views
Glacier Fine Dining (pictured)

Must-try cheese Raclette with a sensational backdrop
Mönchsjochhütte

GETTING AROUND

Train Fast, efficient, scenic SBB trains link Bern to hubs like Thun (20 minutes) and Interlaken (50 minutes).

Driving Hire your own wheels for remoter corners. It's 45 minutes from Bern to Interlaken on the A6 autobahn.

Public transport Bern is well connected by bus, tram and S-Bahn train.

APR-JUN
Blossom and calm days for hiking, cycling and paddling.

JUL-AUG
Outdoor music and folk festivals. Alpine huts open for hikers on multiday treks.

SEP-NOV
Wine festivals. Cows descending from pastures and autumn markets.

DEC-MAR
Snow-frosted peaks, Christmas markets and skiing galore.

10

Rolling on the
AARE RIVER

SWIMS | VIEWS | RIVER BARS

Glacial meltwaters from the Bernese Alps trickle into the Aare River, which wraps around Bern like a perfect ribbon of turquoise. Come summer, locals can't wait to jump right in. Whether you join them for a sunrise dip or to drift past the historic landmarks of the Altstadt, swimming in these invigoratingly cold waters is a rite of passage.

📖 **How To**

Getting here Bus 30 stops close to Marzili Pools or they are around a 10-minute walk from the Altstadt.

When to go Unless you're an ice-bathing fan, jump in during the warmest months from June to August, when water temperatures fluctuate between 18°C and 22°C.

What to bring Bring bathers, a towel and a water-proof swim bag.

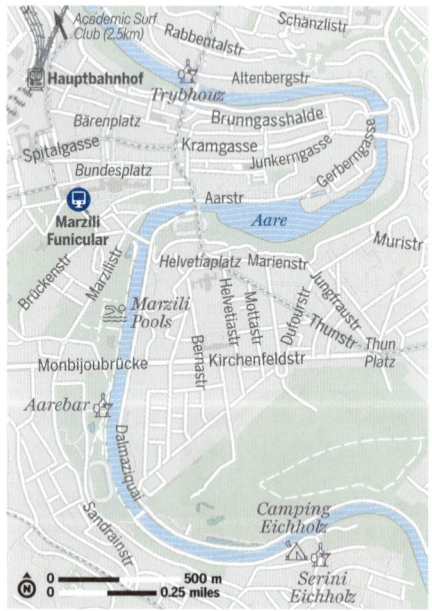

Take the plunge You don't need to be a pro wild swimmer to go for a dip in Bern, where even office workers ditch suits and strip down to their bathers for a re-energising midday swim when the mercury rises. You'll find the odd brave swimmer in the river even in the depths of winter.

Go with the flow Steps lead into the water and red poles mark entrance and exit points. Pop your togs into a waterproof dry bag and try the classic route: hiking 2km upstream from **Marzili Pools** to **Camping Eichholz**, then drifting back with the current to Marzili's brilliant (and free)

lido. Here you can swim laps, sunbathe, play volleyball or grab an ice cream – all with views of the domed Bundeshaus and the Münster's medieval spire.

Up the adventure Kandersteg International Scout Centre (kisc.ch) arranges self-guided, two- to four-hour

🍸 Riverside Bars in Bern

With the first summer rays, bars pop up along the banks of the Aare River, bringing holiday vibes to the city. One of the coolest is **Trybhouz** *(trybhouz.ch)*, a funky little shack reached via steps down from Kornhausbrücke. Here you can grab deli snacks like organic burgers, summer salads and ginger beer, before dipping into the turquoise water. Midway between Marzili Pools and Camping Eichholz, **Aarebar** *(aarebarbern.ch)* is another mellow summer fave, with Bernese flocking to the deck in their bathers for pizza, antipasti and drinks. End your swim with moules-frites, ice cream or a cold beer at parasol-shaded **Serini Eichholz** *(serini.be)*.

river tubing tours from June to August, which begin in Uttigen and take you swiftly floating along the Aare to Bern, with uplifting views of the snow-capped Alps en route. If you're craving bigger thrills, give bungee surfing – surfing in flowing waters with the help of a bungee cord – with the **Academic Surf Club** *(academicsurfclub.ch)* a whirl. Visit the respective websites for details on times, locations and bookings.

Above Marzili Pools

11

Rewinding Time
IN BERN

HISTORY | CULTURE | VIEWS

▬▬▬ On a particularly lovely bend in the Aare River, encircled by gentle hills and with views of the snow-frosted Alps, the city of Bern is a looker. And Switzerland's dinky capital punches high when it comes to history, with a UNESCO World Heritage–listed heart, ⸰ where you can trot in Einstein's footsteps and stroll 6km of arcades.

SAIKO3P/SHUTTERSTOCK

🗺 How To

Getting around Bern's compact Altstadt is a breeze to explore on foot (bring flat, comfortable shoes for the cobbles).

When to go Dodge summer crowds by visiting in the shoulder seasons. Spring brings cherry blossom and autumn colour-changing foliage to parks. December is full of festive Christmas-market sparkle.

Onions galore If you're in Bern in late November, you can't miss the fabulous **Zibelemärit** (Onion Market), a giant farmers market and folk festival. Try *Zibelechueche* with mulled wine.

BUMBLE DEE/SHUTTERSTOCK

Top left Zytglogge
Bottom left Kindlifresserbrunnen

Arcades & Fountains

Medieval heart Bern's flag-bedecked **Altstadt** is an instant heart-stealer, laced with 6km of covered arcades, with cellar shops and bars descending from the streets. Ravaged by fire in 1405, the wooden city was rebuilt in today's sandstone and is crammed with historic big-hitters. Get your bearings at the soaring Gothic **Münster**, with a 100m-tall spire that is Switzerland's highest. Climb the 344-step spiral staircase for views over the snaking Aare River.

Swiss clockwork Bern's eye-catching clock tower, **Zytglogge**, is a focal point. Here crowds gather to watch revolving figures twirl at four minutes before the hour, after which the actual chimes begin. A crowing rooster launches the parade of figures, which include bears (symbol of Bern), a jester and Cronos, god of time. Step inside to gawp at the medieval mechanics and clamber up 130 steps for phenomenal views over the terracotta rooftops, which reach all the way to the snow-crowned peaks of the Bernese Oberland on clear days.

City of fountains You can't turn a cobbled bend in the heart of Bern without stumbling across one of its 100 fountains, all spouting pure drinking water. Most captivating of the lot are 11 decorative fountains dating to 1545, depicting historical and folkloric characters, from marksmen to pipers. The unmissable oddball is the **Kindlifresserbrunnen** on Kornhausplatz, showing an ogre snacking on children. On nearby **Bundesplatz**, 26 water jets (one for every Swiss canton) dance.

📖 Einstein's Bern

Bern has inspired many great minds, not least Albert Einstein, who lived and worked here as a patent clerk from 1903 to 1905. Peering up at the ornate **Zytglogge** clock tower supposedly helped him hone his revolutionary special theory of relativity, our understanding of the universe and how gravity affects mass, time and space.

For an even deeper dive with the genius scientist, visit the **Einsteinhaus** (*einstein-bern.ch*), where the physicist lived with his young family, now filled with photos and heirlooms. He can also be found (in sculptural form) in the **Rosengarten** and **BärenPark**.

12

Waterfall
CHASING

WATERFALLS | ALPS | ADVENTURE

As if cupped in celestial hands, Lauterbrunnen gazes up to the glaciated mountains rising like a theatre curtain above it. This valley mesmerised Goethe, Lord Byron and other romantics, with 72 waterfalls that crash over vertical cliffs in summer and freeze solid in winter. Base jumpers leap fearlessly off its rocky ledges, and trails clamber up through its cow-grazed pastures and dark spruce forest.

EVA BOCEK/SHUTTERSTOCK

 How To

Getting here Lauterbrunnen is brilliantly connected to the wider Bernese Oberland, with trains to Interlaken (22 minutes), Grindelwald (40 minutes) and Wengen (13 minutes).

When to go The falls are accessible from April to October and are at their bang-crash best after the snow melt and heavy rains of spring.

Top tip At the Staubbachfall, be prepared to get wet and wear sturdy shoes for the short but steep uphill walk.

Water, Water Everywhere

Valley of falls It's as though God whipped out the plug in Lauterbrunnen. On a summer's day, the valley is a paradisiacal vision, with pea-green meadows where cows jangle their bells below vertical 400m cliffs splashed with

mist-dashed waterfalls and mountains glinting with glaciers. There are 72 waterfalls nosediving over sheer rock faces in the valley: a view that leaves some speechless and others tutting at smartphone cameras because every photo falls short of the reality.

A drop of romance The wispy **Staubbachfall** inspired Goethe to pen his poem *Song of the Spirits over the Waters*, extolling their ethereal beauty, while Lord Byron compared the falls to the 'long white tail of the pale horse upon which death is mounted in the *Book of*

MELINDA NAGY/SHUTTERSTOCK

Revelations. In the morning light, you can see how this vaporous, 297m-high waterfall captivated their imaginations, with threads of spray floating down the cliffs. What appears to be ultra-fine mist from a distance, however, becomes a torrent when you walk behind the falls.

Gorge walks Make a day of it by strolling to the thun-derous **Trümmelbachfälle** (*lauterbrunnen.swiss*), which roar into a boulder-strewn gorge. Accessed via a series of galleries, tunnels and platforms, the 10 falls drain the Jungfrau Region's biggest glaciers and snow deposits, with 20,000l of water per second corkscrewing through ravines and potholes shaped by the swirling waters.

⊕ Via Ferrata Fun in Mürren

From Lauterbrunnen, hop on a cable car and train to glide along the horizontal ridge to car-free Mürren, where you'll think you've died and gone to Heidi heaven. With its log chalets and ringside mountain views, this cliff-hugging village is Swiss fantasy stuff.

For a thrill, clip onto Mürren's sky-high **Klettersteig** (*via ferrata*), with close-ups of the Bernese Alps as it teeters across sheer cliff faces to Gimmelwald. With its ladders, cables, 80m-long suspension bridge and arresting views of Eiger's gnarly north face, it's breathtaking in every sense of the word. Let a guide from **Outdoor Switzerland** (*outdoor. ch*) show you the ropes.

Left Staubbachfall
Right Trümmelbachfälle

13 Going DOWNHILL

ACTION | EIGER | PICNICS

▬ Rising above the Alpine town of Grindelwald, the 2184m summit of First gets hearts thumping with its up-close views of the Jungfrau Alps and a flurry of ways to thunder, bump and fly downhill at full throttle. Whether you come in summer when the sky is flawless blue and wildflowers freckle the meadows, or in the snowy depths of winter, this peak is adventure mad.

WALKINGMAP/SHUTTERSTOCK

🗺 How To

Getting here From 9am to 5.30pm, cable cars run roughly every 10 minutes from Grindelwald to First, with a journey time of 25 minutes.

When to go Visit from April to October for the full-on downhill adventure package by zip line, mountain cart and scooter. Tickets are sold at the valley station of First cable car.

Lunch stop Unwrap a picnic of local cheese, cured hams and fresh bread on the shores of Bachalpsee.

WATCHARAKUL RONGKAVILIT/SHUTTERSTOCK

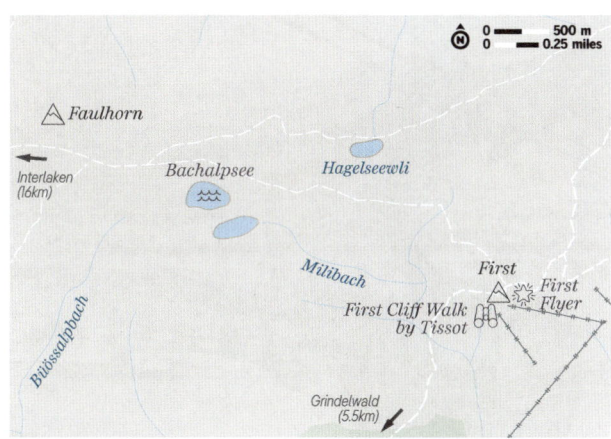

Sky-high views Eiger's ferocious north face and the 4078m fang of Schreckhorn feel close enough to touch from the **First Cliff Walk by Tissot** (*jungfrau.ch*), a gravity-defying lookout platform jutting 45m into the void. Alpine choughs use the lookout as a take-off and landing place.

Alpine hikes A short, insanely scenic hike leads to **Bachalpsee**, at its most entrancing first thing in the morning when its calm sapphire waters mirror snow-polished peaks. The glacial lake is less than an hour's walk from the First cable-car upper station, through high meadows brushed with wildflowers and alive with cowbells.

Hair-raising descents If you want to really let rip, come in summer to whoosh towards Eiger on the **First Flyer** zip line at speeds of up to 84km/h. At midway stop Schreckfeld, switch to a **mountain cart** to bomb downhill through forests and lush pastures. Next stop is Bort, where you switch to a jumbo scooter, or **trotti-bike**, to rattle back down to Grindelwald at speed.

Epic sledge runs In winter, there's fine powder up here for snowboarding and freeskiing. For a more challenging off-the-radar adventure, drag your sledge for 2½ hours on marked trails through the snow up to 2681m-high **Faulhorn**. It's the starting point for the 15km **Big Pintenfritz**, the world's longest toboggan run, which helter-skelters down slopes and through forests all the way back down to Grindelwald. The ride is best tackled in the early morning.

❄ The Velogemel

Skis, snowboards and sleds aren't the only way to zip around on the snow in winter. Cue the **Velogemel** – a single-track, steerable snow bike invented by Grindelwald carpenter Christian Bühlmann in 1911 to make getting around the Alps easier for everyone from postal workers to farmers, doctors and children.

Now this wooden bicycle with runners has cult status and its own world championships held in Grindelwald in February. Rent one out at Grindelwald station and head up to Bussalp to pelt down the final 9km of Big Pintenfritz. It might look scary to begin with, but after a few wobbly minutes, you'll soon be flying down the mountains (dig in your heels to brake).

14

Top of
EUROPE

GLACIERS | VIEWS | ADVENTURE

The train ride up to UNESCO World Heritage–listed Jungfraujoch (3454m) is one of Switzerland's classic experiences. Following an audacious route right through Eiger's frozen heart, the 1912 railway whisks more than a million visitors a year through some of Europe's most staggering high-Alpine scenery.

🗺 **How To**

Getting here Trains depart Interlaken Ost half-hourly; change at Grindelwald to the Eiger Express and at Eigergletcher to the Jungfraubahn. One-way takes 1½ hours.

When to go Avoid peak summer and winter when the summit gets swamped with visitors. Reserve ahead. Depart on the first train (6.30am from Interlaken or 7.15am from Grindelwald) for a Good Morning Ticket with a 15% discount.

Snow time From May to mid-October, ramp up the thrills with summer sledging, zip-lining and tubing at the Snow Fun Park.

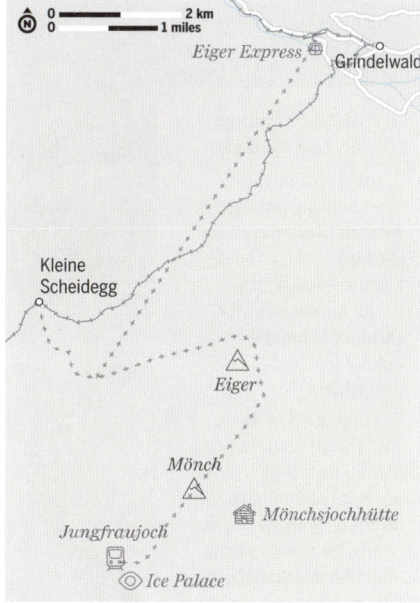

Eiger Express

From Grindelwald, the **Eiger Express** *(jungfrau.ch)*, a fancy, super-fast tri-cable gondola, wings you up to **Eigergletscher** station, using its wheels to generate green power. And the ride? Just wow. You'll be glued to the window as you float above a tapestry of meadows and spruce forests, emerging so close to Eiger's beastly, mile-high north face that you'll feel as though you're about to smash right into it.

Jungfraujoch

At Eigergletscher, you switch to the **Jungfrau Railway** up to **Jungfraujoch** *(jungfrau.ch)*. Bring a warm layer as temperatures plummet and the summit is always wintry white. Top-of-the-world views from the **Sphinx** observation deck stretch across an endless sea of snow-encrusted peaks – many grazing the magic 4000m mark – and the 23km swirl of the Aletsch Glacier, while Germany and France hover in the distance.

Top left Eiger Express **Left** Sphinx

Ice Palace

Tunnels of ice polished as smooth as cut glass lead through the so-called **Ice Palace**, which offers a frosty reception at minus 3°C. Mountain guides wielding saws and pick axes carved the chambers out of solid ice in the 1930s. Now they are adorned with frozen sculptures of bears, ibexes and eagles. Wear sturdy shoes as the glass-smooth ice can be slippery.

Hut Sleeps

Give the madding crowds at Jungfraujoch the slip to trudge through the snow to **Mönchs-jochhütte** (*moenchsjoch.ch*) and you'll be entranced by the views of a never-ending sea of rippling peaks that unfold. You won't be able to suppress gasps of wonder hiking along the trail that threads directly below 4110m **Mönch**, pearl-white glaciers glinting on its rocky flanks. The Aletsch Glacier, **Jungfrau** and **Eiger** are equally dazzling in the snow

Glacier Hiking on the Aletsch

To really appreciate the mind-bending beauty of the **Aletsch Glacier**, consider joining one of the two-day summer hikes across the ice organised by the **Outdoor Mountaineering School** (*outdoor.ch*) in Grindelwald.

The huge ice flow winds 23km down from the peaks of the Jungfrau Alps to Valais. This unforgettable hike takes you properly off the beaten track, with a night at the **Konkordiahütte** at 2850m above sea level. No prior glacier experience is necessary, but you'll need a head for heights, sure-footedness and the ability to walk for six hours with a backpack, sometimes as a roped team.

Aletsch can also be accessed from Fiesch in Valais (p118).

 Eco Rails

The Swiss were racing towards sustainability long before it became a buzzword. Since 1912, a little red train has twisted up to Jungfraujoch, Europe's highest train station at 3454m. Fuelled by hydropower from the outset and blasting through the mountain, the railway is a staggering feat of engineering.

glare. And do you hear that? Silence. Isn't it a beautiful thing?

A favourite of hardy mountaineers who rise bleary-eyed before daybreak to surmount nearby four-thousanders, this is the highest serviced hut in the Swiss Alps at 3657m above sea level. Open from mid-March to mid-October, a stay overnight here is a small taste of the intrepid.

Bring warm layers and a sleeping bag liner and you're good to go. The path is crevasse free and easily accessible. Though recently revamped and solar panelled, the hut is still pleasingly rustic.

The deal is sweet and simple: you'll sleep in a basic dorm, wash in meltwater and eat heartily – dishes like rösti and Valais raclette are paired with regional wines.

It pays to be an early riser, as the clatter of karabiners can be heard at ungodly hours (bring earplugs if you're a light sleeper) and breakfast is served from 2am to 7.30am. It's just as well because you really wouldn't want to miss sunrise...

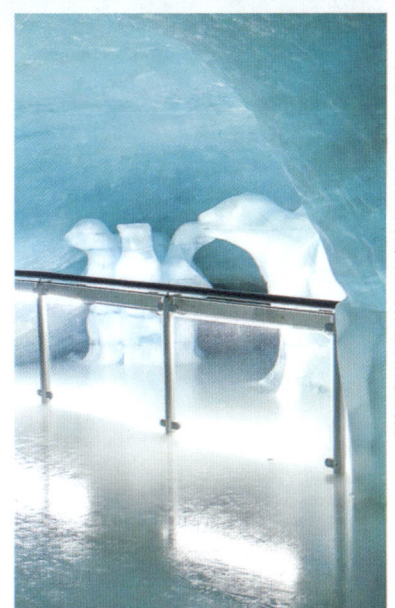

Top Jungfrau Railway **Left** Aletsch Glacier **Below** Ice Palace

15

Interlaken
RUSH

OUTDOORS | VIEWS | EXTREME SPORTS

▬▬▬ Straddling the Aare River, bordering Lakes Thun and Brienz and capped off by Eiger, Mönch and Jungfrau, Interlaken once made the Victorians swoon with ravishing mountain views from its grand hotels. Today it dials up the adventure, with a million and one ways to make the pulse race – in the peaks, on the water and in the sky. Welcome to Europe's biggest extreme-sports hub.

INGOLF POMPE/IMAGE PROFESSIONALS GMBH/ALAMY

🗺 How To

Getting here With excellent rail connections, Interlaken is the springboard for adventures in the wider Jungfrau Region. Outdoor operators arrange pick-ups/drop-offs locally.

When to go Sun or snow? You decide.

Paragliding and skydiving happen year-round (weather permitting), May to September is best for white-water rafting, July and August for high-level climbs.

Top tip Book well in advance. Most outdoor providers supply specialist equipment, but check ahead.

JAN ZAHULA/SHUTTERSTOCK

HAIDAMAC/SHUTTERSTOCK

Far left Rafting, Lütschine River
Below left Eiger
Left Paragliding, Interlaken

On the rocks If you fancy bagging your first four-thousander, hook onto an expedition-style tour with **Outdoor Switzerland** (outdoor.ch). These range from day trips to climb Mönch (4107m) on foot, skis or snowshoes, to winter ski touring the Bernese Oberland Haute Route. If you're mega-experienced and super-fit, the big one is a three-day ascent of the beast that is Eiger (3970m) via Ostegg. If you're not quite ready to scramble up peaks yet, there are taster courses in rock climbing, ice climbing, snowshoeing and ski touring.

Sky high Right in the heart of Interlaken, you'll see paragliders twirl down from towering peaks. You can float in quiet exhilaration above a tapestry of 4000m summits and jewel-like Lakes Thun and Brienz with (phew!) a pro in tow on tandem flights with **Skywings** (skywings.ch). Or take a running jump and catch thermals with **Paragliding Interlaken** (paragliding-interlaken.ch). Tandem flights take off from 1129m Beatenberg, with up to 20 minutes in the air. Transport to the launch spot is included. No prior experience is required.

On the water One look at the foaming, swirling, milky turquoise Lütschine River and you'll be itching to jump right in. Outdoor Switzerland and Paragliding Interlaken arrange exhilarating whitewater rafting adventures that bounce at speed along this gaspingly cold river. Four-hour round trips throw you in at the deep end, with class III-IV rapids to negotiate and a grand finale at Lake Brienz (Brienzersee). You'll need to be a confident swimmer. Bring swim gear, a towel and a backpack.

◇ Skydiving with Eiger

It's a film-set moment as the helicopter buzzes ever higher and you leap out of it, full-on James Bond-style, in front of the shimmering white peaks of Eiger, Mönch and Jungfrau. Terrifying? For sure. Unforgettable? You bet.

Skydive Interlaken (sky diveinterlaken.ch) makes it happen, with tandem HALO (High Altitude – Low Opening) flights that take you up to an ear-popping 5500m before you begin free-falling at speeds of up to 200km/h. Supplementary oxygen is provided. The views are out of this world, ripping across a huge chunk of the Swiss Alps to the valleys and plains beyond. Good weather is essential.

Mountains of Myth

THE BERNESE ALPS HAVE BEEN A FONT OF FASCINATION AND INSPIRATION SINCE TIME IMMEMORIAL
Sharp peaks encrusted with glaciers, the life-affirming crash of a waterfall, the off-the-spectrum blues of an alpine lake, big wilderness on every bend – for centuries the spirit-soaring landscapes of the Bernese Alps have held mountaineers, artists, poets, authors and film-makers in thrall. And they haven't lost their touch.

Alpine Legends

Long before anyone braved taking a rope and karabiner to their heights, the mountains of Eiger, Mönch and Jungfrau swirled with Alpine legend. As creation myths go, theirs is a compelling one. As their German names suggest, the story tells of Eiger being an ogre who endeavours to reach the beautiful, virginal peak of Jungfrau ('young woman'). But in between them is Mönch, the monk, who protects her from his advances.

The enduring allure of the Bernese Alps is not just about what you can see, but the fact that there is a lot up there that you can't. For centuries, these implacable peaks would have struck both fear and wonder into the hearts of farmers and villagers in the valleys below. In the mid 19th-century, hardy climbers battled nature to be the first at their savage summits, with many attempts ending in rope-breaking disaster.

No mountain has more pulling power than Eiger. Marked out by triumph and tragedy, this dark, 3967m-high dagger of a peak strikes fear into the hearts of even hardcore climbers. Eiger has the biggest north face in the Alps – an 1800m-high wall of sheer rock and ice. Its Nordwand ('north wall') was first successfully climbed by Anderl Heckmair and his German-Austrian party in 1938, but 64 climbers have lost their lives on it over the years, giving it the nickname Mordwand ('Wall of Death').

Left Mönch **Centre** Final stand of Sherlock Holmes, Reichenbachfälle Falls
Right Gemmi Pass

Inspiring Heights

Goethe penned an ode to the Staubbachfall in the waterfall-wisped Lauterbrunnen Valley in 1779. Romantic poet Lord Byron was enraptured by the romance of these mountains during his tour through the Bernese Oberland in 1816, detailing 'scenes beyond all description or previous conception' in his journal. Here they found space to breathe and think, reconnect with nature – and let inspiration flow. Many immortalised the region's unfathomable beauty in paint and on paper. Some 200 years later, their wonder endures. British writer Sir Arthur Conan Doyle found Meiringen's soaring cliffs and thunderous Reichenbachfälle fantastically dramatic for pushing Sherlock Holmes and his arch-enemy Dr Moriarty over the precipice in his 1891 *The Final Problem*. The region is said to have been the blueprint for Tolkien's Middle Earth, too. *The Lord of the Rings* author first visited the Lauterbrunnen Valley in 1911, aged 19, and the crashing falls and towering cliffs are said to have inspired his fictional Rivendell.

> The enduring allure of the Bernese Alps is not just about what you can see, but the fact that there is a lot up there that you can't

The region's cinematic looks haven't escaped the notice of film directors either. The rugged peak of Schilthorn shot to fame as the mountaintop lair of 007's arch-villain, Ernst Stavro Blofeld, in the 1969 Bond film *On Her Majesty's Secret Service*. George Lazenby played James Bond, but all of that fancy skiing on breathtakingly steep slopes was done by stunt doubles.

Dawn of Swiss Alpine Tourism

For millennia, traders and travellers have trod the north-south path across the wild, rocky, snow-frosted heights of the **Gemmi Pass**, linking the Bernese Oberland with Valais and Italy beyond. First came the Celts, Romans and medieval muleteers, but it was the dawn of Alpine tourism in the 19th century that really put the pass on the map. In 1863, Thomas Cook included the pass in its first escorted package holiday of Switzerland. So if you think trekking here today is tough, spare a thought for those intrepid Victorian ladies in frocks and lace-up boots. Countless artists and writers followed, seeking inspiration in the wildly romantic terrain – Jules Verne, Mark Twain and Picasso among them.

Listings

BEST OF THE REST

 Art & Heritage

Zentrum Paul Klee

Rising like three rippling waves, this Renzo Piano–designed gallery is Bern's answer to the Guggenheim and an astounding tribute to the colour-charged works of visionary Swiss-German artist Paul Klee.

Ballenberg Swiss Open-Air Museum

Reconstructed farming hamlets present an architectural romp through Switzerland, with 100 century-old buildings from Valasian wooden huts to hip-roofed farmhouses.

Sherlock Holmes Museum

Meiringen's falls inspired Arthur Conan Doyle's Sherlock Holmes tales. Do your detective work to find the re-created sitting room of 221b Baker St.

 Sensational Views

Harder Kulm

Hitch a funicular ride up to this modest summit in Interlaken for front-row views of Eiger, Mönch and Jungfrau, and the piercingly blue lakes of Thun and Brienz.

Brienzer Rothorn

Take a retro ride on a steam-powered cog-wheel train up to 2350m Brienzer Rothorn for long views over Lake Brienz to a parade of snow-dusted 4000m peaks.

Schilthorn

Day breaks in golden glory above Eiger's mile-high north face from 2970m Schilthorn. Its eyrie-like summit, Piz Gloria, wows with wraparound views of 200 peaks, from Titlis to Mont Blanc.

Peak Walk by Tissot

At Glacier 3000, this nerve-splintering suspension bridge links two mountains, with outrageous views of Matterhorn, Mont Blanc, Eiger, Mönch and Jungfrau.

 Rainy Day

Bernatone Alphornbau

The deep, resonant, hairs-on-end sound of the alpenhorn is utterly Swiss. Learn to play one on a full-day course at Heinz Tschiemer's workshop in Habkern.

Funky Chocolate Club

Give chocolate making a whirl at hour-long, hands-on workshops in Interlaken, whizzing from bean to bar. You'll get to mould and temper, decorate and taste like a pro.

Alpine Weinkultur

Delve into Spiez' medieval castle cellars for tours and tastings of Lake Thun riesling and Sylvaner white wines.

Brienzer Rothorn

On Tap

On drizzly days in Bern, swing by this atmospheric vaulted cellar for 12 craft beers on tap and more by the bottle.

 Natural Wonders

Giessbachfälle

Illuminating the fir forest like a spotlight in the dark above Lake Brienz, this wispy torrent plummets 500m over 14 rocky ridges.

St Beatus Caves

Cross foliage-draped cliffs and falls to enter fantastical limestone caves burrowing into the dark heart of the Niederhorn massif. Lore has it they were discovered by Irish monk St Beatus in 100 CE.

 Fine Dining

Glacier Fine Dining €€€

Pepped up with foraged flowers, herbs and berries, chef Paul Cabayé's outstanding tasting menus reflect the mountains on a plate at this Grindelwald restaurant. The signature is Graubünden salmon marinated in gin made from Eiger glacier water.

Wein & Sein €€€

Shining brightly with a Michelin star, this Bern Altstadt stunner puts imaginative riffs on seasonal, regional ingredients in romantically lit brick vaults.

Radius €€€

Michelin-starred wonder, with chef Stefan Beer finessing ingredients sourced within a 50km radius. Meals here are events.

 Winter Warmers

Michel's Stallbeizli €

Back-to-nature dining in a converted barn in Gstaad. In winter, feast on fondue with views of cud-chewing cows.

MARIO KRPAN/SHUTTERSTOCK

St Beatus Caves

Wasserngrat €€

Marvel at views of Diablerets Glacier from this slope-side chalet, where a fire crackles and skiers warm up over fondue on the sunny terrace.

Stallbeizli-Heuboden €€

Go straight to fondue heaven at this gorgeously rustic mountain hut in a converted barn in Grindelwald.

 Mountain Huts

Berghotel Wildstrubel €€

Well-executed Swiss classics come with riveting mountain views at this rustic-chic lodge atop the Gemmi Pass.

Schilthornhütte €

Ski or hike to this timber-clad mountain hut at 2433m, serving cheese and potato-rich specials. Eiger, Mönch and Jungfrau views dazzle from the terrace.

Restaurant Bramisegg €€

High above the Giessbachfälle and Lake Brienz, this woodsy mountain hut delivers dreamy views and Swiss faves like *Älplerrösti* (fried potatoes topped with cheese and a fried egg).

16 Hiking Tour
JUNGFRAU

HIKE | ALPINE VIEWS | HUT SLEEPS

No hike better captures the off-the-charts beauty of the Bernese Alps than the 10-stage, 111km **Tour of the Jungfrau**. Between giddy heights, cute villages and stops at mountain huts, its views of glacier-capped mountains, blue lakes, deep valleys and raging falls make your heart sing as you stride.

NOOR RADYA BINTI MD RADZI/SHUTTERSTOCK

 **How To**

Getting here The Tour of the Jungfrau starts at Schynige Platte and ends just below in Wilderswil. Frequent trains connect Wilderswil with Interlaken, five minutes away.

When to go Late June to early September is prime time for hiking, with long days and warm weather. You should book hut stays well in advance.

Handy companion Grab a copy of Cicerone's helpful stage-by-stage *Tour of the Jungfrau Region* guide, with route details and maps.

DEXTERMELISSA/SHUTTERSTOCK

The Faulhornweg

The hike begins with a drumroll, as the first day's hike from Schynige Platte to First is one of the most spectacular of the lot. A vintage rack railway trundles up to the 2099m plateau of **Schynige Platte**, a natural balcony on the Bernese Alps, with killer views of a host of pearly white summits. At the top, a headily fragranced botanical garden nurtures 600 types of Alpine blooms, including snowbells, arnicas, gentians, anemones and edelweiss.

From here, the 15-km, six-hour, high-level Faulhornweg tosses you in at the alpine deep end, picking its way across rolling pastures, scree slopes, boulder-strewn passes and high moors to the knobbly 2681m peak of Faulhorn ('Lazy Rock'). Here 360-degree views reach across a sea of mountains to the Black Forest in Germany and Vosges in France on cloudless

MARISA ESTIVILL/SHUTTERSTOCK

Navigation Know-How

The hike is immediately dramatic, leading clockwise along ridges and up to vertiginous summits. The trail is well signposted with red-white markings, but don't underestimate the wild terrain – the weather can change at the drop of a hat, paths can be exposed and the walking is challenging (if not especially technical).

Top left Schynige Platte **Left** Schynige Platte funicular vintage rack railway **Above** View from Faulhorn days. Lakes Thun and Brienz glisten far below. Peaks like the dagger-shaped Wetterhorn and the big three of Eiger, Mönch and Jungfrau hover on the horizon. Stop for lunch on the terrace of **Berghotel Faulhorn** *(faulhorn.ch)*, in business since 1830.

Trail Highs

Buoyed by a spectacular start to the hike, you'll be psyched for more phenomenal mountain views in the days that follow. No peak hogs the limelight (and camera lens)

more than 3967m-high Eiger. Getting up-close-and-personal with this monster of a peak, the 6km, three-hour **Eiger Trail** from Eigergletscher to Alpiglen shows off this massive fang of rock and ice in all its glory.

Mürren is a fantastic springboard for hikes. Top billing goes to the **North Face Trail.** Starting at Allmendhubel and ending at the Schilthorn cableway, this 6.5-km, 2½-hour hike is a beauty, weaving through flowery meadows and spruce forest, with heart-pumping views

Best Alpine Villages

Mürren Hovering above the waterfall-wisped Lauterbrunnen Valley, this village is Heidi heaven, with dark-timber chalets and knockout views of the Jungfrau Alps.

Gimmelwald A magnet to hikers and adventurers, this pipsqueak village delivers drop-dead-gorgeous scenery, rural authenticity, flower-bedecked farmhouses and a sense of calm.

Isenfluh Perched on a sunny terrace above Lauterbrunnen, this dinky hamlet, home to just 60 people, feels properly off the beaten track.

Saxeten Pure nature, few crowds and stirring views of the Bernese Alps, and Lakes Thun and Brienz, entice in this mountain hideaway.

Stechelberg See the Lauterbrunnen's falls at their best, as they cascade over perpendicular walls of rock, in this tiny, silent village, long a bolthole for hikers.

Left Mürren
Below Schilthorn

of Eiger, Mönch and Jungfrau on repeat. The highest point on the tour is 2970m **Schilthorn**, a wild, rocky peak that rises like an eyrie above a ripple of snow-encrusted mountains. Most people take the cable car, so you'll be among the very few who arrive breathless at the top. Your reward is sensational 360-degree views stretching from Titlis to Mont Blanc when it's clear.

Hut Sleeps

One of the joys of the Tour of the Jungfrau is unplugging from 21st-century life and going back to basics by spending the night in a pine-scented dorm in a mountain hut. Just bring your gear (including a sleeping bag liner) in a small backpack and book well in advance during the peak summer season when bunks are like gold dust.

Fiery sunsets, starry nights, wildlife encounters and day-break starts await after tough climbs up to the likes of 2317m-high **Gleckstein Hut** (*gleck stein.ch*), at the foot of the ragged 3692m Wetterhorn. Other beauties include the 2039m **Rotstockhütte** (*rotstockhuette.ch*) below Schilthorn, and the 1955m **Lobhornhütte** (*lobhornhuette. ch*) above Lauterbrunnen, with dress-circle Eiger, Mönch and Jungfrau views. After a stiff climb up, you'll be grateful for a cold beer on the sun terrace and simple but hearty grub like rösti potatoes topped with cheese, bacon and a fried egg.

VALAIS

OUTDOOR ADVENTURE | MOUNTAINS | WINE
RESEARCHED BY NICOLA WILLIAMS

VALAIS
Trip Builder

The story of Valais is one of rags to riches, of changing seasons and celebrities, of outdoor life so fantastic it never goes out of fashion. The unfathomable Matterhorn, Aletsch Glacier, the Rhône Valley's gravity-defying vineyards: landscapes here leave you dumbstruck.

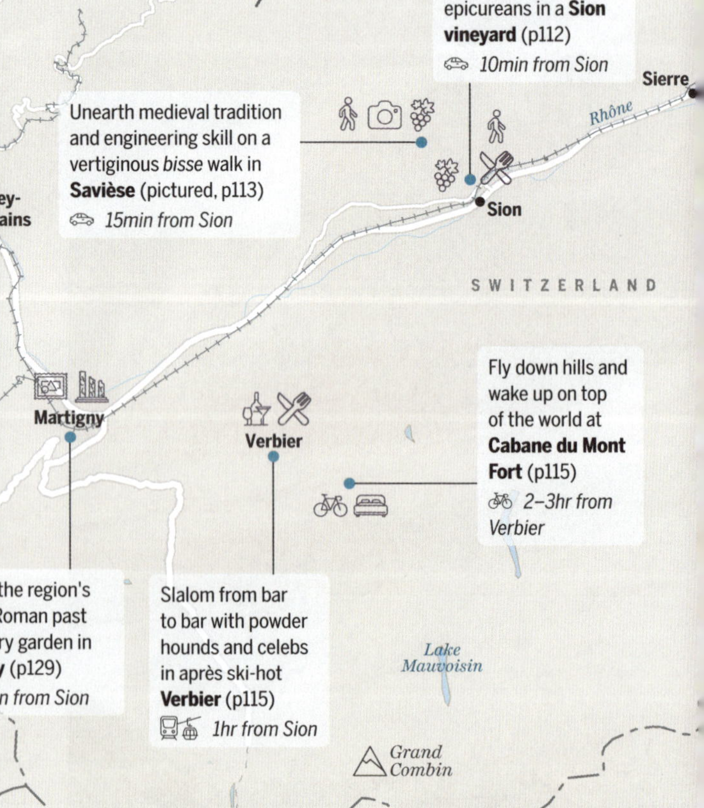

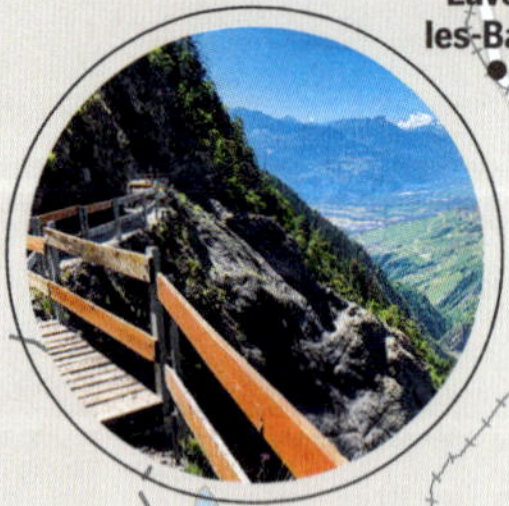

Monthey
Bex
Lavey-les-Bains
Sion
Sierre
Rhône
SWITZERLAND
Martigny
Verbier
Lac de Barberine
Lake Mauvoisin
Grand Combin
Chamonix

Feast on good food and fine wine with epicureans in a **Sion vineyard** (p112)
10min from Sion

Unearth medieval tradition and engineering skill on a vertiginous *bisse* walk in **Savièse** (pictured, p113)
15min from Sion

Fly down hills and wake up on top of the world at **Cabane du Mont Fort** (p115)
2–3hr from Verbier

Unearth the region's ancient Roman past in a gallery garden in **Martigny** (p129)
15 min from Sion

Slalom from bar to bar with powder hounds and celebs in après ski-hot **Verbier** (p115)
1hr from Sion

CLOCKWISE FROM LEFT: INGRID VERTESSEN/SHUTTERSTOCK, PHILLIP RICHTER/SHUTTERSTOCK, SIMON DANNHAUER/SHUTTERSTOCK. PREVIOUS SPREAD: JAKSUTHEP TEEKUL/SHUTTERSTOCK

Stride out on a big-thrill ice hike on the Alps' mightiest glacier, **Aletsch Glacier** (p118)

🚆 *45min from Brig*

Fiesch

Live the Swiss alpine dream – on skis and sledges – in **Bettmeralp** (pictured, p117)

🚆🚠 *45min from Brig*

Bettmeralp

Mörel

Brig

Visp

I T A L Y

Ride Europe's highest open-air cogwheel railway up to **Gornergrat** (p122)

🚆 *30min from Zermatt*

Lake Moiry

Dent Blanche

Zermatt

Matterhorn (Monte Cervino)

Swim, bronze and enjoy alpine beach life at altitude at **Leisee** (pictured, p121)

🚠🚶 *20min from Zermatt*

Macugnaga

Join the jet set on bucket-list ski slopes in **Zermatt** (p129)

🚆 *2hr from Martigny*

Dufourspitze (Monte Rosa)

I T A L Y

Parco Naturale Alta Valsesia

N

0 ——— 10 km
0 ——— 5 miles

Practicalities

STERLING IMAGES/SHUTTERSTOCK

ARRIVING

Geneva Airport Direct trains *(sbb.ch)* run from the region's primary international entry point along the valley to Sion (2 hours), Martigny (2 hours) and Le Châble–Verbier (2½ hours). For Zermatt (4 hours), change trains in Visp.

Furka Base Tunnel At the Valais' eastern end, trains and car-shuttle trains come through the Furka Base Tunnel from Andermatt in Central Switzerland. In summer you can drive over the Furka Pass from Andermatt or the Grimsel Pass (p171) from Meiringen in the Bernese Oberland.

HOW MUCH FOR A

Gornergratbahn train ticket Chf66/132

Cheese fondue Chf30

Mountain-bike Chf50–70 per day

GETTING AROUND

Car & Motorcycle Your own wheels are useful for navigating deeply rural folds of this mountainous canton, void of major cities. Roads to mountain ski resorts are steep and serpentine. Winter tyres are essential, November to April. Zermatt-bound motorists must park in the Matterhorn Terminal Täsch *(matterhorn terminal.ch)* and take a shuttle train *(mgbahn.ch)* up the mountain.

Trains & Cable Cars Trains traversing the Rhône Valley connect with cable cars up to ski resorts. Find large car parks to leave your car in Le Châble and at Bettmeralp's bottom station.

Hiking & Biking Consult SwitzerlandMobility *(schweiz-mobil.ch)* for trail ideas and map. wanderland.ch for maps. Club Alpin Suisse *(sac-cas.ch/en)* is the definite planning tool.

WHEN TO GO

MID-DEC–MID-APR
Ski season, mixing snowfall with blue-sky days. January is extra-cold.

JUN-AUG
Cable cars open in the Alps for hikers and bikers. Expect blistering-hot days.

SEP-OCT
The tail end of hiking season, with cooler weather. Grapes are harvested.

NOV-MID-DEC
Grey days. Mountain resorts hibernate.

EATING & DRINKING

Valais is a gourmet land of vineyards, fruit orchards and alpine pastures. Sparkling AOC Fendant wine and wafer-thin slices of *viande séchée* (pictured; air-dried beef) are perfect partners to creamy Tomme de Verbier cheese, tangy mature Vieux Bagnes or golden puddle of melted AOP Raclette du Valais. Alfresco dining in summer vineyards closes with autumnal banquets celebrating the grape harvest. Dining in valley towns is traditional Swiss and top-drawer; in mountain resorts, glitzy, glam and international.

Best modern Swiss cuisine
Potato (pictured; p129)

Must-try trompe l'oeil apricot cake Cabane du Mont Fort (p115)

CONNECT & FIND YOUR WAY

Wi-fi Free hotspots keep you connected in towns, but in rural areas and in the mountains, even a phone signal can be non-existent.

Navigation Before hitting the trail, download motoring and hiking maps to ensure offline access in the wild. Road trippers, September to June, always check if *cols* (mountain passes) are open.

WHERE TO STAY

Valais sports stunning alpine resorts with equally stunning places to stay: sleep up high beneath stars, next to the lifts or overlooking slopes.

Town	Pro/Con
Martigny	Valley town with functional, good-value hotels. Good transport links.
Sion	In-town options can be cookie-cutter; appealing auberges in surrounding vineyards.
Verbier	Luxury Heidi chalets and contemporary hotels ooze charm. Cheaper summer rates lure a less-glitzy crowd.
Zermatt	Masses of lux hotels in a world-famous ski resort; some winter-only.
Bettmeralp	Handful of traditional village hotels; car-free, pricey and enchanting.

ALPINE PASSES

Check *cols* (mountain passes) before setting out: Col du Grand St Bernard (into neighbouring Italy) and the Furka Pass to central Switzerland close in winter.

MONEY

In Zermatt, under 9s staying one night in a hotel with their parents, receive a Wolli Card covering free travel year-round on all Zermatt cable cars and railways. Some summertime cable cars are free with Verbier's VIP Pass (included in hotel accommodation, June to October).

17 Medieval WATERWAYS

HISTORY | WALKING | FOOD & WINE

As glaciers shrank from the 13th century, water on steep slopes around sun-blazed Sion became scarcer. Villagers built *bisses* (waterways) to irrigate their parched vineyards and agricultural pastures, engineering gravity-defying channels from wooden planks to divert glacial milk and alpine springs from their natural course. Exploring the incredulous web of *bisses* (waterways) still used today around Sion is a powerful lesson in human ingenuity and survival.

OLEG LOPATKIN/SHUTTERSTOCK

📍 How To

Getting here/around
Trains between Lausanne (50–80min) and Brig (35–45min) stop in Sion, a small valley town easy to explore on foot. You'll need your own wheels – two or four – to access most *bisse* walks.

When to go April to October, when trails are open.

Hot date August's *tavolata* when locals feast in vineyards around long shared tables. September/October's *La Brisolée* feast celebrating the close of the grape harvest.

FIKOVA/SHUTTERSTOCK

Top left Bisse de Savièse Torrent Neuf
Bottom left Bisse de Clavau

Vineyard Escape Cicadas, buxom fig trees, sun-drenched vines and bottles of white or rosé on ice ... such is the vibe on a hot summer's day along Sion's **Bisse de Clavau** (*les-bisses-du-valais.ch*) that you'd be forgiven for thinking you're in the south of France. Built in 1450 to carry water between Sion and St Léonard, 8km east, the mini canal saunters through steeply terraced vineyards. From the trailhead in Parking Bisse de Clavau, off Route de Sion above town, it takes two to four hours to walk the 8km waterside trail. Make a day of it by stopping for a summer lunch alfresco at **La Guérite Brûlefer**, a cottage on Maison Bonvin's south-facing vineyards. Foodie lunches end with lemon sorbet soaked in a glass of sweet, fruity, gently sparkling white Le Must wine. Views across Sion in the valley floor to Dente Blanche (4357m) beyond are equally punchy.

Cliff-Edge Encounter The prize for high drama goes to **Bisse de Savièse Torrent Neuf** (*torrent-neuf.ch*), built in 1430 to transport water across hills in Savièse and functional until 1934. Walking its scenic length (11km return, 3-4 hours) through forests, across five suspension bridges and along vertiginous cliff edges is an evocative lesson in the crazy risks farmers took while building these channels. Pick up the trailhead in Parking Torrent Neuf, 10km north of Sion.

✕ 🍴 The Soul of Sion

My favourite summer spot for Raclette is Sion's Friday's market in the old town. On Rue du Grand-Pont at No 44, Philippe Savioz runs Cave Les Futailles, a very old wine cellar from the 13th century. He sells Raclette and wine.

For Raclette in winter go to La Cambuse. It's on the ski slopes in Les Collons and you have a real chalet ambiance.

AOC Fendant is a Valais unmissable. The best is Les Murettes which is a bit sparkling. Red Cornalin is made from one of the oldest grape varieties.

■ **By Sabine De Kalbermatten -Van Vliet**, *a Sion native ever faithful to her Valaisian home town's deeply rooted cheese and wine culture.*

18

Bike
CENTRAL

CYCLING | OUTDOORS | SCENERY

Ritzy Verbier has dazzled accomplished skiers and celebrities alike since the 1950s when the first lifts whisked ski fiends up the mountain. Increasingly these days, it is the chic mountain town's fast-growing biking culture that is turning heads – and filling its squares, streets and grassy slopes with two-wheel riders out for a spin and speed fix. Here's how to join the summer peloton.

© VERBIER 4VALLÉES

🗺 How To

Getting here/around
Trains connect Geneva (2¼ hours) and Lausanne (1½ hours) with Le Châble in the valley, from where a cable car glides up to Verbier in 16 minutes; cheaper buses take 25 minutes.

When to go June to mid-October.

Nuts & Bolts The Médran cable car and La Chaux Express chairlift transport bikes. Bike Park day passes cover lifts. Single-trail (*singletrailverbier.com*) and École Suisse de VTT (*ecole-suisse-vtt.ch*) are recommended bike schools.

© VERBIER 4VALLÉES

RHKAMEN/GETTY IMAGES

Top left Verbier Bike Park
Below left Fat-tyre scooters, Verbier
Left Cabane du Mont Fort

Verbier Bike Park The bike park's trail hub is Les Ruinettes, reached from Verbier by the Médran cable car from also transports bikes. Just like ski runs, 19km of downhill descents and technical jumps are colour-graded by difficulty. Beginners can cut their teeth on the easy green Tsenelle flow trail (1.9km) from Fontanet to La Chaux, and the fun Tsopu blue (2.4km) from trail hub Les Ruinettes. European downhill championships are frequently held on official competition track Tire's Fire, and four enduro trails (7.7km to 18.8km) wind beyond Verbier to Le Châble (822m) in the valley. Download trail maps at verbierbikepark.ch.

Up to Cabane du Mont Fort Pair a scenic mountain-bike ride along intermediate tracks from Verbier (30km, 2–3hr) with an overnight at the resort's most legendary mountain hut. Teetering atop a craggy rock at 2457m, sunset and sunrise from the terrace above the clouds or cosy wood-panelled dorms sleeping two, three or six is unforgettable. Ditto for the perfect croissants and trompe l'oeil apricots crafted on-site by baker–pastry chef Fabien Navilloux in what must be Switzerland's highest bakery.

Family Fun Tear down the mountainside on a chunky *trottinette* (hairnet and helmet included in fat-tyre scooter rental; from 8yrs) from the top of the Savoleyres or Les Ruinettes cable cars.

Verbier Bike Festival Pair e-biking with gourmet snacking and music during Verbier's headline biking fest *(verbierbikefestival. com);* four days in mid-August.

🚲 Top Rides

Intermediate-Hard:
Verbier – Col de Mille
(12km / +1500m climb)

A big alpine climb on gravel and trail up to the Col de Mille (2472m) where you can have a well deserved beverage. The reward is a huge panoramic view over the Val de Bagnes, Mont Blanc Massif and Rhône Valley. I love the sense of wilderness and the epic descent- fast, rocky, and grin-inducing all the way back down.

Easy: **Verbier – La Tzoumaz** (5km descent).

A smooth, purpose-built flow trail winding through alpine forest with endless berms and rollers. You can cruise it at any pace, and the trail through the forest makes it a joyful ride all the way down.

■ **Recommended by Sascha Panayotopoulos,** *biker & chalet B&B owners @ rideinnverbier*

19 Ice
AGE

GLACIER | SPORTS | ENVIRONMENT

In the Upper Valais, Aletsch's spectacular 23km-long superhighway of a glacier unearths action adventures in spades. Shimmering glacier views from hiking trails and ski pistes above are soul-soaring, but for the hardest hitting adrenalin surge, get stuck in between crevasses on the UNESCO-listed ice.

BRUNOKI/SHUTTERSTOCK

VALAIS EXPERIENCES

🔖 How To

Getting here/around
Head by car or regular SBB train to old-world village Fiesch, 20km north of Brig in the valley; or the car-free mountain villages of Riederalp (accessed by gondola from Mörel) or Bettmeralp (gondola from its valley station). Onward cable cars from all three villages transport you closer to the ice.

When to go June to September for hiking and climbing, December to April for snowy ski adventures.

PETER MOULTON/ALAMY

Panoramic Highs

Floating on Air Activate your head for heights to tackle the ultimate panoramic platform from which to stare dumbstruck at the Aletsch Glacier: the **Aletschji–Grünsee Hängebrücke**. This 124m-long suspension bridge straddles the 80m-deep **Massa Gorge**, at the foot of Aletsch. Pick up the summer-only walking trail (11.4km, five hours) on alpine pastures in Riederalp (1925m) or Belalp (2100m, reached by PostBus from Brig).

Glacier World With its whitewashed chapel on a hill and quaint main street where kids and luggage are pulled along in wooden sledges in winter, car-free **Bettmeralp** (1900m) is the stuff of Swiss alpine dreams. Eagle-eye glacier views from its Bettmerhorn cable-car top station are the icing on the cake. Summer or winter, exiting at an icy 2647m, follow the walkway

YUESTOCK/SHUTTERSTOCK

⚜ Belle Époque Glamour

The walking trail from Fiescheralp to Märjela passes ruins of Hotel Jungfrau (1871), an alpine oasis of sophistication during the belle époque. Fiesch's **Hotel du Glacier** (aletsch-duglacier. ch) from 1866, still provides shelter and nourishment to guests in search of winter snow, summer ice and crisp mountain air.

Top left Aletschji–Grünsee Hängebrücke
Left Bettmeralp **Above** Hotel du Glacier

to Glacier World to unravel 19th-century glacier exploration and natural life on the glacier (fleas, crevasses, caves, how it takes 10 years for 1m of fresh snow to become 1cm of glacial ice, etc) inside the bunker-style exhibition space.

Summer Trails Signposted walking trails in front of the top Bettmerhorn cable-car station include the **Unesco Höhenweg** (3km, three hours), a tough scramble across rocks to Eggishorn (2869m) where a mind-blowing panorama unfolds. The easier, more accessible approach to Eggishorn is by cable car from **Fiesch.** Signposted walking trails in front of the top Bettmerhorn cable-car station include the Unesco Höhenweg (3km, three hours), a tough scramble across rocks to Eggishorn (2869m) where a mind-blowing panorama unfolds. The easier, more accessible approach to Eggishorn is by cable car from Fiesch village (1049m), with a change of cable car in Fiescheralp (2212m). At the summit, a family-friendly circular path (one hour) ensnares nine 'glacier lounges' with

ⓘ Need to Know

■ Walking with crampons or ski touring on the Aletsch Glacier is only allowed with a guide and the correct equipment.

■ Don't underestimate the physical effort of glacier hiking. A reasonable level of fitness, agility and surefoot-ed-ness is essential.

■ Glacier hikes with a mountain guide don't require any mountaineering experience, but you will be provided with crampons and a harness, and will be roped.

■ Wear gloves and long trousers on glacier hikes to protect your hands and knees. Should you slip or fall, razor-sharp ice crystals can shred your skin like glass.

■ Bring sunglasses, sun protection, plenty of water. Hiking poles are handy for summertime walks.

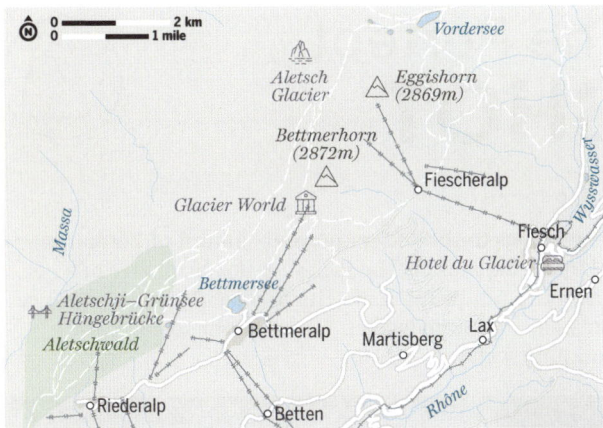

Left Aletsch Glacier
Below Konkordiahütte

telescopes and 'fun fact' panels about the Alps' longest ice flow.

Down on the Ice

Guided summer treks Day hikes led by mountain guides at **Bergsteigerzentrum Aletsch** *(bergsteiger zentrum.ch)* in Fiesch are a dramatic encounter with a retreating glacier. On a sunny day in July on the Aletsch Glacier, 80 cu metres of ice are said to melt every second. Squatting on a rock to picnic on the apocalyptic rubble of the Kranzberg moraine – one of two moraines ribboning down the Aletsch Glacier – is unforgettable. Knowing that ice plunges 400m deep beneath your feet is humbling; contemplating the 30% of its ice mass that this phenomenal glacier has lost since 1860 and the further 90% it's predicted to lose by 2100 is simply unsettling.

Glacial Sleepover More challenging two-day treks with a guide overnight at the legendary **Konkordiahütte** *(konkordiahuette.ch)*, at a breathtaking 2800m above Konkordiaplatz (itself, a spectacular 'platz' or square of ice on the glacier spanning 6 sq km). When the mountain hut was built on a rocky spur in 1869, it bordered the ice. Today, you have to stagger up 526 metal steps (increased from 450 steps in 2023) from the fast-retreating glacier to access it. In winter ski-touring treks here, likewise led by guides across the snow-covered glacier, are breathtakingly magical.

20 The Perfect **SHOT**

HIKING | MATTERHORN | PHOTOGRAPHY

A puff cloud invariably clings to the 4478m hooked summit of Zermatt's absurdly perfect, one-of-a-kind peak, making the jack-in-a-box brilliance of a cloudless Matterhorn all the more wondrous. Enjoy its spectacular omnipresence on this high-drama circular hike around five lakes. Count 3–4hr to cover the 10km of relatively easy, mountain walking.

MUMEMORIES/SHUTTERSTOCK

📷 Photo Op

The Matterhorn (pictured) has repeatedly become a powerful backdrop to commissioned assignments. Early morning and before/after sunset are my favourite times to shoot, obviously. In past years I've have been able to shoot in winter at **Zermatt Unplugged** (*zermatt-unplugged.ch*) – go if you can! One of the acoustic stages is at Riffelhaus where you have an amazing view onto the Matterhorn.

■ *Recommended by Melanie Uhkötter, Swiss photographer @mell.melanieuhkoetter*

🗺 Trip Notes

Getting here/around Funicular train from Zermatt's **Sunnegga–Rothorn valley station** to **Sunnegga** Funicular train from Zermatt's Sunnegga–Rothorn valley station to Sunnegga (2288m), then onward bubble to Blauherd (2571m). On the mountain, follow yellow '5 Seeweg' (5 Lakes Trail) signs.

When to go May to September when cable cars run and skies are blue. June is a riot of wild flowers. August gets busy and can be stormy.

Refuel Matterhorn-swoon over coffee or cheese fondue on the spectacular terrace of mountain restaurant **Fluhalp** (2620m), immediately above Stellisee.

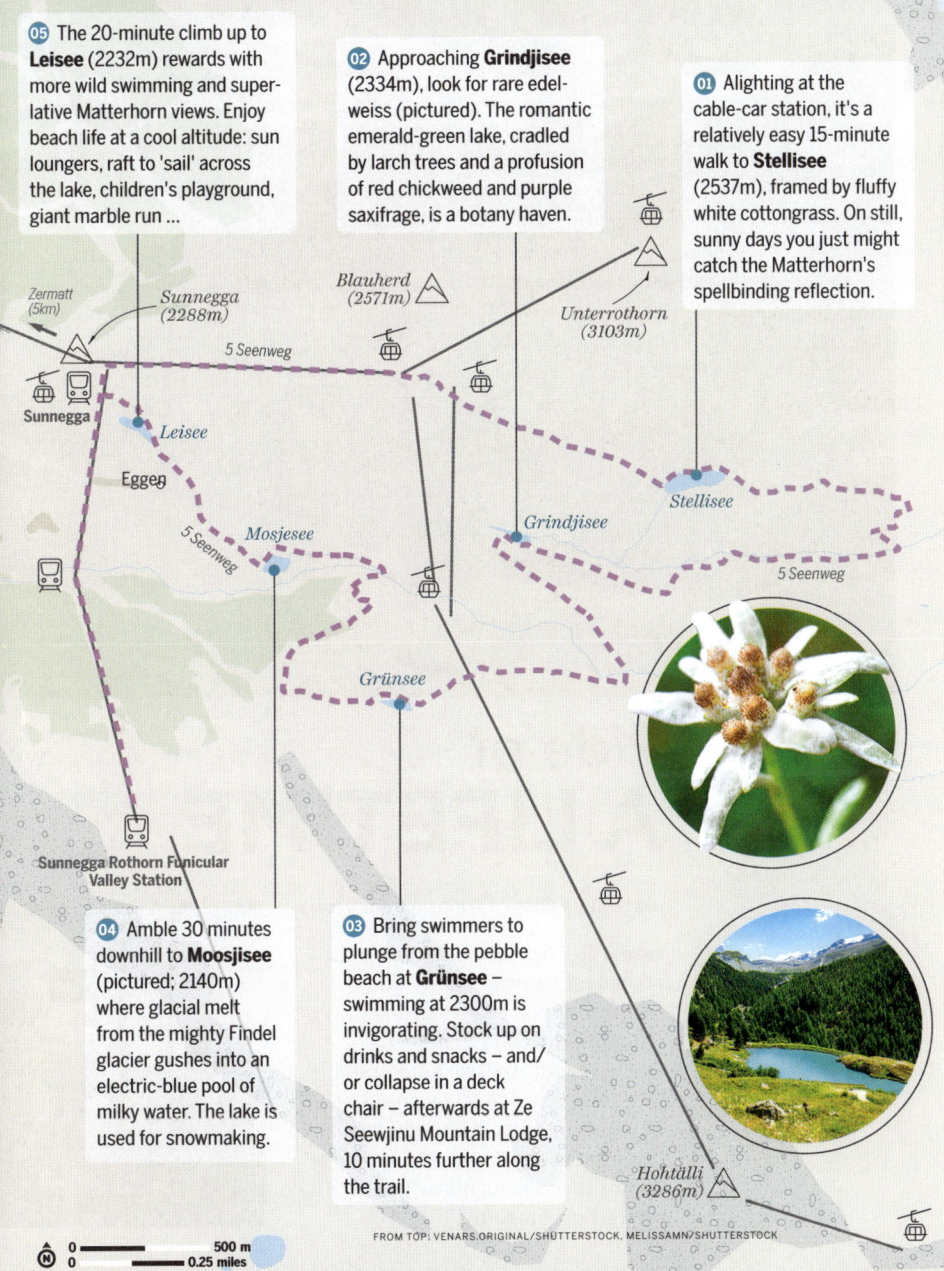

05 The 20-minute climb up to **Leisee** (2232m) rewards with more wild swimming and superlative Matterhorn views. Enjoy beach life at a cool altitude: sun loungers, raft to 'sail' across the lake, children's playground, giant marble run ...

02 Approaching **Grindjisee** (2334m), look for rare edelweiss (pictured). The romantic emerald-green lake, cradled by larch trees and a profusion of red chickweed and purple saxifrage, is a botany haven.

01 Alighting at the cable-car station, it's a relatively easy 15-minute walk to **Stellisee** (2537m), framed by fluffy white cottongrass. On still, sunny days you just might catch the Matterhorn's spellbinding reflection.

Zermatt (5km)

Sunnegga (2288m)

Blauherd (2571m)

Unterrothorn (3103m)

5 Seenweg

Sunnegga

Leisee

Eggen

5 Seenweg

Mosjesee

Grindjisee

Stellisee

5 Seenweg

Grünsee

Sunnegga Rothorn Funicular Valley Station

04 Amble 30 minutes downhill to **Moosjisee** (pictured; 2140m) where glacial melt from the mighty Findel glacier gushes into an electric-blue pool of milky water. The lake is used for snowmaking.

03 Bring swimmers to plunge from the pebble beach at **Grünsee** – swimming at 2300m is invigorating. Stock up on drinks and snacks – and/ or collapse in a deck chair – afterwards at Ze Seewjinu Mountain Lodge, 10 minutes further along the trail.

Hohtälli (3286m)

0 ___ 500 m
0 ___ 0.25 miles

FROM TOP: VENARS.ORIGINAL/SHUTTERSTOCK, MELISSAMN/SHUTTERSTOCK

21

Ride of
A LIFETIME

HISTORIC RAILWAY | HIKING | BIG VIEWS

Europe's highest open-air cogwheel railway has climbed through picture-postcard scenery from downtown Zermatt to Gornergrat (3089m) since 1898. Needless to say, the impossibly bewitching, diva Matterhorn dominates the train ride. Make a day of it – tickets allow you to hop on and off en route.

BERNSTEIN/SHUTTERSTOCK

🗺 **How To**

Getting here/around

Trains depart daily year-round from Gornergrat train station, opposite Zermatt's SBB railway station on Bahnhof-platz. Journey time up to Gornergrat is 30 minutes.

When to go Summer

for hiking; winter for snowshoeing, skiing and 'snow globe' romance. Whatever the season, the weather changes fast on the summit. Bring layers.

Buying tickets

Tickets don't sell out *(gornergrat.ch/en);* buy on the day (or when you're certain of a good weather forecast), to ensure superlative views.

JENNYWONDERLAND/SHUTTERSTOCK

The Ascent

ALEXANDRE ROSA/SHUTTERSTOCK

Inching slowly and noisily uphill aboard Zermatt's rattling storybook **Gornergratbahn**, it's not difficult to time-travel back to 1898. Larch forests and the Vispa River give way to lime-green meadows, Swiss stone pines, rocky peaks and blinding white snow fields as the rust-coloured train staggers up gradients of up to 20% for 9.4km. It's impossible not to be transfixed by the kaleidoscope of alpine grandeur framed by carriage windows. Spot black-nosed, woolly white sheep grazing on green pastures at Riffelberg – or, simpler still, track the flock in their summer habitat with the aid of GPS sheep collars. Higher up in snowy scapes, 'just-married' couples posing in their wedding attire for photographers is a common sighting.

📖 **Best Foot Forward**

Originally intended as a summer-only leisure railway, it was not until 1909 that the Gornergratbahn was extended to its current top-of-the-world perch. Until then, trains arrived 71m below the current station. Porters were at hand to carry rich visitors to the summit in sedan chairs. Everyone else walked.

Top left and left Gornergratbahn
Above Gornergrat train station

Summiting

Alight at the top to a hypnotic panorama of the Monte Rosa massif, the retreating tongue of the **Gornergrat glacier** set like a diamond in a ring of 29 peaks above 4000m. Spot Switzerland's highest peak Dufourspitze (4634m) among them. At sunrise and sunset all this natural grandeur is extra magical.

Ramen turkey and gyoza bowls cooked up at Asian fusion restaurant **Tiger Bowl** fuel the overwhelmingly international tourist crowd that ventures up here. Your train ticket includes admission to the summit's virtual-reality **Zooom the Matterhorn** exhibition and **3D cinema** which sees you paragliding around the Matterhorn and battling icy winds, autumnal storms and other wild elements.

The neighbouring whitewashed chapel **Kapelle Bernhard von Aosta** was built in 1950 for guests from the summit's landmark **Kulmhotel Gornergrat** (gornergrat-kulm. ch) to attend mass – until then it was held in

🚆 Train Tips

Avoid morning rush hour
If you're only planning on a leisurely stroll around the summit, catch a late-morning train to avoid the early-morning crush of day hikers using the Gornergrat-bahn to access high-altitude trails.

Priority boarding
Assuming you'd prefer not to stand for the duration of the 30-minute journey, it's worth paying the extra Chf7 for 'priority boarding'. Not only does this guarantee you a bum-numbing seat in a rickety old carriage – it also means you get first dibs at bagging one by the window. Sit on the right (when facing up the mountain) for the best views.

Cheap tickets Cut costs by embarking on the trip after 3.30pm when reduced fares kick in.

the hotel dining room. Toast your successful ascent with a glass of bubbly Fondant and a cheese or Toblerone chocolate or fondue on the sun-soaked (invariably very very windy) terrace of huge, century-old hotel, built in 1910 for Zermatt's first summer tourists. Stay overnight to to soak it all up. Once the crowds leave for the day, the solitude and panoramas at Switzerland's highest hotel is off-the-charts magical. **Star-gaze** here, with or without a guide – astronomers accompany guests to the hotel's 'dome room' observatory to observe the night sky through a telescope.

The Descent

Ride the train down to **Rotenboden** (2815m). From here it is a 10-minute walk, through an alpine garden and along a rocky footpath – wear trainers or sturdy shoes – to **Riffelsee** (2770m). On sunny days, see the Matterhorn famously reflected in the lake's mirror-like waters.

Walk downhill for 40 scenic minutes (3km) to **Riffelberg** (2583m), from where you can hop back on the Gornergrat train to Zermatt (or continue walking down). Grab drinks or lunch on the sun-drenched terrace at the eponymous self-service restaurant – all to swoon, of course, over more glorious views of the Matterhorn and, on the mountainside in the foreground, the bijou **Bruder Klaus Chapel** famously shaped like the Weisshorn peak across the valley.

FROM LEFT: PANDORA PICTURES/SHUTTERSTOCK, FELIX LIPOV/SHUTTERSTOCK

VALAIS EXPERIENCES

Left Kulmhotel Gornergrat and observatory
Above Bruder Klaus Chapel

NIX DORF, CC BY-SA 4.0,
VIA WIKIMEDIA COMMONS ®

Changing Topography

**CLIMATIC
ENCOUNTERS:
A LANDSCAPE
ON THE MOVE**
Living in harmony
with nature – and
the world at large
– has always been
something the
famously neutral
Swiss have always
been enviably good
at. No gorge or
mountain has ever
really proven too
deep or too high. Yet
as planet Earth heats
up, change is in the
air.

Herculean Feats

Given the country's extreme topography (the unfathomable
Matterhorn that defies trigonometry, for starters), you'd
think geography would have the upper hand in Switzerland.
Yet the infallible, cool-headed Swiss have long risen to the
challenge its physical diversity presents. No other small
country boasts such Herculean feats: Europe's highest train
station (Jungfraujoch, 3454m), the world's steepest funicular (Stoosbahn, 110% gradient), the longest deepest rail
tunnel (Gotthard Base Tunnel, 57km). Kilometres of tunnels
and caverns were dug inside a mountain on the St Gotthard
Pass (2106m) to build a secret fortress during WWII,
created to defend the country against attack from Italy and
an official military secret until 2021. On the nearby Grimsel
Pass (p171), when a crack appeared in the 113m-high wall
of the Spitallamm Dam in the 1960s, engineers simply set
about designing a new wall to replace the 1920s original
which, at the time, was hailed as the world's highest. The
new mega wall – 220,000 cubic m of glittering white concrete – went into operation in 2025.

Trouble in Paradise

On 11 August 2025 the daily weather balloon released by
MétéoSuisse north of Lake Geneva in Payerne, measured a
troubling 5113m as the altitude at which temperatures drop
below zero. Warming temperatures might make snow cover
at lower altitudes frustratingly uncertain for the country's
over-zealous winter skiers, but far more sinister is the risk
the warming climate poses to Switzerland's mountain set-
tlements. In June 2024, a cloudburst sent millions of tons of
rock crashing down into Ticinio's remote Val Bavona, wiping

Left Stoosbahn
Centre Spitallamm Dam
Right Blatten

MAHG/SHUTTERSTOCK

MICHAEL BUHOLZER/EPA/SHUTTERSTOCK

out part of the village of Bignasco and killing five people. In May 2025, the village of Blatten in the Valais was destroyed after the Birch Glacier collapsed, triggering a devastating avalanche of rock, rubble and mud – an estimated 9 million cubic metres – that buried the village. The few houses left standing were then flooded by the nearby Lonza River, dammed by the debris. Geologists, monitoring the glacier for months previously, had advised the 300 people living in the village to evacuate days earlier. It is doubtful they will ever return, such is the devastation of their once picture-postcard alpine hamlet of dark timber chalets and geranium flower boxes.

> A cloudburst sent millions of tons of rock crashing down into Ticinio's remote Val Bavona, wiping out part of the village of Bignasco and killing five people

On the Watch

Monitoring mountains and evacuating villages at risk is not new. In Graubünden, the 70 or so villagers living in the Grisons hamlet of Brienz have been ordered to leave on numerous occasions in the past few years. In August 2025 it was still forbidden to enter the ghost village, empty of inhabitants since its evacuation due to high rockfall risk the previous November. An electronic surveillance system above the village detects and measures unnatural movement in the mountain. Scientists know that accelerated rock erosion is due to melting permafrost, a geological gluey layer formed by ice, rock and earth above altitudes of 2500m and covering – or rather stabilising – 5% of Swiss land. As the ice within it melts, so its natural glue-like super power diminishes.

🏠 The Power of Prayer

Each year on St Ignatius Day (31 July) villagers in Fiesch and Fieschertal walk at dawn up to the bijou Maria Hilf chapel (1693) deep in the Ernernwald (forest). In the 17th century the intention of this 'glacial procession' was simple: to summon up divine intervention to stop the almighty Aletsch Glacier swallowing up alpine pastures, agricultural land, all sorts, with its uncontrollable tongues of ice. The prayer has since changed. The intention now, officially logged with Pope Benedict XVI in 2010, is to protect the dangerously receding glacier and so safeguard the villagers' prime water source and lifeline.

Listings

BEST OF THE REST

 ### Long Lazy Lunches

Le Cube Varone €

Overlooking vines irrigated by the 15th-century Bisse de Clavau, this 'cube' of a winegrower's hut pairs Maison Barone wines with air-dried beef on a parasol-shaded terrace above Sion.

Fluhalp €€

One of Zermatt's easiest mountain restaurants to access, reached by cable car and a 15-minute walk along a footpath to its dramatic perch at 2620m. Spend hours Matterhorn-swooning over coffee or fondue on its spectacular terrace.

L'Enclos de Valère €€

Game (goat, chamois, venison) dominates the menu at this institution of a traditional restaurant in Sion. The cottage garden is a delight on sunny days – make no plans for the afternoon.

Chez Dany €€€€

Heidi's Switzerland is alive and well at Verbier's most iconic mountain restaurant, aka this geranium-strewn chalet at 1720m. In winter, ski here, or snowmobile up and sledge home.

Chez Vrony €€€

In Zermatt ride the Sunnegga Express funicular to 2288m, then ski or summer-hike to Zermatt's iconic piste-side address for cheese dishes, sausage from Vrony's own cows, and burgers.

Mountain Highs

Matterhorn Glacier Paradise

Little competes with the 360-degree panorama atop Klein Matterhorn (3883m), accessed from Zermatt town by three cable cars culminating with this iconic ride. Admire 14 glaciers and 40-odd peaks over 4000m, including the Matterhorn.

Matterhorn Alpine Crossing

Glide across the world's highest alpine border by cableway, linking Zermatt's Klein Matterhorn (3883m) with Cervinia's Testa Grigia (3458m) in Italy without a single supporting pylon. It links two of Europe's most prized ski resorts.

Mont 4 Zipline

From Verbier, ride the cable car up to Mont Fort to admire 4000m-plus peaks and dip into Europe's highest-altitude cheese fondue at Igloo Mont Fort. Harness the daredevil in you for the descent: fly back down on a zip line.

Hospice du Grand St Bernard

Follow in the footsteps of ancient Via Francigena pilgrims to this high-altitude hospice and museum on the remote Col du Grand St Bernard. Plan a scenic road trip in summer, unforgettable ski-touring expedition in winter.

 ### Downtown Verbier Dines

Fer à Cheval €€

A decades-old HQ for local mountain guys, The Horseshoe is as popular for daytime drinks as it is for tasty salads, burgers and grilled meats. Great people-watching outside, a fascinating collection of Verbier ski memorabilia inside.

Milk Bar €€

This 1930s icon in Verbier is famous for its hot chocolate, milkshakes, crepes and ice-cream sundaes, served in a cosy interior. Flowers and mountains views festoon its summer rooftop.

Arctic Juice & Cafe €

Organic coffee, juices squeezed to order, bowls, punchy salads and brunch pull in a chic set at this new-gen coffee shop by the Medran cable car. Music, books to browse, sofas and sun terrace make it an appealing all-day hangout.

Le Caveau €€

Eyeball mountain peaks from the terrace of Verbier's historic fondue restaurant, with summer terrace and doorway fashioned like an oak wine barrel. The ultimate splurge: a pot of bubbling cheese laced with champagne and truffles.

Good-Value Skiing

Ovronnaz

With eight lifts and 30km of downhill runs, this bijou 1950s resort is a family-friendly day flit from Martigny.

Nendaz

In the world-renowned 4 Vallées ski area, this village offers more bang for your buck. Cheaper ski passes cover 220km of slopes in neighbouring Veysonnaz and Thyon–Les Collons.

Le Tzoumaz

Ski Verbier 'on the cheap' by staying in this low-key village. Additional tasty perks: a heart-pounding sledge run with a 700m vertical descent and potence (a tower of marinated beef chunks) at Restaurant Les Trappeurs.

Crans-Montana

Skiing is intermediate paradise, with, almost exclusively south-facing slopes and 360-degree vistas from the Matterhorn to Mont Blanc.

Cultural Riches

Musée Valaisan des Bisses

Gen up on the fascinating history and prized backstories behind the Valais' unique *bisses* (irrigation channels) at this museum, in a frescoed 17th-century house in Botyre, 8km north of Sion.

Fondation Pierre Gianadda

Roman temple ruins tango with one of Switzerland's best modern sculpture collections at Martigny's celebrated modern-art gallery. Don't miss Rodin's *Le Baiser* (1886), the second of four 'kisses' by the French sculptor.

Foire du Valais

Pair October's grape harvest with the Foire du Valais, a 10-day fair, showcasing local cuisine, viticulture, music, culture and *combat des reines* (cow fight) in Martigny's Roman amphitheatre.

Château de Tourbillon

It's a steep 15-minute walk through vines to the beautiful ruins of Sion's episcopal palace, used until 1371. Rhône Valley views are equally sweeping from sister castle Château de Valère.

Barryland

Devour historical anecdotes and everything there is to know about Switzerland's most loveable icon, the St Bernard dog, at this address designed like a paw print in Martigny.

Laiterie de Verbier

July to September, learn how wheels of creamy Raclette du Valais with are made with father-and-son cheesemakers Roger and Marc at Verbier's cheese dairy. Book a hotly contested spot at Verbier tourist office (*verbier.ch*).

Zermatt Crawl

Fuch's €

Grab a snack or picnic at Zermatt's bakery: go for a Chf5 Bäcker hot dog or sandwich, protein-packed fruit-nut loaf or quarkini (donut ball).

Snowboat

Chill with a cool crowd on a rooftop overlooking the rushing glacial waters of the Vispa River. Tasty international fare, DJ sets and live music.

Stefanie's Crêperie €

This hole-in-the-wall icon whips up crepes with sweet or savoury (cheese fondue with cherry brandy!) toppings. A queue marks the spot.

Potato €€€

With produce sourced within 99km and ceiling lamps crafted from wooden veg crates, you'll don't get more local – or brilliantly creative than this neobistro on Bahnhofstrasse. Dinner only.

Train Trip
GLACIER EXPRESS

22

ALPINE ICON | TRAIN TRAVEL | GLAMOUR

▬▬▬ One of those irresistible 'champagne picnic' train journeys, this mythic trip has been in the discerning traveller's little black book since the 1930s. Allow eight hours – or savour it slowly, interwoven with overnights in some of Switzerland's most fashionable alpine resorts.

VIACHESLAV LOPATIN/SHUTTERSTOCK

🗺️ **How To**

Getting here Board in Zermatt's central train station. Count on eight hours to the end of the line in St Moritz.

When to go Winter for snow-globe romance, May to September for green landscapes. Whatever the season, a clear blue sky is imperative.

Tickets Reserve tickets up to 93 days in advance (glacierexpress. ch). Everyone pays the Chf49 reservation fee on top of the ticket (1st/2nd class Chf159/272). Swiss rail cards, Eurail and InterRail pass discounts apply.

I VIEWFINDER/SHUTTERSTOCK

Vintage Slow Motion

Gorging on one cinematic shot after another of peaks, lakes, gushing white water, deep gorges and other natural landscapes through oversized panoramic windows is what riding this bucket-list red train is about. Pulled by steam engine when it first puffed out of Zermatt in 1930, the iconic Glacier Express traverses 91 tunnels and 291 bridges on its gloriously slow journey in to ritzy St Moritz.

Creeping along at 10km/h at times, the average speed on this 290km-long journey is just 42km/h. Throughout the trip, listen for a gong indicating relevant audio commentary on headphones provided to every passenger on the train's modern 'infotainment' system. Connect your device to the free wi-fi, follow your train journey in real time on a map, and get in the right headspace with two music

AARONCHENPS2/SHUTTERSTOCK

📷 **Photography Hack**

Panoramic windows on Glacier Express carriages don't open. Photographers can clamour for a spot at an open window between carriages or ditch the glamour train for cheaper, regular SBB trains. In Andermatt and elsewhere, don't board the Glacier Express by mistake.

Top left Landwasser Viaduct (p133)
Left Glacier Express
Above Zermatt train station

channels playing Swiss folk songs or 1980s Swiss pop classics.

Tech tip off: power points, next to window seats only, are Swiss plug sockets – bring an adaptor for non-Swiss plugs should you need to charge your phone.

Natural Highs

If you can't bear the thought of sitting all day in a carriage full of strangers – love it or hate it, socialising is an unavoidable part of the experience – consider doing just one section of the route instead: the highest point of the journey is the Disentis to Andermatt leg (one hour) across the breathtaking **Oberalp Pass**.

It's easy to know when the train hits the expansive pass. At 2044m above sea level, it's the incongruous location for a lighthouse. The red-and-white beacon is a smaller replica of the lighthouse that once stood at the mouth of the Rhine at the Hook of Holland, the Netherlands. Erected close to the Rhine's source at Lai da Tuma, it champions the start of

ⓘ Good to Know

Dining

There is no dining car. Formal waitstaff zip through 2nd-class carriages balancing trays of ordered drinks; count on Chf6.50/7 for a cappuccino/Zermatt craft beer. Lunch (2-/3-/4 course Chf42/49/54) can only be pre-ordered online. If you do this, your table (rather inconveniently) will already be laid when you board the train, leaving you very little space to spread out in the hours preceding your lunch arriving.

Excellence Class

Given the price tag – a 1st-class ticket, plus Chf490 for a seat reservation – not all Glacier Express trains include this luxe carriage with a champagne welcome, five-course gastronomy and personal concierge.

Left Glacier Express
Below Oberalp Pass

this major European waterway. Each year a local celebrity or media personality is named honorary lighthouse keeper, receiving an oversized key at an annual ceremony.

If you've been on the train since Zermatt, quaint **Disentis** is a great spot to stretch your legs. Passengers briefly hop onto the station platform here while the train switches from the cogwheel engine it needed for the climb up to the Oberalp Pass. On the platform, drink in the attractive village's unique Romansch vibe. Look up to admire the Benedictine monastery, with a lavishly stuccoed baroque church (1683), towering on a hillside above.

The Final Leg

The dazzling jewel in the crown on the final leg between Chur and St Moritz, just before the village of **Filisur**, is the emblematic **Landwasser Viaduct**. This six-arch, 65m-high aqueduct pre-dates the Glacier Express and is the single manmade sight every passenger on the train is impatient to see. It does not disappoint.

Natural Hurdles

The Glacier Express doesn't run at all between mid-October and mid-December. Remember too, that it's a mountain train: last-minute cancellations due to lines blocked by snow or rockfall happen with surprising frequency (your reserved journey will still take place, but on regular lines).

TICINO

PEAKS | LAKES | VALLEYS

RESEARCHED BY MARC DI DUCA

0 10 km
N
0 5 miles

Gaze in awe at the power of the Foroglio (pictured; p149) **waterfall**
🚌 40min from Locarno

SWITZERLAND

Have a game of giant marbles in wonderful Val Verzasca (p148)
🚗 15min from Locarno

Biasca

Verzasca

Scramble around the high ramparts of Bellinzona's Castelgrande (p139)
🚶 20min from Bellinzona station

Take a scenic train trip into Italy on the Centovalli Railway (p151)
🚆 Depart from Locarno train station

Bellinzona

Ascend Monte San Salvatore (p144) **for a forest hike down to Morcote**
🚡 15min from Lugano

Maggia

Locarno

Ascona

Lago Maggiore

ITALY

Hike Lugano's Olive Trail along the soothing shores of Lake Lugano to the pretty village of Gandria (p140)
🚌 20min from Lugano

Lugano

Lago di Lugano

TICINO
Trip Builder

The Italian-speaking canton of Ticino in Switzerland's far south is like a breathe of warm, Mediterranean air. Palm-fringed lakes Lugano and Maggiore provide a shimmering contrast to the Alps while the lost-in-time valleys are revelations for those looking for less-touristed alpine adventures.

Practicalities

ARRIVING

Very few arrive in Ticino by air. The train stations in Bellizona, Locarno and Lugano are all in the town centre and all three cities have good bus networks.

MONEY

The Ticino Ticket is handed out by 500 accommodation providers and gives free access to transport and discounts at countless attractions.

FIND YOUR WAY

Calling and data plans from all other countries simply switch to potentially ruinous roaming in Switzerland. Get a local or e-SIM.

WHERE TO STAY

Town/Village	Pro/Con
Lugano	Lots of hiking possibilities. Lake views. Cramped centre.
Locarno	Wonderful lake setting. Access to the Western Valleys. Less going on.
Bellinzona	Central location with historical interest. No lake setting.

EATING & DRINKING

A grotto restaurant is a rustic tavern serving typical Ticino cuisine. Some are seasonal affairs.

Locally produced cheese and occasionally other dairy products can be purchased from outdoor fridges at strategic points in the valleys. Payment is via an honesty box (pictured below left).

Best grotto restaurant Grotto Cà Rossa

Must-try Ticino wines at Alpe Vicania (pictured top left)

GETTING AROUND

Train Locarno, Lugano and Bellinzona are all linked by Switzerland's famously efficient train system.

Bus Ticino's valleys are accessible by bus and it's the best way to get around the large towns.

Car This is the best mode of transport for exploring Ticino's valleys.

TICINO FIND YOUR FEET

JAN-MAR

Valleys are essentially closed for business though skiing keeps Bosco/Gurin lively.

APR-JUN

Valleys open up, flowers reappear in Locarno and Lugano, and the first hot days arrive.

JUL-SEP

While the lake towns swelter in the humid air, snow remains in some high spots.

OCT-DEC

The mixed forests of the valleys burst into fiery autumnal hues.

23 History in
BELLINZONA

CASTLES | HISTORY | ARCHITECTURE

Ticino's least well-known town is its capital, Bellinzona, a sprawl of 45,000 souls situated in the heart of the canton. Lacking a dramatic lakeside settings of Locarno and Lugano, Bellinzona makes up for its shortcomings with knockout views of snowcapped mountains and a trio of magnificent UNESCO-listed medieval castles – Castelgrande, Castello di Montebello and Castello di Sasso Corbaro – the main reasons to come here.

ISIDRO LOPEZ/SHUTTERSTOCK

📍 How To

Getting here The Ticinese capital is linked with the rest of Switzerland and northern Italy by regular trains.

When to go Bellinzona is a great place to visit year-round.

Tickets Before you click that 'online ticket' button on the castle website, it may be good to know that most of Castelgrande is free to scramble around at will. The ticket is only valid for the museum.

ANTONIO FILIPPI/SHUTTERSTOCK

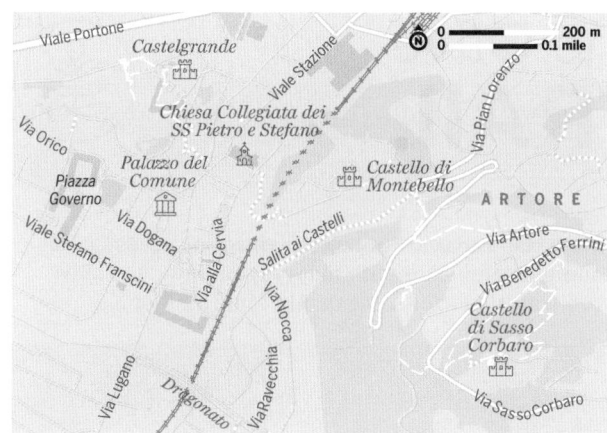

Top left Castelgrande
Bottom left Palazzo del Comune

Castles & Cobblestones

Town centre While the castles are the town's big attractions, its historic centre is also worth a stroll with its Renaissance churches, flower-draped alleys, arcaded streets and cafe-rimmed piazzas brimming with life. On Piazza Collegiata you'll find the **Chiesa Collegiata dei SS Pietro e Stefano**, an exquisite church lavishly adorned with frescoes and baroque stucco. The cobblestone square outside is framed by 18th-century patrician houses, many with decorative wrought-iron balconies. The well-preserved Renaissance **Palazzo del Comune** has a three-storey inner courtyard of loggias and frescoes showing historic scenes of Bellinzona.

Castelgrande The best thing about Bellinzona's UNESCO-listed fortress are its towers and ramparts, which can be climbed and scaled for great photo ops. Be aware that some of the towers have very narrow flights of steps that can get claustrophobic at busy times. The line of defensive walls that barrels out for 450m to the west resembles a stretch of the Great Wall of China, and affords panoramas of the town and mountainscape beyond.

Castello di Montebello and Castello di Sasso Corbaro
Bellinzona's 'other' castles are worth the legwork to reach them, if only to say you've bagged the trio. On the other side of the valley to Castlegrande, Castello di Montebello has drawbridges, climbable towers and fascinating archaeological exhibits. From there it's a long climb up switchbacks to high-perched Castello di Sasso Corbaro which flaunts an austere beauty.

 Tibetan Bridge

If you've still got the legs for more hiking, why not take locals' advice and head up into the mountains to the **Tibetan Bridge** (Ponte Tibetano). This swing bridge is high in the hills around 5km west of Bellinzona, rising 130m above the gorge of the Semeitina stream, and stretches over 270m in length, with a walkway approximately 1m wide made of larch wood. Crossing it represents a knee-weakening challenge for some, but safety measures guarantee a risk-free crossing. It is accessed via the Monte Carasso–Curzútt–Mornera cable car from the suburb of Monte Carasso, alighting at Curzútt. From there it's a 2km walk.

24 The Olive TRAIL

HIKING | NATURE | VIEWS

▬▬ This high-rise day out on the trails east of Lugano encapsulates the best the region has to offer – mountains and lakes with many a panorama to enjoy along the way. So pull on your trail shoes for some quality time on foot.

TOBIAS THOMANN/SHUTTERSTOCK

🗺 Trip Notes

Getting here The Funicolare Monte Brè *(montebre.ch)* departs from Cassarate near the lakefront and ascends in two stages to the top of Monte Brè.

When to go This route is best in spring and autumn as even at over 1000m summer temperatures can be too much for comfortable hiking.

All about olives The Olive Trail has 18 multilingual panels on the cultivation of olives and local history.

> ⛰ **Monte Boglia**
>
> An alternative to descending back down to Lake Lugano is to head up from Monte Brè to a second peak, Monte Boglia (pictured; 1516m) which is shared with neighbouring Italy, around a three-hour (5km), quite steep slog. From the top you can see the whole of Lake Lugano.

Lugano

01 Lugano's delightfully old-fashioned **Funicolare Monte Brè** (pictured) makes the journey from Cassarate to the summit in just over 10 minutes, passing over steep stone viaducts and even through a tunnel en route.

02 At 925m, **Monte Brè** is not much of a mountain by Swiss standards but more than makes up for its altitude with incredible lake views from several points around the sprawling summit.

03 It's a 4km downhill hike to lakeside **Gandria**, a shore-hugging village that's one of Switzerland's prettiest. Scramble through the narrow, stepped and arched lanes to find tiny shops and cafes.

Monte Brè (925m)

Via Ruvigliana

Via Aldesago

Via Brè

Via Massago

Via Cantonale

Castagnola

Strada di Fulmignano

Strada di Gandria

Via Riviera

Lago di Lugano

04 From Gandria, the way back on foot to Lugano follows the **Olive Trail** (pictured), a route lined with sub-tropical greenery, olde-worlde hotels, lake views and swimming spots.

05 One of the dreamiest places to take a cooling dip in Lago di Lugano is the **Lido di San Domenico** around halfway along the Olive Trail. Bathers enjoy the shade of chestnut trees between dips.

N
0 — 500 m
0 — 0.25 miles

The Swiss Italians

ANSIPHOTO/SHUTTERSTOCK

ITALY OR SWITZERLAND? THE TICINESE PREFER TO TAKE THE BEST OF BOTH WORLDS

Switzerland is often cited as a country where three (or sometimes four) languages are spoken, but the country only actually has one fully Italian-speaking canton: Ticino. While the Francophone west and German-speaking east dominate Swiss life, Ticino sunnily ambles to a different beat, that of the *bel paese*.

Emerging from the Gotthard Tunnel or descending from the San Bernardino Pass, everything is suddenly different. The tidy flower boxes of red geraniums have been replaced with sprawling bougainvillea, palm trees rustle in a subtropical breeze, there are red terracotta roofs instead of pine shingles and perhaps not quite so many white crosses on red backgrounds. Welcome to Ticino, a little piece of Italy in the Swiss Confederation.

Why is Ticino in Switzerland?

This question crosses the mind of every visitor to Lugano and Locarno as they caress their morning cappuccino under the palm trees of Lake Lugano or Lake Maggiore, listening to the Italian chatter and observing the quite un-Swiss gesticulations of the locals. It may come as something of a surprise to learn that Ticino wasn't part of Italy for almost six centuries. Until the 15th century, the region was part of Lombardy and was ruled over by various northern Italian powers such as the Dukes of Milan. Over the course of the 15th century, the valleys of Ticino were conquered by the Swiss Confederation and from 1512 the region was overseen by a several other cantons. It wasn't until 1803 that Ticino became a fully fledged canton in its own right and it only officially joined the Swiss Confederation in 1815.

But why did the Swiss see Ticino as prized territory? There are many reasons; the Dukes of Milan were a formidable European military power and Ticino formed a buffer zone south of the Alps just in case the Milanese got any big ideas. Also, the Swiss wanted to control the passes (Gotthard and Bernadino) over the Alps for obvious

Left San Bernardino pass
Centre Lake Maggiore
Right Rösti

strategic reasons. They could also set up customs posts and collect revenue from all goods coming through the only two passes north of wealthy Milan.

You might imagine 'reunification' would be a topic in Ticino but you'd be dead wrong. Since 1803, the Ticinese have enjoyed political and economic stability that the rest of the

> You might imagine 'reunification' would be a topic in Ticino but you'd be dead wrong. Since 1803, the Ticinese have enjoyed political and economic stability that the rest of the Italian-speaking world can only dream of.

Italian-speaking world can only dream of. Throughout the 19th and 20th centuries, Italy was much poorer and largely a political basket case, which led to the Ticinese clamping the province ever tighter to Switzerland's underbelly. The canton even became a safe haven for Italian liberals during the *Risorgimento* (Unification of Italy).

Swiss-Italian Identity

Mussolini had his eye on Ticino as part of his *Italia Irredenta* rhetoric - this claimed all Italian-speaking lands for Italy. The Italian fascists tried to infiltrate Ticino newspapers and cultural institutions but the Ticinese were having none of it. Fearing annexation of the canton, the Swiss government promoted the idea of the Swiss-Italian identity, emphasizing to the populace that Ticino was both proudly Italian-speaking *and* Swiss. That idea prevails today, and most Ticinese agree that it has served them pretty well so far.

Where Is my Rösti?

Food is the obvious big difference between Ticino and the rest of Switzerland. Gone is the raclette from most restaurant menus, replaced by polenta and game. Asking for rösti in a typical Ticino grotto restaurant may be met with an awkward silence from your waiter.

But Ticino cuisine is no bland pizza-pasta blow out – as in all regions of Italy 'proper', local cooking can differ greatly to what many consider 'Italian'. Ticino's cookbooks reflect the seasonality of the local landscapes with chestnuts, freshwater fish, game, mountain cheeses and Alpine herbs playing leading roles.

25 Mount San **SALVATORE**

HIKING | VIEWS | FOREST

▬▬▬ This full day out takes you from Lugano's sun-splashed promenade high up into the chestnut forests of Mount San Salvatore, only to descend again for a boat ride back to town. Bring sturdy footwear and a picnic to make the most of the route.

SEARAIN/SHUTTERSTOCK

🗺 Trip Notes

Getting there The Funicolare Monte San Salvatore (*montesansalvatore.ch*) starts in the Paradiso suburb of Lugano. There's plenty of parking at the lower station.

Getting back The Società Navigazione del Lago di Lugano (*lakelugano.ch*) operates the boats back from Morcote to Paradiso.

Short cut If you don't fancy tackling the whole route, from Carona a steep, zigzagging path descends to Meride from where there are trains, buses and boats back to Lugano.

📖 Hermann Hesse

Though a German born near Stuttgart, the writer Hermann Hesse lived the last 43 years of his life in the village of Montagnola on the western slopes of Monte San Salvatore where he died in 1962. It was here that Hesse wrote some of his best-known works including *Siddharta* and *Steppenwolf*.

01 Start the day at the lower station of the **Funicolare Monte San Salvatore** (pictured) in the Paradiso suburb of Lugano. The first train leaves at 9am and you should be on it.

02 The two-stage funicular journey delivers you swiftly to the top of **Monte San Salvatore** (pictured opposite page; 912m) where there's a lot going on in the shape of several viewing points, a cafe and a museum.

03 From the top, take the rocky, steep, downhill trail heading south through the forest. The first stop is the miniature village of **Ciona** with its cobbled streets, tiny squares and church.

04 Another 1.6km brings you to Carona where the botanical gem of **Parco Botanico San Grato** has an exquisite collection of rhododendrons, azaleas and conifers.

05 The trail's finale is a picturesque stretch of chestnut forest, cascading down what seems like a million steps towards beautiful, lakeside **Morcote** (pictured) which you first see from high above, an impressive spectacle.

Lugano

Via Ponte Tresa

Paradiso

Caprino

Via Pian Scairolo

Monte San Salvatore (912m)

ITALY

Via Cantonale

Centro Lugano Sud

Campione d'Italia

Ciona

Via Cantonale

Via Principale

Carona

Melide

Parco Tosi

Strada Cantonale

Parco San Grato

RivaLago Olivella

Lago di Lugano

SWITZERLAND

Alpe Vicania

Riva da Buro

Riva da l'Indipendenza

ITALY

Morcote

N

0 ———— 1 km
0 ———— 0.5 miles

26 Val VERZASCA

HIKING | KIDS' FUN | RIVER SWIMMING

▬ The highlight of any trip to Ticino for many is Val Verzasca extending for 24km northeast of Locarno. Lined with steep walls of limestone rising to 2500m, the valley is speckled with attractions, picturesque villages and natural wonders. It can come as no surprise that this is a rare place in Ticino where you may have to jostle for a parking space.

EVA BOCEK/SHUTTERSTOCK

🗺 How To

When to go The best times to journey up Val Verzasca are between spring and late autumn. In winter, businesses close and transport is limited.

Getting there At least 12 buses a day make the run from Tenero train station to Sonogno in summer.

Parking The day parking card for Chf12 allows you to park anywhere in the valley and saves a lot of messing around with parking meters.

PIXEL CREATOR/SHUTTERSTOCK

IMAGEBROKER.COM/SHUTTERSTOCK

Top left Ponte dei Salti
Below left Verzasca Dam
Left Sonogno

Valley of Emotions

The first emotion Val Verzasca might induce is unease at the sight of the 220m-high **Verzasca Dam** (the world's 36th tallest) that caps the lower end of the valley like huge grey concrete curtains drawn across the show beyond. The dam's claim to fame is that it formed the striking backdrop for scenes in the Bond movie *Golden Eye*.

Arriving in the pint-sized hamlet of **Corippo**, a sense of wonder comes over visitors as they imagine bedding down in Switzerland's smallest village, half of which has been turned into accommodation. But just 3.5km further up the valley comes the joy-inducing highlight of the entire area, the **Ponte dei Salti** (Jumper's Bridge). This delicate, double arched stone hop over the emerald-flowing waters of the River Verzasca is one of the most famous places in the canton. Either side of the bridge, the river's waters have smoothed long channels in the solid rock. These are ideal for swimming though the glacial water is numbingly cold, even in summer.

Fun for the kids and adults awaits between Lavertezzo and Sonogno. The **BoBosco Trail** (*bobosco.ch*) is essentially an XXL marble run and just about the best thing for children to do in Ticino. Val Verzasco comes to an emotional crescendo in pretty **Sonogno** – the main attraction here is the **Wool Centre** (*proverzasca.ch*) where local women spin and knit local fleece into attractive sweaters and blankets.

The BoBosco Trail

Top Ticino kids' attraction, the BoBosco Trail (*bobosco.ch*) 'hiking by stealth' attraction is the work of a genius. Basically, this is a monster marble run, a series of channels, swings, water features, tunnels, mazes and pulleys spread out between Lavertezzo and the bridge at Brione, and then from Gerra to Sonogno (a total distance of 11km).

The large wooden marbles (Chf9), pleasingly heavy in the palm and a great souvenir, can be bought from vending machines at Brione bridge, and several shops and tourist offices along the valley. The XXL marble run is the work of local artists and uses only natural materials.

27 Locarno to Lago di ROBIÈI VALLEY

VIEWS | MOUNTAINS | LAKES

▬ This eclectic journey through the Ticino Alps takes you from the sunny lakeside of subtropical Locarno to the reservoirs fed by Ticino's biggest glacier. Wander ancient villages, gaze up at high-tumbling waterfalls, ride a cable car to 2000m – and still be back in Locarno for dinner.

ROLF E. STAERK/SHUTTERSTOCK

⚠ Tragedy in Val Bavona

Around pretty Fontana, five minutes beyond the bridge at Bignasco, you may notice the road is a temporary affair here, boulders piled up everywhere and no trees. On the last day of June 2024, a cloudburst sent millions of tons of rock down into the valley, wiping out part of the village. Five died.

🗺 Trip Notes

Getting around You can get all the way to Funicolare San Carlo by PostBus with a change in Bignasco. Buses are timed to coincide with cable car departures.

When to go Valle Maggia is open year-round, but snow can block Val Bavona in winter, and almost all business, facilities and accommodation close between October and Easter.

Parking The only place where you have to pay for parking is in Foroglio.

05 **Lago di Robièi** is one of Ticino's biggest reservoirs and can be admired from the dam near the cable car station. Take the path from there to Lago Bianco, another picturesque reservoir.

04 After Val Bavona's rural, almost tourist-free hamlets, the modern **Funicolare San Carlo-Robièi** comes as a surprise. The single, large gondola runs approximately hourly, swinging high above the steep valley.

03 Val Bavona's is dotted with ancient, stone-built villages set against a backdrop of moody Ticino peaks. Arguably the most dramatic is **Sonlerto** (pictured opposite page) that straddles a ridge over which the road humpbacks.

02 The highpoint of Val Bavona, **Foroglio** is an incredibly well-preserved stone village clustered around a historic 15th-century church. Beyond rises the **Cascata di Foroglio**, a 110m-high waterfall, Ticino's tallest and most dramatic.

01 **Locarno**'s sunny setting by Lago Maggiore creates a subtropical scene, a far cry from the cold limestone of the Alps just beyond. The lakefront is a soothing place to stroll, ice cream in hand.

Lago di Robiei

San Carlo

Ri d'Antabia

Buzong

Foroglio

Via Bavona

Bosco Gurin

Piscina di Bignasco

Sonogno

Gerra

La Cantonál

Ri d'Ateasca

Someo

Giumaglio

Moghegno

Aurigeno

Gordevio

La Cantonál

Ribo

Vergeletto

Spruga

Isorno

I T A L Y

Stradón

Via Arbigo

Melezza

Via Cantonale

Locarno

Lago Maggiore

0   5 km
0   2.5 miles
N

Listings

BEST OF THE REST

 Water Fun

Lido di Lugano

On hot days, head to the popular lido in Lugano across the river from Parco Ciani, where there are pools, cafes, a sandy beach and lots of lawn space for tanning.

Splash & Spa Tamaro

Just 13km southwest of Bellinzona, this aquapark and sauna centre is Ticino's top place to make a splash. There are slides, whirlpools, indoor and outdoor pools, and refreshments to enjoy.

Lido Locarno

Locarno's lido has several pools, including an Olympic-sized one, children's splash areas and waterslides, and fabulous lake and mountain views. The huge complex uses solar and hydropower.

 Art & Museums

Museum of Fossils

Revamped and expanded by Ticinese architect Mario Botta, Meride's Fossil Museum showcases petrified creatures found on Monte San Giorgio, a World Heritage Site. You're welcomed by a 2.5m long replica of a Ticinosuchus.

Swissminiatur

At Swissminiatur in Melide you'll find 130 meticulously detailed models of Switzerland's most famous landmarks. It's the quick way to see Switzerland in a day but perhaps less interesting for children than parents might imagine.

Museo Hermann Hesse

This museum showcases German-born Swiss poet, novelist and painter Hermann Hesse's personal objects, including some of the thousands of watercolours he painted in Ticino, plus books and other odds and ends that help recreate something of his life.

Museo d'Arte della Svizzera Italiana (MASI)

The showpiece of Lugano's striking LAC cultural centre, the MASI zooms in predominantly on 20th-century and contemporary art – from the abstract to the highly experimental, with exhibitions spread across three spaces.

Museo Comunale d'Arte Moderna

Housed in the late-16th-century Palazzo Pancaldi, this museum showcases paintings by artists connected with the town, among them Paul Klee, Ben Nicholson, Alexej von Jawlensky and Marianne von Werefkin.

 Grotto Restaurants

Grotto Morchino   €€

Located in the Paradiso suburb of Lugano, this rustic retreat offers hearty Ticinese specialities in tranquil surroundings.

PAOLA MARTINI/SHUTTERSTOCK

Fossil found on Monte San Giorgio

Grottino Ticinese €€

In Ascona on the other side of the River Maggia to Locarno, this grotto has a stone-walled interior and local flavours that echo Ticino's culinary heritage.

Grotto Cà' Rossa €€

Spilling onto a flower-strewn garden in summer and with a log fire blazing in winter, this Gordevio-Ronchini grotto is an atmospheric spot for tasty Ticinese specialities and wine.

Alpe Vicania €€

In a lonely spot high above Morcote on the trail across Monte San Salvatore, this summer grotto restaurant serves dishes made with ingredients from the neighbouring farm and local wines.

Great Views

Santuario della Madonna del Sasso

A 20-minute walk out of Locarno up the chapel-lined via Crucis brings you to this spectacularly located pilgrimage site high above the town with impressive views of Lago Maggiore.

Monte San Giorgio

Rising in a pyramid above Lake Lugano, 1097m Monte San Giorgio commands fine lake views from the summit, reached via forested paths from Meride. Look out for (but don't collect) fossils en route.

Capanna Grossalp

A steep hike from Bosco/Gurin takes you to the hut at Grossalp from where views back down to the village and across the huge mountain amphitheatre open up.

LAC cultural centre, home to MASI

ROBSON90/SHUTTERSTOCK

Valleys & Islands

Centovalli Railway

The Centovalli Railway takes 1¾ hours to make the journey from Locarno into Italy, twisting and bucking its way through some spectacular landscapes that can be admired from the carriages' panoramic windows.

Valle Rovana

Travel the lonely Valle Rovana to Bosco/Gurin where timber architecture, skiing, hiking and snowshoeing await the adventurous in Ticino's most remote spot.

Brissago Islands

Marooned in the glimmering waters of Lake Maggiore, this tiny pair of islands is famous for its botanic gardens designed in the 19th century. Hundreds of tropical and sub-tropical species flourish here.

Valle Onsernone

For total peace and big wilderness, make a detour to Valle Onsernone west of Locarno. Once known for its granite mines, this valley of shaggy, densely wooded mountains is dotted with stone-built hamlets.

CENTRAL
SWITZERLAND

HIKING | BUNKERS | CHERRIES

RESEARCHED BY CAROLINE BISHOP

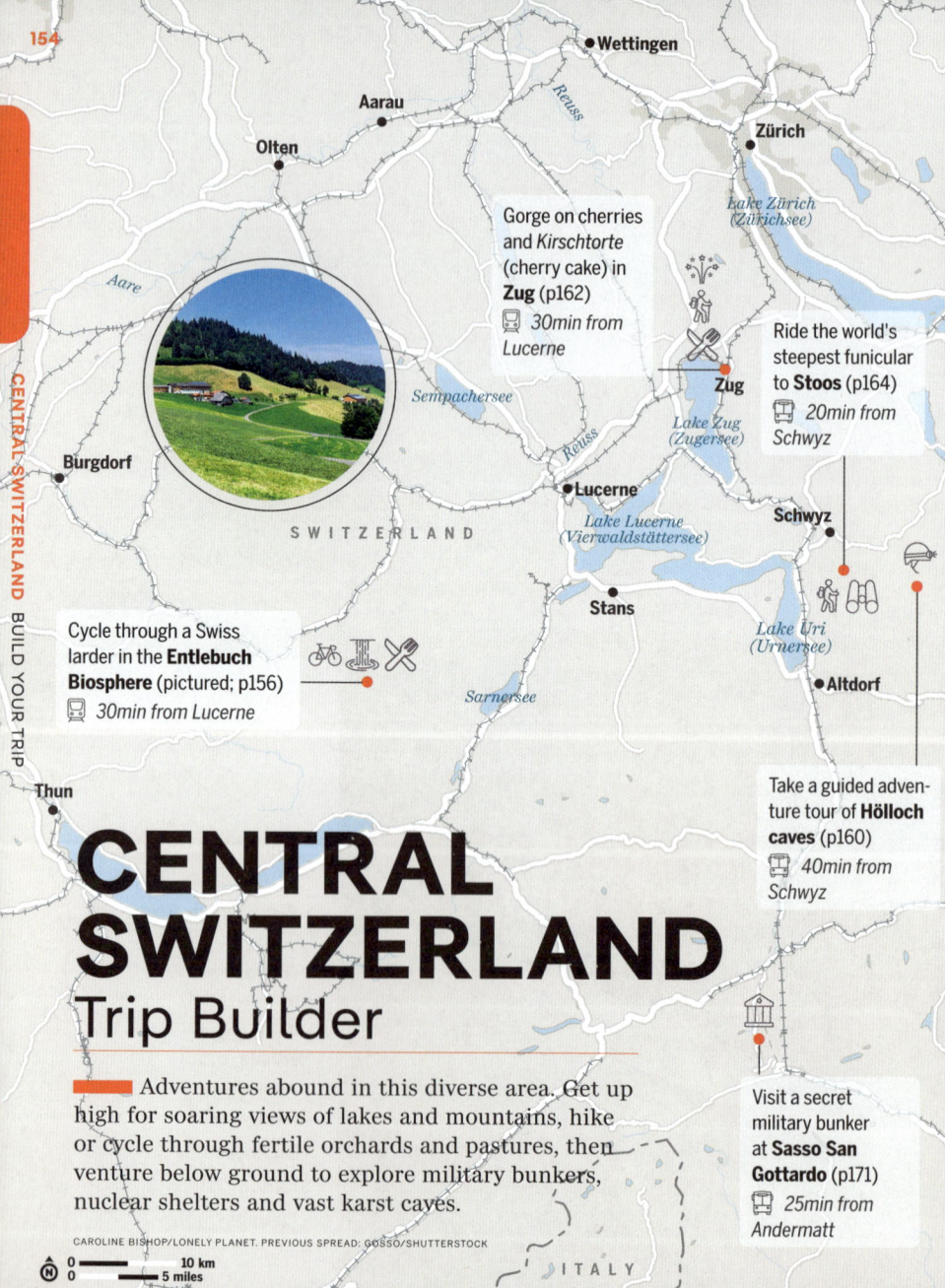

Gorge on cherries and *Kirschtorte* (cherry cake) in **Zug** (p162)
🚆 *30min from Lucerne*

Ride the world's steepest funicular to **Stoos** (p164)
🚆 *20min from Schwyz*

Cycle through a Swiss larder in the **Entlebuch Biosphere** (pictured; p156)
🚆 *30min from Lucerne*

Take a guided adventure tour of **Hölloch caves** (p160)
🚌 *40min from Schwyz*

CENTRAL SWITZERLAND
Trip Builder

Adventures abound in this diverse area. Get up high for soaring views of lakes and mountains, hike or cycle through fertile orchards and pastures, then venture below ground to explore military bunkers, nuclear shelters and vast karst caves.

Visit a secret military bunker at **Sasso San Gottardo** (p171)
🚆 *25min from Andermatt*

CAROLINE BISHOP/LONELY PLANET. PREVIOUS SPREAD: GOSSO/SHUTTERSTOCK

0 — 10 km
0 — 5 miles

Practicalities

ARRIVING

Zürich Airport About 70km from Lucerne, this is the closest airport. Regular direct train services (single ticket Chf31) run to Lucerne main station.

MONEY

The Tell Pass *(tellpass.ch)* could save you money if you're planning extensive travel in the area.

FIND YOUR WAY

Lucerne's tourist office, on platform 3 of the train station, can help with excursion advice and transport tickets.

WHERE TO STAY

Town /Village	Pro/Con
Lucerne	A gorgeous city with tons of accommodation, albeit at stiff prices.
Zug	Small lakeside town with a lovely medieval centre. Limited appeal for more than a day or two.
Andermatt	Charming mountain village southeast of Lucerne. A little far from rest of the region.

EATING & DRINKING

Jam, sausages, schnapps and cake are just some of the products infused with cherries in Zug, thanks to its abundant orchards. The Entlebuch valley is a UNESCO Biosphere Reserve producing cheese, meat, ice cream, schnapps, herbs and much more, all used to gourmet effect by the area's many excellent restaurants.

Best local spirit
Edelwhite gin (pictured)

Must-try
Kirschtorte (pictured) at Treichler

GETTING AROUND

Train Services connect efficiently with buses and cable cars, making driving unnecessary.

Bicycle Well-signed routes crisscross the region. Entlebuch and Zug are particular hotspots; use a mountain bike for Stoos.

Boat SGV ferries cross Lake Lucerne to meet mountain trains for Rigi, Pilatus and more.

CENTRAL SWITZERLAND FIND YOUR FEET

JAN-MAR
Blue-sky snow days above the valley clouds

APR-JUN
Blossoming cherry orchards and early-season hiking

JUL-SEP
Sunny days, busy trails and lakeside buzz

OCT-DEC
Crowd-free hiking, pleasant temperatures and golden trees

28 Biosphere by BIKE

CYCLING | WATERFALLS | FOOD

Lush green hills, hidden waterfalls and a secret pond: the tranquil valley of Entlebuch feels a world away from busy Lucerne. As a UNESCO Biosphere Reserve, its fecund farmland is nurtured in a sustainable, respectful way. Pedal through countryside rich with the pong of manure, birds of prey wheeling overhead, and discover small producers making a living from the land with top-quality produce.

🗺 How To

Getting around Hire wheels on rentabike.ch for pick up at the **Landgasthof Drei Könige** hotel in Entlebuch village.

When to go Time your trip around seasonal produce: spring for asparagus, summer for berries, autumn for game meats.

Extend your trip Sörenberg to Entlebuch is stage 5 of the 300km e-bike route 1291, which starts and ends in Lucerne. Use schweizmobil.ch to navigate.

Map area:
0 — 5 km
0 — 2.5 mile

Entlebuch • — Würzig
Landgasthof Drei Könige
• Schüpfheim
UNESCO Entlebuch Biosphere
Wiggen
Kneippanlage Schwandalpweiher
Flühli
Chessimätteli suspension bridge
Chessiloch
Waldemme
Schrattenfluh (2092m)
Sörenberg
Emme

Hillside and riverside

Numerous cycle trails wind their way through the hills either side of Entlebuch village. Take route 24 or 399 towards Schüpfheim, from where route 4 follows the Waldemme River to Flühli. From here, the challenging circular route 817 loops up and around the Schrattenfluh and then down to Sörenberg and back to Flühli.

A peaceful pit stop

Near Flühli is a secret oasis. The **Kneippanlage Schwandalpweiher** (Schwandalp Pond) is a Kneipp cold-water therapy centre inspired by the teachings of 19th-century German naturopath Sebastian Kneipp. Don't expect a swanky Swiss health spa – it's literally a pond. Different facilities encourage you to douse your feet, arms and face in the 6°C water, while a tactile barefoot path surprises the soles of the feet with pinecones, pebbles, woodchips and more.

🏔 Ode to Entlebuch

To me, this region is exactly the Switzerland visitors dream of: rolling hills, grazing cows, tidy farms, geraniums in every window, and a simple, grounded lifestyle. People live with a real connection to the land, and sustainability is part of daily life.

For example, local woodworker BühlmannART uses reclaimed, regional wood to create cheeseboards, home decor and custom furniture. His craftsmanship is top-notch and it's all local. Then there's herb-growing cooperative Kräuteranbau Genossenschaft, run by 15 local farming families, which produces an incredible variety of herbal teas. It's where I source many of the botanicals for my gin.

■ *Insights by Barb Grossen-bacher, owner of Entlebu ch gin distillery Edelwhite Gin @ edelwhitegin*

On foot to the falls A short way south of Flühli is the **Chessiloch** waterfall. Leave your bike at the Kragen carpark and hike 15 minutes through the woods to reach this elegant horsetail of water swishing over the rock into a small pool. Nearby is the **Chessimätteli suspension bridge**, hanging 45m high above the valley.

Biosphere treats Back in Entlebuch village, pick up locally made cheese, jams, herbal teas and spirits at **Würzig**, and round off your day with dinner at the **Landgasthof Drei Könige**, where every dish is lovingly crafted from local, seasonal produce.

Above Entlebuch

29 Fortresses & **BUNKERS**

HISTORY | MILITARY SECRETS | MUSEUMS

The serene beauty of Switzerland's mountains covers some serious secrets. Explore the huge hidden military fortress on the St Gotthard Pass and tour a nuclear bunker designed for thousands in Lucerne for insights into the fear and turmoil of the 20th century. You'll emerge very glad that your subterranean stay was only temporary.

How To

Getting here Sasso San Gottardo is 25 minutes by bus from Andermatt. For Sonnenberg, meet your guide in Lucerne city centre.

When to go Sasso San Gottardo opens daily, June-October. English public tours of Sonnenberg are held on the last Sunday of the month, April to August; reserve in advance.

More fortresses Visit the **Festung Vitznau** in the village of the same name, and the **Festung Fürigen** near Stansstad.

What to wear Closed-toe shoes and warm clothes; however hot a day, it can be chilly inside.

Hot war Switzerland's neutral status in WWII didn't allay its fears of invasion by neighbouring Germany and Italy. Its response was to secure the Swiss Alps with secret military fortresses armed against potential attack. Built inside a mountain on the St Gotthard Pass, the vast

Sasso San Gottardo (now a museum) is entirely hidden from the outside, but venture inside and you'll find a tunnel 2km long, a staircase with 475 steps and rooms where hundreds of soldiers would have slept, washed, cooked and eaten. If this doesn't already tell you that the Swiss

were deadly serious about protecting themselves, check out the huge cannons aimed at the Italian side of the pass far below.

Cold war Switzerland's fears didn't dissipate after VE Day. As the Cold War became ever chillier, the Swiss decided to provide every citizen with a

ETHAMPHOTO/ALAMY

Inside History

It's so important not to forget history and a tour of the Sonnenberg shelter helps people get a better understanding of the Cold War. Switzerland has been neutral forever so visitors often find it surprising that the country feels such fear and paranoia as to build shelters. They were initially intended for use in the event of nuclear attack. Today, they could also come into play during a more conventional war or to house people who have lost their homes in a natural disaster. Their primary purpose is to give people a sense of hope and security.

■ *Insights by Zora Schelbert,*
Chief Operating Officer, guided
tours of the Sonnenberg shelter
unterirdisch-ueberleben.ch

spot in a nuclear shelter – a law that still stands today. The **Zivilschutzanlage Sonnenberg** (Sonnenberg Civil Protection Facility) was built in 1976 to house 20,000 people in two motorway tunnels beneath the Sonnenberg mountain in Lucerne. A good idea in theory,

but a guided tour reveals the nightmarish reality: rows of bucket-style toilets, thousands of cramped bunks, and a prison and hospital for eventualities it's best not to think about. It's now been downsized but could still house 2000 people if required.

Above Sasso San Gottardo

30 Exploring a HELLHOLE

ADVENTURE | CAVING | OUTDOORS

▬▬▬ Unfathomably vast, **Hölloch** is a karst cave network stretching 212km in length and 1km in depth – and that's just what's been explored so far. Discovered in the late 19th century, it was formed over millions of years by water carving the limestone rock into channels, potholes and great caverns. Bring your sense of adventure and follow your guide into its pitch-black depths.

MARCEL MURRI

🗺️ **How To**

Getting here Trekking Team, which runs guided tours of the caves, is a five-minute walk from the nearest bus stop, which links Muotathal with the town of Schwyz.

When to go Short tours are offered year-round; come in winter for longer tours and multiday expeditions.

What to expect Visit trekking.ch for a description of each tour and the physical ability required. English-speaking guides are available on request.

GEORG TAFFET

HÖLLOCH CENTER

Far left top and bottom Hölloch cave
Left Hölloch Cave centre

Going underground There is dark and then there is *dark*. Switching your headtorch off inside **Hölloch** (meaning 'hell-hole') is a humbling experience. Your eyes won't adjust to glimmers of light, because there are none to be found – the blackness is molasses-thick. It's just one of several moments during an adventure tour of this labyrinthine cave network that make you feel insignificant in the face of nature. Get lost in here and you'd never find your way out. Thankfully, you're in safe hands. Trekking Team's guides know every nook and cranny, and the darkness demonstration is only temporary. Headtorches back on full beam, your tour continues in the chilly cave air.

Adrenaline rush A few times a year, water floods Hölloch's channels and caverns, making tours impossible, but outside these times, they are safe to explore. Winter, when snow above ground means there's no risk of sudden flooding, allows for longer, multiday expeditions. Apart from a short section of concrete path created by early explorers with an eye to tourism, the caves remain in their natural state. You'll scramble over water-rippled rock, inch your way through narrow passageways, lower yourself into caverns with the help of fixed ropes or chains, and emerge exhilarated, sweaty (the humidity below ground is almost 100%) and with a new respect for the power of nature.

 A Subterranean Adventure

Almost nothing has changed in these caves for 100,000 years. They are so diverse, from small crawling passages to big halls with waterfalls, and it feels incredible to be so close to nature. It's dirty, it's silent, it's dark and almost a bit spiritual. There's no mobile phone signal down there, so it's a chance to really step away from daily life and out of your comfort zone. To get the most out of it, be open-minded, be brave and have a sense of adventure. The short tours are for nearly everyone, but for longer day tours or multiday expeditions, you need to be pretty fit.

■ *Insights from Sandra Betschart and Sonja Ulber, co-Managing Director s, Trekking Team @hoelloch_ center_muotathal*

31 Cherryland **TASTING**

SCHNAPPS | HIKING | FESTIVALS

Cherry orchards have adorned the farmland around Zug since at least the 17th century, resulting in no end of tasty cherry-infused creations, from schnapps to syrup to sausages. Hike under the blossoming trees, gorge yourself on freshly picked *Chriesi* and help celebrate the region's cherry traditions with a *Kirschwasser* (cherry schnapps) or two at Zug's annual festival.

🗺 How To

Getting here Zug is half an hour by train from Lucerne, with easy onward connections.

When to go Spring for the cherry blossoms, late June for the festival, year-round for cherry treats.

Pack your swimsuit On a hot day, a dip in the lake at **Seebad Seeliken** is a must, particularly after a hike. Open daily in summer; free entry.

Cherry hiking Work up an appetite with a hike in the hills above Zug. Phone the so-called *Chriesitelefon* (cherry telephone; actually Zug Tourism) to find out when the trees are in full bloom (usually mid-late April) and then walk up towards Menzingen, Walchwil or Goldau for gorgeous views and peaceful trails past blossoming cherry orchards. For a downhill alternative, take the **Zugerbergbahn** funicular up to Zugerberg and descend to Allenwinden. Back in town, enjoy a well-deserved slice of *Kirschtorte* at **Treichler** bakery. This delectable kirsch-laced cake was invented here by Heinrich Höhn in 1915 – a small exhibition in the bakery commemorates this history.

Right Cherry trees

YUESTOCK/SHUTTERSTOCK

Cherry Eating & Drinking

Apart from fresh cherries – nothing beats sun-ripened fruit picked just hours earlier – here are my top picks:

Chriesiglocken

Chocolate bells filled with cherry jam, inspired by the *Chriesigloggä*. Find them at **Confiserie Speck**.

Kirsch

Restaurant Guggital serves Zuger Kirsch by Etter, Röllin and Heiner. Stop by **Aeschbach Chocolatier** for *Kirschstängli* (kirsch-filled chocolates), and head to **Wirtschaft Brandenberg** for Zuger *Kafi*, black coffee with kirsch and whipped cream.

Syrup

Look out for cherry syrup on Saturdays at the **Landsgemeindeplatz** farmers market or at local farm shops.

■ *By Kristin Reinhard, photographer, writer and founder of Swiss lifestyle blog z'Nuni. z-nuni. com @kristin_reinhard*

Cherry running Every year on a Monday in late June, Zug celebrates its cherry heritage with the Chriesisturm, a light-hearted fun run through the lanes of the medieval old town. The action kicks off at noon with a peal of the *Chriesigloggä* (cherry bell) on St Michael's church – in days gone by this signified the start of the cherry harvest. Crowds line the streets to cheer on teams of runners racing down the middle carrying wooden ladders or cherry-picking baskets. Afterwards, everyone heads to the cherry market on **Landsgemeindeplatz** to tuck into grilled cherry sausage with cherry chutney, buy fresh cherries from the farm stalls and toast the harvest with a kirsch.

32 Up Above STOOS

RIDGE HIKING | VIEWS | FUNICULAR

▬▬ The tiny car-free mountain village of Stoos has several aces up its sleeve. Arrive on the world's steepest funicular and then ascend further by chairlift to hike a ridge between two mountains (pictured) for dreamy bird's-eye views of Lake Lucerne and beyond.

MELISSAMN/SHUTTERSTOCK

🗺 Trip Notes

Getting here Catch bus 501 from Schwyz to Schwyz Stoosbahn Talstation (20 minutes). Cars can park on-site.

When to go The ridge is open and secured with chains June to early Nov. Summer brings peak crowds; a sunny, midweek autumn day is perfection.

Be prepared Allow two to three hours to complete the trail, which ascends nearly 400m elevation (and a similar amount down) over 4km. Sturdy footwear and water are essential.

🚆 Eco-Train

Opened in 2017, the current, eye-catching **Stoosbahn** replaced an older funicular railway that had been swooping up to Stoos since 1933. Wasteful it is not: heat from the engine room is harnessed by the top station and **Stoos Lodge**, while water in the latter is heated using the funicular's recuperative braking energy.

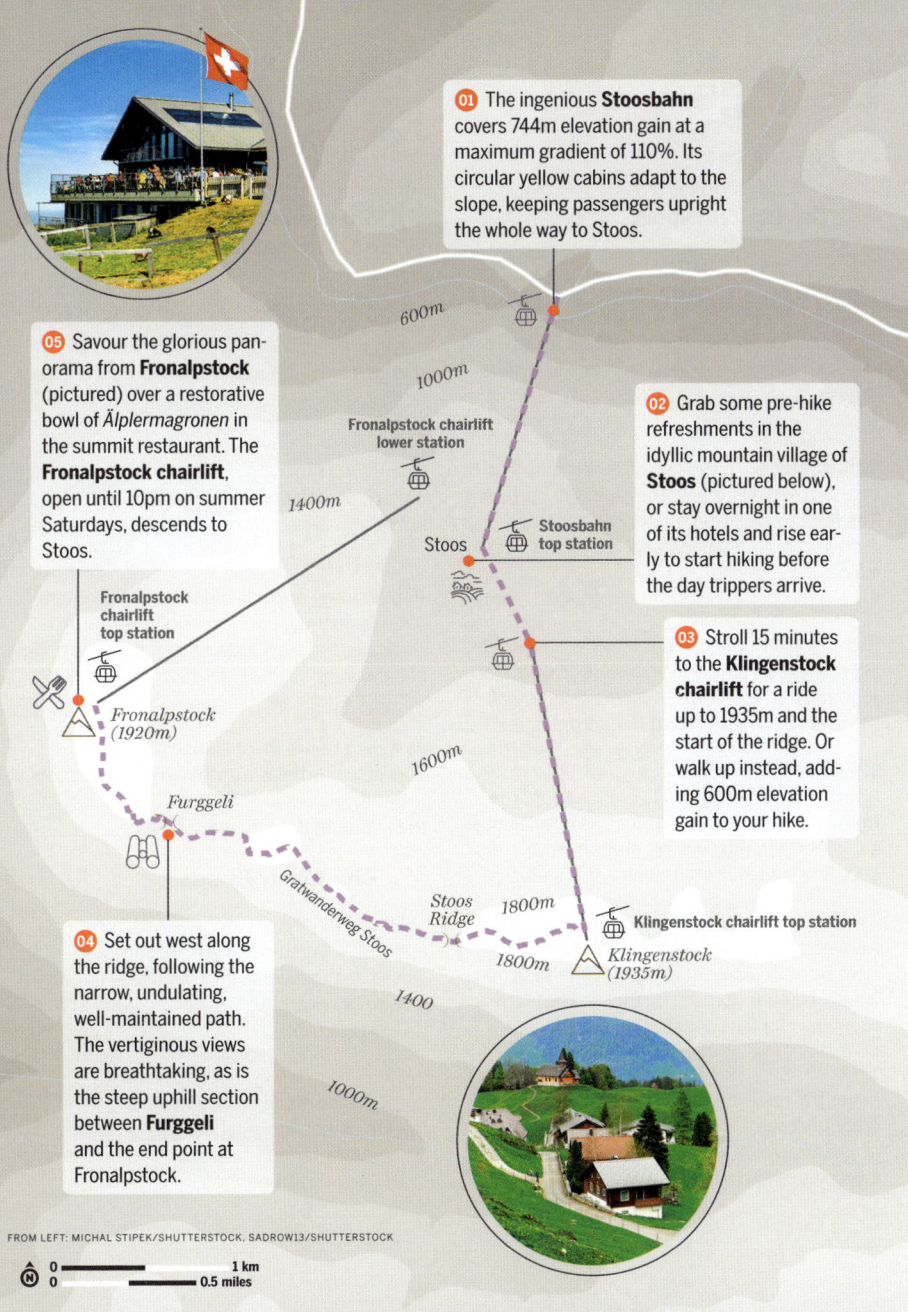

01 The ingenious **Stoosbahn** covers 744m elevation gain at a maximum gradient of 110%. Its circular yellow cabins adapt to the slope, keeping passengers upright the whole way to Stoos.

05 Savour the glorious panorama from **Fronalpstock** (pictured) over a restorative bowl of *Älplermagronen* in the summit restaurant. The **Fronalpstock chairlift**, open until 10pm on summer Saturdays, descends to Stoos.

600m

1000m

Fronalpstock chairlift lower station

1400m

Stoos

Stoosbahn top station

Fronalpstock chairlift top station

Fronalpstock (1920m)

02 Grab some pre-hike refreshments in the idyllic mountain village of **Stoos** (pictured below), or stay overnight in one of its hotels and rise early to start hiking before the day trippers arrive.

03 Stroll 15 minutes to the **Klingenstock chairlift** for a ride up to 1935m and the start of the ridge. Or walk up instead, adding 600m elevation gain to your hike.

Furggeli

1600m

Gratwanderweg Stoos

Stoos Ridge

1800m

1800m

Klingenstock chairlift top station

Klingenstock (1935m)

04 Set out west along the ridge, following the narrow, undulating, well-maintained path. The vertiginous views are breathtaking, as is the steep uphill section between **Furggeli** and the end point at Fronalpstock.

1400

1000m

0   1 km
0   0.5 miles

Listings

BEST OF THE REST

 ## Terrific Transport

CabriO

The original Swiss open-topped cable car provides an obstacle-free view of the magical landscape around Lucerne as it glides up to the Stanserhorn, an easy-to-reach peak near Stans.

Rigibahn

Dating from 1871, the cogwheel railway from Vitznau up to Mt Rigi is the oldest in Europe. The fleet ranges from historic steam locomotives and open carriages to sleek modern trains.

Pilatusbahn

With a maximum gradient of 48%, the steepest cogwheel railway in the world travels from Alpnachstad to Pilatus-Kulm, the saddle of the craggy mountain that backdrops Lucerne.

Rotair

Another epic feat of Swiss engineering, the Rotair gondola slowly revolves as it takes passengers up to the summit station of Mt Titlis (3028m) above the ski village of Engelberg.

Hammetschwand lift

Above the Bürgenstock Resort, itself accessible by funicular, is the highest lift in Europe, which ascends 152.8m further to the Hammetschwand for spectacular views.

Verkehrshaus

In central Lucerne, the Swiss Museum of Transport pays homage to transport in general and Switzerland's superlative engineering capabilities in particular. Great family fun.

 ## Waterside Coffee, Wine & Cocktails

Sunset Bar

On the lakeshore east of Lucerne, this large outdoor bar is the best place to watch the sun go down with a cocktail and a pizza. Only open in good weather.

Seebistro LUZ

Come for a morning coffee on the balcony terrace over the water and watch the ferries arrive and depart from Lucerne's main quay.

Fischerstube

Tucked away in Zug's old town, this cosy bar has an imaginative menu of signature cocktails and a secluded terrace on the edge of Lake Zug.

Di Alt Apothek

Attached to the River House hotel in Andermatt, this bar's trump card is its rooftop terrace overlooking the river. Sip a spritz to the sound of the Reuss rushing by.

 ## Live Music Events

Lucerne Festival

Lucerne's flagship event is its summer classical music festival, a five-week line-up of international orchestras and soloists at the KKL arts centre.

Luzern Live

Local, Swiss and international bands and DJs take to stages around Lucerne for 10 days in July, while market stalls and food trucks add to the festive atmosphere.

StadtFest

The last weekend in June sees Lucerne taken over by local street musicians performing on multiple open-air stages, showcasing the best of the city's local talent.

Fasnacht

Lucerne's most anticipated annual event, this historic carnival fills the streets with confetti, outlandish costumes and *Guuggenmusigen* brass bands for three days starting on the Thursday before Ash Wednesday.

 Thrills & Spills

Windsurfing Urnersee

Make the most of Lake Uri's superb conditions for windsurfing, windfoiling and sailing by taking lessons with this watersports centre and campsite based near Flüelen.

Erlebniswelt Muotathal

Hang out with huskies at this lodge and adventure sports centre where winter escapades on offer include mushing courses and dog-sled tours (in German only).

Andermatt Guides

Hit the ski slopes around Andermatt with a guide who knows all the best pistes, freeride terrain and ski touring routes.

Diavolo Via Ferrata

A head for heights and decent physical fitness is required on this fixed climbing route that starts near the Teufelsbrücke (Devil's Bridge) just outside Andermatt.

Skywalk

Accessed by revolving gondola from the village of Sattel, the Mostelberg is popular with families for its Skywalk, a delightfully wobbly 374m-long suspension bridge hanging 58m above the ground.

 **Long-Distance Hiking**

Tell Trail

An eight-stage, 156km route through the Lake Lucerne region, starting in Altdorf and taking in six of the region's biggest peaks: Pilatus, Rigi, Stanserhorn, Fronalpstock, Titlis and the Brienzer Rothorn.

Swiss Path

Created in honour of Switzerland's 700th birthday in 1991, this four-stage trail around Lake Uri starts at Rütli meadow, where the country's founding oath was signed in 1291.

 Mountain Food

Gasthaus zum Sternen   €

Rösti to rival the best at this traditional restaurant in Andermatt's old town. Finish with a warm apple strudel.

Alpwirtschaft Brunegg   €

Veal sausage, Cordon bleu and house speciality *Capuns* (dumplings typical of eastern canton Graubünden) at this tranquil farm restaurant on the panorama trail between Unterägeri and Zug.

Restaurant Ochsen   €

Settle down for a traditional fondue in the cosy wood-panelled dining room of this Andermatt restaurant, which specialises in the hot cheese dish.

Gipfel Restaurant Rothorn   €

Simple but tasty alpine dishes in this self-service restaurant at the top of the Sörenberg gondola. Tuck into *Älplermagronen* while enjoying stunning views.

33 Road Trip Mountain
PASS LOOP

ROAD TRIP | ALPINE SCENERY | VINTAGE GLAMOUR

█████ It's no coincidence that you might find yourself cruising with classic cars, Harleys and Porsches out for an afternoon spin on this glorious 140km trip over four mountain passes in central Switzerland. Expect jaw-dropping scenery of Herculean proportions, hairy hairpins and ice.

DESTINOLIBRE2025/SHUTTERSTOCK

OCTAVIAN LAZAR/SHUTTERSTOCK

 How To

Getting here Begin the circular itinerary in Gletsch, 50km north of Brig in Upper Valais. Pick up route info at the hamlet's visitor centre (*infopoint-gletsch.ch*).

When to go June to September, when mountain passes are open and snow-free.

Top tips Tap 'Andermatt' into the Météo-Suisse app to check weather conditions; clear skies are essential for this panoramic trip. En route, stop at roadside farms to buy *Alpkasë* (summer cheese).

Golden Age Allure

CARL DEABREU PHOTOGRAPHY/SHUTTERSTOCK

The village of **Gletsch** is an alluring starting point. Early tourists stayed from 1830 at the **Grand Hotel Glacier du Rhône** (*glacier-du-rhone.ch*), closed for renovation until 2027, dominating the riverside hamlet. In the 1920s, arriving in Gletsch by steam train was the hot attraction. The Furka cogwheel railway (*dfb.ch*) – 18km of metre-gauge rack-and-pinion line between **Oberwald** and **Realp**, stopping en route at Gletsch's toy-like train station – is run by volunteers today.

Immortalised in a car chase in the 1964 James Bond classic *Goldfinger,* the vertiginous **Furka Pass** (2431m) is Switzerland's king of alpine passes. Open since 1867, the now-comfortably wide road chicanes from Gletsch around white-knuckle hairpins up to the **Hotel Belvédère**. An iconic photo stop,

Vintage Motoring Must

Thank the time-travel gods you're not navigating the **Tremola** road in a 19th-century stagecoach. Paved with square granite cobbles, this narrow mountain road spirals down the southern side of the St Gotthard Pass in 24 dizzying concertina folds to Italian-speaking Airolo. It was built in the 1820s to access the pass.

Top left Furka Pass
Left Grand Hotel Glacier du Rhône
Above Hotel Belvédère

this derelict hotel was famously built in one of the bends in 1882 and closed in 2015. Park opposite and walk through the souvenir shop to access the dazzling **Rhône Glacier**. This fast-retreating tongue of ice quite literally licked the doorstep of Gletsch's hotel in the 1830s. Allow two hours to explore the fragile landscape on foot, a 1km hike (20 to 30 minutes) along rocks and moraine from the car park.

Military Secret

Corkscrew 2.7km to the top of the Furka Pass, then 21km down to **Andermatt**. Some 3km before of the town, follow southbound signs to Airolo in Ticino to the **St Gotthard Pass** (2106m). This famous mountain pass raises the curtain on far more than jaw-dropping mountain views. Beyond its windswept summit, the mountain conceals a massive WWII military fortress. Learn its extraordinary history in the **Museo Nazionale del San Gottardo**

⛰ Swiss Village Gold

If you love mountains, **Guttannen** is paradise. You can walk, look for mushrooms in the forest and crystals in the mountains. The coolest thing about the village below the Grimsel Pass is it's not crowded. Here you can still find a real 'Swissness': in two words, **Faceplant Gin** and fondue.

We make 12 gins, three seasonal using the springtime tips of fir and Scots pine. I forage wild blueberries in summer, juniper in autumn.

The best fondue is at **Hotel Bären** (baeren-guttannen. ch), a really simple address from 1803 with good prices and excellent game in autumn.

■ *Recommended by Davide Tiraboschi, artisanal gin distiller at Faceplant @faceplant_gin*

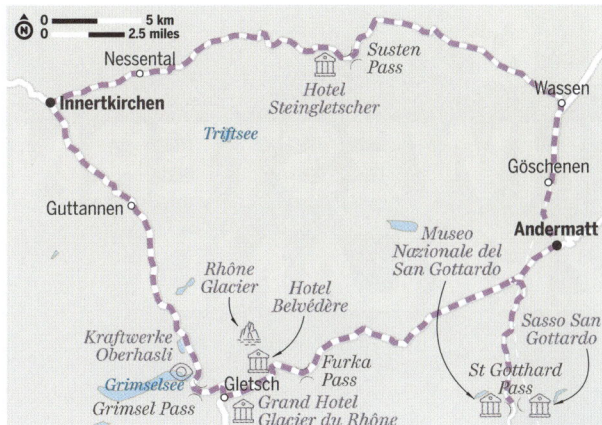

Left Hotel Bären
Below Tremola road

(museonazionalesangottardo.ch), inside the pass' old staging post and customs house, then tour the once top-secret **Sasso San Gottardo** with a guide. History lesson complete, head back the way you came to continue to Andermatt, or bone-rattle your way down and back up the breathtaking **Tremola** road.

Ice & Water

North of **Andermatt**, road tunnels conjure up jack-in-the-box views of the storybook baroque chapel in **Wassen**. Ribbon west towards the **Susten Pass** (2224m), past farmsteads and cow-specked pastures. Beyond the summit, pull up at **Hotel Steingletscher** to look back at the road: admire the waterfall gushing across the tunnel (one of 26 on the pass) you've just navigated. Overnight here and hike next morning to the retreating Stein Glacier – the ice reached the hotel a half-century ago.

The final leg of the loop corkscrews back to Gletsch, 30km south of **Innertkirchen**, across the mighty **Grimsel Pass** (2164m). Drive across the top of a dam wall James Bond–style for an underground tour of hydroelectric power station **Kraftwerke Oberhasli** *(grimselwelt.ch)* and precious insight into sustainable 'controllable' energy.

BASEL & NORTHWESTERN SWITZERLAND

ART | HISTORIC TOWNS | HIKING & CANOEING

RESEARCHED BY ANTHONY HAYWOOD

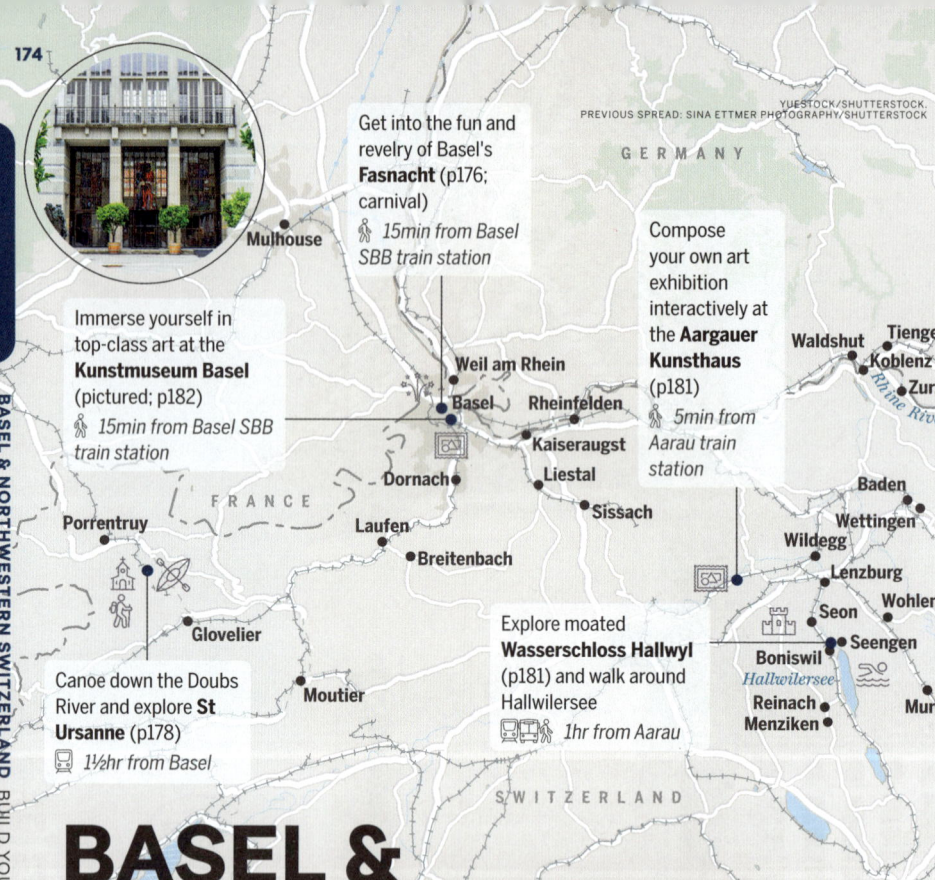

YUESTOCK/SHUTTERSTOCK.
PREVIOUS SPREAD: SINA ETTMER PHOTOGRAPHY/SHUTTERSTOCK

GERMANY

Get into the fun and revelry of Basel's **Fasnacht** (p176; carnival)
🚶 *15min from Basel SBB train station*

Compose your own art exhibition interactively at the **Aargauer Kunsthaus** (p181)
🚶 *5min from Aarau train station*

Immerse yourself in top-class art at the **Kunstmuseum Basel** (pictured; p182)
🚶 *15min from Basel SBB train station*

Canoe down the Doubs River and explore **St Ursanne** (p178)
🚆 *1½hr from Basel*

Explore moated **Wasserschloss Hallwyl** (p181) and walk around Hallwilersee
🚌 *1hr from Aarau*

Mulhouse

Weil am Rhein

Basel

Rheinfelden

Kaiseraugst

Liestal

Sissach

Dornach

Laufen

Breitenbach

Porrentruy

Glovelier

Moutier

FRANCE

Waldshut

Tiengen

Koblenz

Zurzach

Rhine River

Baden

Wettingen

Wildegg

Lenzburg

Seon

Wohlen

Boniswil

Seengen

Hallwilersee

Reinach

Menziken

Muri

SWITZERLAND

BASEL & NORTHWESTERN SWITZERLAND
Trip Builder

Explore the stunning art museums in Basel, or jump feet first into festive culture during Basel's wild Fasnacht (Carnival). Outside Switzerland's third-largest city, dip into Swiss art, hike a shoreline and swim in a lake, or canoe down a meandering river.

Sarnersee

Lungernsee

Meiringen

Innertkirchen

0   10 km
0   5 miles

Practicalities

ARRIVING

EuroAirport Basel-Mulhouse-Freiburg
The small regional airport on the borders of Switzerland, France and Germany. Take the Swiss exit and 20-minute trip by bus 50/taxi (Chf6.60/50) to Basel Swiss Railway Station (Basel SBB).

MONEY

As elsewhere in Switzerland, it gets expensive here. Hopping across the border to France or Germany reduces costs significantly.

FIND YOUR WAY

Basel's **tourist office** (basel.com) is just off Barfüsser-platz. **Aarau Info** is in Metzgergasse (aarauinfo.ch). Both have excellent online info.

WHERE TO STAY

Town	Pro/Con
Basel	In the heart of the region, wide range of hotels and hostels. Can get heavily booked.
St Ursanne	Tranquil, with a quaint centre and spectacular church. Few options.
Aarau	Historic atmosphere in old town, good places to eat and drink. Limited nightlife.

EATING & DRINKING

Though low on local specialities, Basel has an excellent range of restaurants. Lörrach (Germany) and Huningue/St Louis (France) have less expensive eats. In Basel, Markthalle (pictured below left; p187) and Klara have international food stalls, and La Huninguoise (Huningue) has great wine.

Best bar with a view
Kulturbeiz 113

Must-try elegant afternoon tea Les Trois Rois (pictured top left; p187)

GETTING AROUND

Tram and city bus Basel is well served, with trams and some buses running into the early hours Friday to Sunday; Aarau and St Ursanne are walkable.

Train and rural bus Basel has a Swiss station (Basel SBB) and a German station (Basel Badischer Bahnhof). Aarau and St Ursanne trains leave from Basel SBB. Take buses for some Aargau castles (or drive if you can).

MAR
Basel Fasnacht (Carnival) starts on the first Monday after Ash Wednesday

MAY
Spring sunshine, streetside tables and seasonal sights are open

JUN-EARLY SEP
Museums open, all activities possible, including swimming

NOV-APR
Christmas markets in December, and mostly indoor pursuits

34 Three Crazy DAYS

CARNIVAL | OFF-KEY MUSIC | STREET LIFE

They call these the craziest three days of the year. Basel's **Fasnacht** (Carnival) begins in the early hours of the morn on the first Monday after Ash Wednesday. Colourful masks known as *Larven*, lanterns and quirky off-key brass music that drags its heels – this annual UNESCO Intangible Cultural Heritage festival promises late nights, red eyes and lots of fun.

ANDREAS MANN/SHUTTERSTOCK

📷 How To

Getting here Reaching the top spots around town itself is easy on foot. Some city tram and bus routes are re-routed.

When to go Fasnacht starts at 4am on the Monday after Ash Wednesday, and ends at 4am on the Thursday morning.

Best spots to be Claraplatz or on Clarastrasse in Kleinbasel (less crowded), Barfüsserplatz and Marktplatz (both in Grossbasel) are favourites for the cortège (procession). See basel.com for the cortège route.

ANDREAS MANN/SHUTTERSTOCK

ANDREAS MANN/SHUTTERSTOCK

Top far left Morgenstraich parade
Bottom left Confetti throwing
Left *Gugge* music group

🎵♪ **Clique Cellars – Fasnacht Culture Up Close**

Clique cellars are the heart of Basel's Fasnacht. They're where the Fasnacht cliques rehearse, store their things, and craft their costumes, masks and other props – and above all, where the cliques get together throughout the year to socialise over a drink. Each year, cliques on both sides of the Rhine throw open their cellar doors to the city at large during the *Kellerabstieg* (cellar descent). And during Fasnacht itself, visitors can drop by for a fascinating glimpse behind the scenes. Expect lovingly decorated underground spaces, historical artefacts and a very lively atmosphere. It's a must for fans of Fasnacht and culture as a whole.

■ *Recommended by Dominic Stöcklin, Fasnacht Fan & Marketing Head at Tourismus Basel.*

Basel's Fasnacht (Carnival) is said to be the largest of its kind, and dates back to the 14th century, and possibly to Celtic and Germanic times.

It begins with Morgenstraich Take position by 3.30am for the 4am start, when lights are extinguished on the fourth chime of St Martin's Church and the fun starts, with colourful themed lanterns illuminating the streets. The cliques (carnival associations), in grotesque Fasnacht masks, emerge from their cellars around town and fill the morning air with the trill of piccolos and the rhythmic beating of drums.

Along comes the cortège Catch 40 winks and get up for the Monday and Wednesday afternoon *cortège* (procession) from 1.30pm to 6pm. Lanterns lead the cliques, masks galore, brass *Gugge* music fills the air with warped tones, piccolos trill again, drummers thud, and floats and carriages roll by. Position yourself along the set route; check out the themed lanterns, on display on Münsterplatz since Monday evening.

Good for kids Tuesday afternoon is when the kids hit the streets in costumes, casting sweets, confetti (*Räppli*) and amusing self-penned ditties.

Pack your earplugs Tuesday evening the *Guuggemusik* bands show their chops with brass, complemented by other instruments. It lurches ever-so-slightly off-key, resounding through packed streets.

And then you ask: 'What on Earth was that?' After Wednesday's second Cortège, the action peaks as you and fellow revellers celebrate until the *Endstraich* (closing parade) at 4am Thursday.

35

Paddle Through
ST URSANNE

ROMANESQUE CHURCH | HISTORIC TOWN | CANOEING & HIKING

▬▬▬ Situated in the picturesque Jura region, some 60km southwest of Basel, St Ursanne is famous for a collegiate church that crosses architectural genres and a quaint medieval old town. The snaking Doubs River runs through town and is perfect for canoeing or riverside hiking among the rolling green hills of the region. Extending southwest along the river is the picturesque Doubs Nature Park.

🗺 How To

Getting here Trains run from Basel SBB station to St Ursanne, but your own car or bike is best for exploring the nature park.

When to go Summer if you want to enjoy the outdoors, but exploring

St Ursanne in also nice in winter.

Cheese Dreams If you love cheese and have your own wheels, take a 30-minute drive to **Fromagerie Antony** (*fromagerieantony.fr*) in Vieux-Ferrette (France).

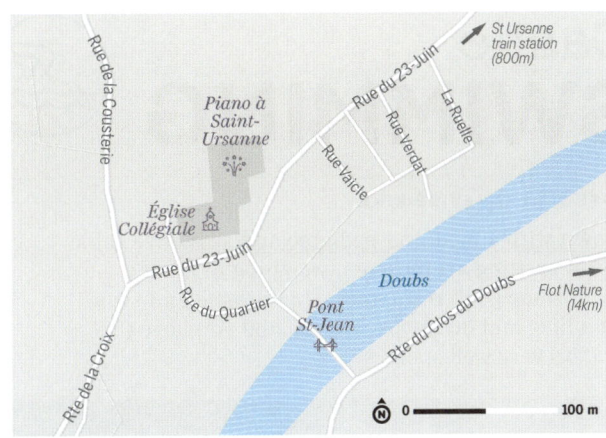

Top left Pont St-Jean
Bottom left Kayaking
on the Doubs River

Explore St Ursanne A monastery was built in St Ursanne on the grave of the hermit Ursinus (later St. Ursinus) in the 9th century. Today, its **Église Collégiale** (Collegiate Church) captures the transition from the Romanesque style to the Gothic during the late 12th century. Stroll through the church and magnificent **cloisters** at leisure before taking a walk among fine medieval buildings to soak up local history.

Walks & hikes There is no shortage of walking trails in and around town. The 9-km **Parcours de St Ursanne** (trail 464) starts at **St Ursanne train station** and winds into the centre, with a river detour. Or set out along a Section 2 of the **Trans-Swiss Trail** from **Pont St-Jean** (1728; St John's Bridge) on a four-hour hike upstream to the village of Soubey, following the course of the river most of the way, until you reach the limestone-slate roofed **Saint-Valbert church** (1632) in the town centre. The trail eventually leads to Neuchâtel and beyond.

Paddling the Doubs River The Doubs River winds and snakes between picturesque forests and hills, making it perfect for canoeing. Several outfits at different points along the river rent out canoes, kayaks or both, and **Flot Nature** (*flotnature.ch*) does trips taking in St Ursanne and the Doubs Nature Park. It's based in Soubey, 15km southwest of town.

♫♪ Piano à Saint-Ursanne

A fine time to visit St Ursanne is during the Piano à Saint-Ursanne. This series of piano concerts has been held for over two decades, taking place in August over 10 days. The concerts focus on classical music, staged the afternoon or evening, or both, in the beautiful cloisters of the collegiate church.

The series is organised by Crescendo (*crescendo-jura.ch*), which sells tickets from its website, but you can also buy them on site from one hour before the events. Crescendo organises a similar two-day event in March in the town of Porrentruy.

36 Castle SWIMMING

ART MUSEUM | OLD-TOWN STROLL | LAKESIDE HIKE

▬ Aarau is a historic town with a medieval pedigree and attractive gable decorations, but it also has an exciting art museum, weighing in among the best in Switzerland. Throw in some good restaurants, hit a castle and swim outside town, perhaps rent a bike and do the backroads, and you have the ingredients for a couple of days very well spent.

🗺 How To

Getting here Aarau is well under an hour from Basel by train, and **Wasserschloss Hallwyl** 45 minutes by train and bus from Aarau.

When to go Winter is possible, but summer is best for activities; avoid Monday, when the museum and most castles are closed.

Wheels and walks The region has great bike and hiking trails. Rent bikes from **Veloservice Aarau** at the train station; plan using the Aargau Tourismus website (*aargau tourismus.ch*).

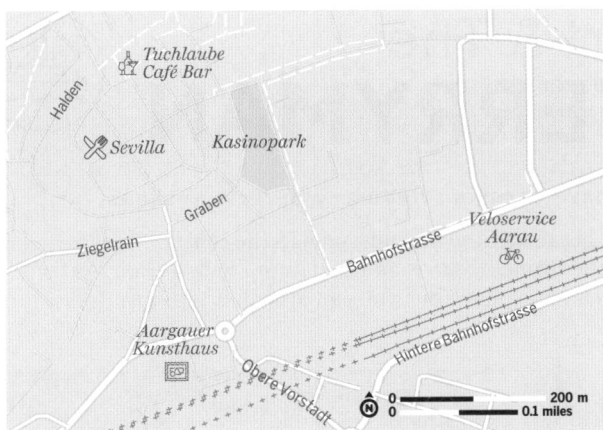

An aimless stroll through Aarau's walled **Altstadt** takes you through streets packed with historic houses, many with overhanging roofs and timber undersides colourfully decorated. Metzgergasse has one of the best cafes and nightspots in town, **Tuchlaube Café Bar**, alongside the local theatre. If a meal is on the agenda, consider **Sevilla**, a popular tapas bar.

This is the capital of Aargau canton. Though small, the canton has one of Switzerland's best art exhibitions in the **Aargauer Kunsthaus**. There's so much, in fact, that only a selection is on show at any one time, but downstairs you can get creative and concoct your own gallery on the walls using an interactive screen.

Aargau is also famous for its many castles. One that you can combine with a hike or bike ride around a lake (with swimming) is **Wasserschloss Hallwyl**. This moated castle has a small museum showcasing the lives and lifestyles of former inhabitants, but in summer don't miss **Hallwilersee**, located a 10-minute walk from the castle along a meadow path. Once at the lake, you can pick up a 22-km walking and cycling track around the entirety, and if you bring swimming gear you can dip into the waters at one of the bathing areas. And, of course, this is perfect summer picnic territory.

Top left Wasserschloss Hallwyl
Bottom left Aargauer Kunsthaus

Exploring Castles Ruins

Aargau canton is the 'Land of the Castles', with over 100 – mostly castle ruins – sprinkling the countryside. Apart from **Wasserschloss Halwyl**, a couple of the better ones are 11th-century **Schloss Lenzburg**, **Schloss Wildegg** and **Schloss Habsburg**. The first two are intact and now museums, and Schloss Habsburg is a ruin and free museum.

Search 'burgruinen' on the canton's ag.ch website for a map to create your own bucket list. And if you're both a castle ruin fan and Rhine swimmer, head to **Inseli**, a Rhine island close to Basel in Rheinfelden (in Aargau canton), with village swimming also suitable for kids.

37 Art & The FERRYMAN

KUNSTMUSEUM BASEL | FERRY CROSSING | TINGUELY & BEYELER MUSEUMS

Visit two of Basel's 'big three' fine art museums in the centre, Basel's towering cathedral, cross the Rhine by ferry, and then jump onto a tram for Fondation Beyeler in Riehen on explorations you can also split into two days with extras.

TALIAT DAVID/SHUTTERSTOCK

📍 Trip Notes

Getting here & around Start at the Kunstmuseum tram stop. You will need to take steps down to the ferry dock. The ferry operates 9am-8pm during summer hours, and 11am to 5pm otherwise.

When to go Any time of year. Check out the museum free-entry times to reduce costs.

What's more Late in the month, **Museum Jean Tinguely** has a free concert, often experimental and off-beat jazz.

👁 View to the Alps

If you decide to visit the Riehen leg of the itinerary on a separate day, you might also follow marked hiking trails from there to the 15th-century hilltop **Church of St Chrischona**. Climb the steps to the enclosed tower, or enjoy the panorama on a clear day to the Alps from the outside terrace.

05 Backtrack and make your way from **Mittlere Brücke** by tram 6 to the **Fondation Beyeler** art collection in Riehen, just down from the pretty **Dorfkirche Riehen** (Riehen Village Church).

Lörrach

G E R M A N Y

F R A N C E

04 **Museum Jean Tinguely** (pictured), in a building designed by leading Ticino architect Mario Botta, is dedicated to the contraptious motion art of Basel's favourite son. The top floor also has temporary exhibitions by other artists.

Weil am Rhein

Wiesenmatt Nature Reserve

Dorfkirche Riehen

Riehen

03 Descend the steps for the **Münsterfähre** (cathedral ferry; pictured opposite page) and cross the Rhine, pushed quietly or sometimes briskly by the current. Alternatively, walk across **Mittlere Brücke** (Middle Bridge).

Riehenring

Schwarzwaldallee

Aeussere Baselstrasse

Rhine River

Clarastrasse

Riehenstrasse

Tram 6 stop

Mittlere Brücke

Grenzacherstrasse

02 Basel's **Münster** (cathedral; pictured above) is the city's signature landmark, rising over the Rhine. After looking inside, climb a tower for sensational views. Walk around the side for terrace views and river gazing.

Steinengraben

Steinenring

St. Alban-Anlage

Basel

G E R M A N Y

01 The **Kunstmuseum Basel** has a fantastic collection of old masters, 19th-century art and classical modern. Also dive into the **New Building** (pictured right) across the road for late modern art.

S W I T Z E R L A N D

Muttenz

0   1 km
0   0.5 miles
N

Listings

BEST OF THE REST

 Green City Lungs & Beaches

Garten der alten Universität

Spread over several levels and with a small pagoda and seating, these historic gardens in Basel might be small but they are easily the most attractive, offering a great view over the Rhine.

Tinguely Beach

A Rhine River beach? Sure. This pebble stretch of shoreline in front of the Tinguely Museum in Basel is perfect for sitting and watching the river flow (or setting out on a swim).

Lange Erlen

You can walk this roughly 5km promenade along the Wiese River in Basel or through forest to Riehen in little over an hour, taking you to Fondation Beyeler (p183) art museum.

Kaserne (Basel)

The small patch of lawn at the heart of the former barracks is a lively space to sit around, picnic and perhaps even strum a song or two. Flanked by a couple of bars.

 Contemporary Design & Ancient History

Vitra Campus

Located just across the border in Weil am Rhein (Germany), contemporary furniture and applied arts feature here, set in a campus with stunning architecture.

Jüdisches Museum der Schweiz

In Basel's old town, recently revamped and in a new location, tracing the history of Judaism in Switzerland, its rituals and artefacts.

Augusta Raurica

Explore Roman ruins, and the museum artefacts and historical displays about 17km upriver from Basel in Augst, with a splendid ampitheatre and other sites nearby.

 Taking the Cure

Sole uno

Float your way around the 'Dead Sea' in salt water pools in Rheinfelden (Switzerland), where you also find aroma steam baths and saunas, and lots of wellness offerings.

Fortyseven° Wellness-Therme

Baden is famous for its hot springs, and this complex has the advantage of having been completely revamped, with indoor and outdoor areas, along with saunas and stream baths.

 Pop-up & Summer Bars in Basel

Holzpark Klybeck €

This industrial wasteland has temporarily morphed into a dense constellation of bars and spaces for cultural events; some constructions are matchstick-like, others look more permanent. Patschifig and Landestelle are popular, but the choices are many.

Basel's Buvetten €

The best of these small, often wooden summer bars flank the Rhine in Kleinbasel, and have outdoor seating. Walther Buvette is a larger, popular one.

Das Viertel & Viertel Dach €€

It looks pop-up, and it's in an industrial area just outside the centre of Basel, but it's built to last. This rooftop bar is among the most popular, and the affiliated Viertel_Klub is a late-night party venue.

♪♪ Views, Music or the River

Rhybar Buvette €

Situated in Stadtpark in Swiss Rheinfelden; enjoy drinks and snacks on the leafy promenade in one of the best *Buvettes* (refreshment kiosks) while watching the Rhine swirl by.

Kulturbeiz 113 €€

Climb the external, iron designer stairs into the dizzy heights of this former inner city brewery (there's also a lift), with stupendous views over Basel from the terraces. Cosy vibe indoors.

Cargo Bar €€

On the Rhine, with a friendly, everyone-welcome vibe, a pokey toilet with lots to read on the walls, and in warm weather chairs outside with the river flowing at your feet.

La Huninguoise €€

Your first choice for a great selection of French wines in Huningue (France), with outdoor seating on warm days and a view over the Rhine and Passerelle des Trois Pays (Three Countries' Bridge), 3km outside Basel.

Atlantis €€

This central Basel institution has lots of live music and other events, including film, as well as a restaurant that is coordinated with the various events.

Parterre One €€

Open mic, poetry slam, comedy and club nights – a lot happens at this place, located in the Kaserne cultural complex in Basel.

Les Trois Rois €€€

In the old town hotel, with large windows in the lounge section, a river-view terrace, nibbles, and a lounge piano player tinkling keys at strategic times.

🥢 International Food Flavours

Baaz Indian Restaurant €€

Upstairs, a short hop from Aarau train station, with an extensive range of pan-Indian meats and vegetarian dishes, including tandoori, fish, chicken and lamb. Something for everyone.

Tenmanya €€

Skip across the border to Lörrach (Germany) to this bustling pan-Asian, with dishes ranging from grills to Chinese, sushi and beyond; enjoy the enormous buffet or order from the menu.

Markthalle €€

From Abyssinian cuisine to Zoe's Sri Lankan dishes, Markthalle is a large food hall packed with eateries in the centre, and several cafes and bars, along with hang-out spaces like 'Wohnzimmer' (Living Room).

Klara €€

In Kleinbasel, a smaller version of the Markthalle, with eateries and a main bar serving drinks and coffee. Outdoor and streetside seating means you won't miss any of the action.

Miake Izakaya €€

One of the top Japanese restaurants in Basel, with sushi but a good range of other specialities. Reserve a table to avoid disappointment.

✨ Mulled Wine & Christmas Tidings

Adväntsgass Rheingasse

From late November to just before Christmas, Rheingasse in Kleinbasel fills with patrons sipping mulled wine, snacking and buying crafts at this Christmas market.

Christmas Market Münsterplatz

The towering cathedral forms the backdrop as the square is transformed into an enormous Christmas market.

ZÜRICH & NORTHEASTERN SWITZERLAND

SCENERY | OLD TOWNS | ART

RESEARCHED BY SIMON RICHMOND

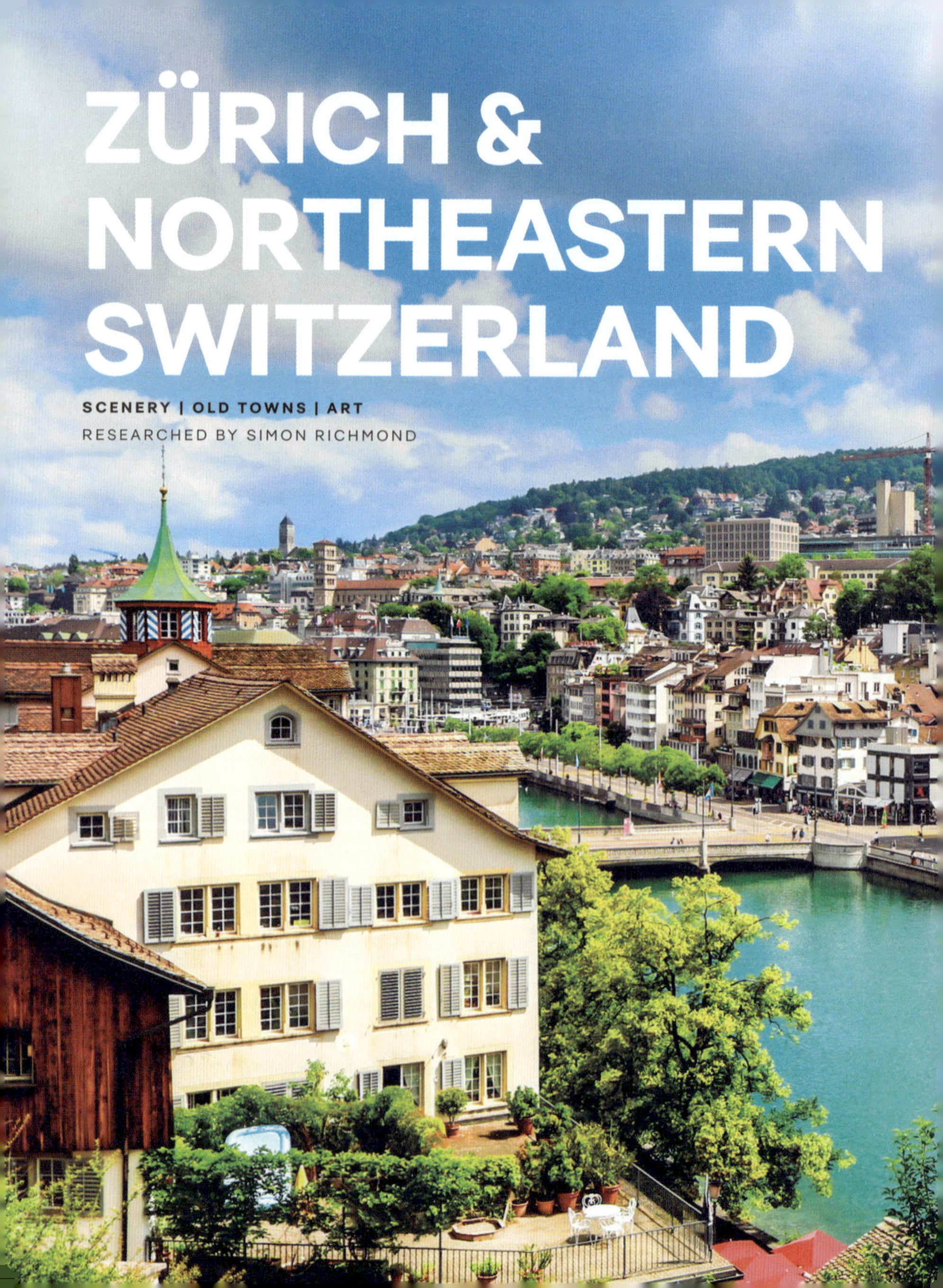

ZÜRICH & NORTHEASTERN SWITZERLAND
Trip Builder

Rich in culture, money and scenic beauty, Zürich is the jumping-off point for adventures along the Rhine, around serene Bodensee (Lake Constance) and the historic city of St Gallen with its UNESCO-listed abbey, and access to lofty mountains and lush alpine landscapes.

Take in views over Schaffhausen from the **Munot** (p201)
🚶🚂 *45min from Zürich*

Singen

Schaffhausen
Neuhausen

Koblenz

Zurzach

Rhine River

Sail up to the thundering waters of **Rheinfall** (p202)
🚆 *55min from Zürich*

Aare

Brugg Baden

Wettingen

Winterthur

Admire the best of Swiss design at **Museum für Gestaltung** (p197)
🚆 *10min from Zürich station*

Wildegg

Aarau

Dietikon

Zürich

Explore **Kunsthaus** (pictured top right; p195), Switzerland's largest art museum
🚆 *5min from Zürich station*

Contemplate Chagall's stained-glass windows at **Fraumünster** (pictured; p193)
🚆 *5min from Zürich station*

Mutschellen

Hallwilersee

Muri

Reinach

Menziken

Lake Zürich (Zürichsee)

Rapperswil

Baldeggersee

Zug

Lake Zug (Zugersee)

Einsiedeln

GERMANY

GERMANY

Lake Constance

Meersburg

Stein am Rhein

Konstanz

Steckborn

Gottlieben

Kreuzlingen

Friedrichshafen

Lake Constance (Bodensee)

Pedal along the southern shore of Bodensee (Lake Constance) (p208)
20min from St Gallen station

Romanshorn

Amriswil

rauenfeld

Arbon

Lindau

Bregenz

Wil

Gawp at the baroque splendour of Stiftsbibliothek (p207)
10min from St Gallen station

St Margrethen

Lustenau

SWITZERLAND

Gossau

St Gallen

Herisau

Appenzell

AUSTRIA

Ride the cable car (pictured) up Ebenalp (p210)
1½hr from St Gallen station

Feldkirch

Rhine River

Werdenberg

Buchs

LIECHTENSTEIN

FROM LEFT: FEDOR SELIVANOV/SHUTTERSTOCK, NICK FOX/SHUTTERSTOCK, SAIKO3P/SHUTTERSTOCK. PREVIOUS SPREAD: BERM_TEERAWAT/SHUTTERSTOCK

Niederurnen

Walensee

Walenstadt

Vaduz

10 km
5 miles

Practicalities

TOM-5400/SHUTTERSTOCK

ARRIVING

Zürich Airport 9km north of the city centre with flights around the world. Several trains an hour run to Zürich station (15 minutes). A one hour/24 hour ticket is Chf7/14, both covering all public transport in the city.

Zürich HB The main train station (pictured) is centrally located with many services to and from the region, and beyond. Right outside are trams that can get you to most parts of Zürich.

HOW MUCH FOR A

Kunsthaus ticket Chf24

Grilled sausage roll Chf15

Ebenalp cable car Chf24/36

GETTING AROUND

Trams, trains and buses You can get most places easily in Zürich on public transport with trams having the edge – see zvv. ch for details. St Gallen also has excellent public transport – see vbsg.ch for details.

Walking and cycling Both Zürich and St Gallen are very walkable cities. *Züri rollt* is the city's public bicycle scheme – for a Chf20 deposit (Chf30 for e-bikes) you can rent bicycles for free. Bicycles can also be rented at most major train stations. In Kreuzlingen download the Donkey Republic app to access bicycles there.

Boats From spring through late autumn cruise boats operate on Zürichsee (Lake Zürich), Bodensee (Lake Constance) and Walensee.

WHEN TO GO

APR-MAY
Spring sees the flowers in bloom and Zürich's spectacular Sechseläuten festival.

JUN-AUG
Take cooling dips in lakes and rivers. Join in Zürich's Street Parade.

SEP-NOV
Ideal weather for countryside and mountain hikes, bicycle rides and wine tasting.

DEC-FEB
Wrap up for the Christmas markets then head to the mountains for fun in the snow.

ZÜRICH & NORTHEASTERN SWITZERLAND FIND YOUR FEET

EATING & DRINKING

There's an astounding range of places to eat and drink in Zürich and St Gallen. Traditional cuisine is very rich, as epitomised by Zürich's signature dish, *Zürcher Geschnetzeltes* (pictured below right; sliced veal in a creamy mushroom and white-wine sauce). You can't leave St Gallen without sampling its *Olma* bratwurst, a white veal sausage flavoured with spices and bacon, and served plain in a *Bürli* (bun). Also try the various spicy Appenzeller cheese made around Appenzell. Schaffhausen is well known for its Pinot noir wines produced from vines in the Klettgau region (pictured above right).

Best coffee
Mame

Must-try schnitzel
Weisser Wind

CONNECT & FIND YOUR WAY

Wi-fi At Zürich airport and many hotels, restaurants and businesses across the city you can access free wi-fi.

Navigation Zürich spreads around the northwest end of Zürichsee (Lake Zürich), from where the Limmat River runs further north still, splitting the city in two. The city's districts are called Kreis, with Kreis 1 covering the old town.

WHERE TO STAY

Zürich is easy to get around, so choose a neighbourhood further from the centre for lower rates. St Gallen is a great alternative regional base.

City/Town	Pro/Con
Zürich	Major transit hub. Widest range of options but rates tend to be higher here than elsewhere in the region.
Schaffhausen	Some good-value places to stay in a compact historic town. Close to the Rheinfall.
Kreuzlingen	Right on the border with Germany. Largest of the Bodensee towns.
St Gallen	Handsome, walkable city with a decent range of accommodation. Good transport links.
Appenzell	Small, charming countryside town. Great access to nearby mountains.

BODENSEE CARD PLUS

This good-value card *(bodensee.eu/en/bcp)* covers entry to 160 attractions (including ones in Liechtenstein) plus free travel on lake and Rhine liners.

MONEY

A Zürich Card (valid either for 24 or 72 hours) covers all public transport around the city (including short river and lake cruises), free admission to many sights and lots of other discounts.

38 Tour Zürich's
OLD TOWN

VIEWS | CHURCHES | ART

Crisscross the Limmat River on this easy amble through Zürich's wonderfully preserved and picturesque old town. Cobbled streets lead to leafy parks, historic churches and cosy cafes as well as the city's main police station, which hides an artistic marvel.

TODAMO/SHUTTERSTOCK

🗺 Trip Notes

Getting around This is an easy walk of around 1.5km. There are cobblestone streets and alleys, and small hills along the way.

When to go Year-round. Sundays are quieter as all shops are shut that day.

Top tip The **James Joyce Foundation** holds Europe's largest collection of books, papers and other items related to the legendary Irish writer. It hosts English-language readings of his work, usually on Thursday evenings.

Giacometti's Murals

The dazzling *Blüem-lihalle* (Hall of Little Flowers) by Augusto Giacometti consists of frescoes entirely covering the entrance hall of **Amtshaus 1**, a building that today houses the city's police station. To see them, bring your ID and join one of the free guided tours between 2pm and 5pm Wednesday to Saturday.

Zürich Hauptbahnhof

01 The terrace in tree-shaded hilltop park **Lindenhof** (pictured) offers gorgeous views across the Limmat and the rooftops and church spires of the old town. Fill your water bottle from its ornamental fountain.

05 Tuck into hearty Swiss grub (think sausages and rösti) and local beers at **Zeughauskeller** (pictured), an atmospheric 15th-century hall, decorated with arms including anti-tank guns.

02 In 1916, **Cabaret Voltaire** was the birthplace of the deliberately nonsensical art movement Dada. Drop in to see quirky art exhibitions and to have a drink at the bar.

04 The **Fraumünster** is famous for its luminous stained-glass windows designed by Marc Chagall. The five vibrantly coloured designs were installed in 1970 in the presence the 83-year-old artist.

03 The twin-towered cathedral **Grossmünster** (pictured opposite page) contains stained-glass windows by Augusto Giacometti and German artist Sigmar Polke. Climb the 190 steps of the southern tower for a great views.

39 City of Art
& DESIGN

MUSEUMS | ARCHITECTURE | ARTS

Zürich's arts scene covers everything from old masters to dazzling contemporary installations. The city's home to Switzerland's largest art museum, as well as the main branch of the Swiss National Museum. In Züri-West, once-mighty factories have been transformed into galleries and art centres.

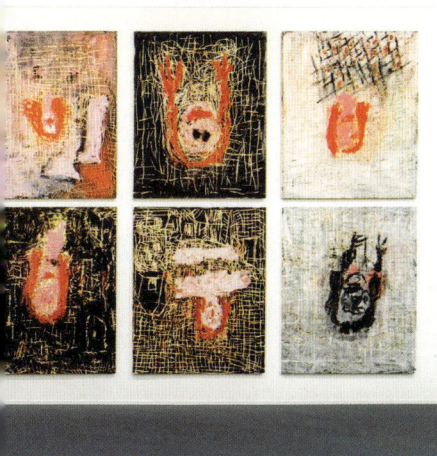

🗺 How To

Getting around Take trams between Zürich's city-centre museums and galleries, and those in Züri-West.

When to go Any time but check individual museum closing days.

Pit stop Drop by **Mame**, a stylish coffee shop that serves some of the best brews in town.

Top tip A Zürich Card (24 or 72 hours) is a great deal, covering all city transport and entry to most museums.

Admire Switzerland's Largest Art Collection

The **Kunsthaus** (*kunsthaus.ch*) has an unparalleled collection of works by titans of the Swiss art world, including Augusto and Alberto Giacometti, and Ferdinand Hodler, as well as some dazzling contemporary installations. The museum is split between two buildings joined by an underground corridor, and curates its artworks in a thought-provoking way.

Works in the original **Moser Building** range from Middle Ages religious icons to installations by Bruce Nauman. Ponder the symbolic works of Ferdinand Hodler, including some monumental-scale paintings along the main staircase. And look out for contemporary artists in the museum's ReCollect! initiative.

In the modern **Chipperfield Building** highlights include the colourful Merzbacher collection of 19th- and 20th-century paintings, and the Emil Bührle collection with a focus on impressionist art and including three of Monet's *Waterlily* paintings. The controversy surrounding this collection (Bührle made his money selling arms and bought art that once

Top left Kunsthaus **Left** Chipperfield Building (p198)

belonged to Jewish collectors persecuted by Nazi Germany) is fully explained.

Storehouse of Swiss History & Culture

National history and culture are celebrated in style across the **Landesmuseum Zürich** (*landesmuseum.ch*). Exhibits at the main branch of the Swiss National Museum are beautifully presented. Look out for elaborately carved and painted sledges, traditional costumes and impressively reconstructed histori-cal rooms. In the contemporary extension find exhibits on archaeology, Zürich's history and national identity. The gift shop has one of the city's best ranges of souvenirs.

Design Destinations

The **Museum für Gestaltung** (*museum-gestaltung.ch*) is Switzerland's premier design and visual communication museum. It's particularly strong on graphic art, with an incredible collection of some 380,000 posters from around the world. To view 2500 key

🖼 Art Insider

Scratch Zürich's surface and you'll find a very dynamic art scene, from the most established to the most progressive. There's the beautifully curated collection at **Museum Rietberg**, while **Shedhalle** (*shedhalle.ch*) at alternative arts centre **Rote Fabrik,** showcases mostly perfor-mance-based pieces. Check out local dealers such as **Galerie Gregor Staiger** (*galerie.gregorstaiger.com*) and **Karma International** (*karmainternational.ch*) rep-resenting artists including Monster Chetwynd, Nicolas Party and Nora Turato. And there over 100 'off-spaces', which might be as simple as art in a window between a hairdresser and a kebab shop.

■ *Recommended by Charlotte von Stotzingen, founding Director of Zürich Art Weekend* (*Zürichartweekend.com*).

🏛 **Pavillion Le Corbusier**

Under the curatorial umbrella of Museum für Gestaltung, **Pavillion Le Corbusier** is the final building by the seminal Swiss-born architect. It's located in the lovely lakeside park Zürichhorn, where you'll also find the beautiful **Chinagarten Zürich** and Jean Tinguely's huge kinetic sculpture **Heureka**.

works from the permanent collection head to the **Toni-Areal** branch. There's some fun activities here for kids and families. The **Ausstellungs-strasse** branch hosts excellent temporary exhibitions and has a cafe with outdoor seating beside a serene carp-filled pond.

In the Former Brewery

The old brewery **Löwenbräukunst-Areal** (lowen braukunst.ch) has been transformed into one of Zürich's hottest art locations, hosting both commercial and public galleries. **Museum Haus Konstruktiv** showcases concrete, constructivist and conceptual art from the 1920s onwards, including a permanent exhibit of Fritz Glarner's colour-blocked *Rockefeller Dining Room*.

Global Art Jewels

Based across three villas in the lush, hillside Reitpark, **Museum Rietberg** (rietberg.ch) presents an outstanding collection of global ethnographic art and cultural objects from Africa, Asia and ancient America. Look out for the expressive Swiss carnival masks.

Top Pavilion Le Corbusier **Left** Museum Rietberg **Above** Landesmuseum Zürich

Made in Switzerland

FROM SWATCHES TO SNEAKERS, SWISS DESIGN IS EVERYWHERE.

It's not just on product packaging, magazine pages or billboards that Swiss design has made an international impact. In the last century, product design has come to the fore. Swiss army knives, Swatch watches and, since 2010, On running shoes are all Swiss-designed items that have been global consumer hits.

Time for Design

Hanging above the concourse of Zürich's Hauptbahnhof is a familiar-looking clock. This is the original location of the official Swiss Railways (SBB) clock, designed in the 1940s by railway engineer Hans Hilfiker and launched in its current form in 1955. The clock's most distinctive feature is the lipstick red second hand with its circular end, modelled after the red signalling paddles used by train staff. When the seconds hand reaches 12 it pauses for a second and a half before the minute hand leaps forward as it receives an electronic impulse from SBB's central master clock. In this way, trains are perfectly synchronised.

Swiss timepiece company Mondaine, which has held the production licence for the clock since 1986, produces a wristwatch version that has been selected by both the London Design Museum and New York's MoMA as one of the most noteworthy examples of 20th-century design.

Zürich's **Museum für Gestaltung** is Switzerland's leading museum for design and visual communication. It has been gathering both utilitarian and sophisticated design objects since 1875 and has amassed a collection of over half a million pieces – one them being the Rex vegetable peeler. Designed in 1935 by Alfred Neweczerzal in his Zürich garage, the aluminium gadget's ergonomic form, ability to keep peelings thin (thus maximising each piece of food) and low price point made it an instant hit. It's something that you'll find in nearly every Swiss kitchen and further afield, as over 70 million Rex peelers have been sold worldwide.

Left Museum für Gestaltung
Centre Rex vegetable peeler
Right Helvetica typeface

PETER WIEGEL, CC BY-SA 3.0, VIA WIKIMEDIA COMMONS

GLOBAL PIXEL/SHUTTERSTOCK

HELVETICA
ABCDEFGHIJKLMN
OPQRSTUVWXYZ

Architecture & Sustainability

For Swiss design on a larger scale, look no further than **Pavilion Le Corbusier** in Zürich. This was the Swiss-born architect Le Corbusier's final flourish, commissioned in the early 1960s by Heidi Weber, a gallerist who also successfully relaunched the production of iconic furniture, such as the LC2 armchair, created by Le Corbusier, Pierre Jeanneret and Charlotte Perriand in 1929.

Other notable Swiss architects include Mario Botta, whose distinctive buildings can be seen in the Ticino region; and Jacques Herzog and Pierre de Meuron of Basel-based Herzog & de Meuron – their Roche Tower 2, which opened in 2022, is Switzerland's tallest building.

Herzog & de Meuron also designed the restaurant buildings, cable cars and cable car stations at Chäserrugg, a mountain resort with a sustainability focus. In the 21st century, sustainability has also become one of the hallmarks of contemporary Swiss design. Slightly ahead of the curve were brothers Markus and Daniel Freitag. In 1993, Markus had an idea to recycle old truck tarpaulins, seatbelts and bicycle inner tubes into a waterproof bag modelled on those used by bicycle couriers. Today the brothers' Freitag company sells around 500,000 bags and accessories a year, each one unique and made from recycled materials. Their original bag is also part of MoMA's permanent collection. And they're not alone. Qwstion is another successful Swiss bag manufacturer, who developed Bananatex, a natural banana-fibre canvas that's water-resistant without reliance on plastics.

 What's My Type?

Named after the Latin for the Swiss Confederation, Helvetica is one of the most popular san serif typefaces in the world, used on countless posters as well as for the logos of international brands including American Apparel and Lufthansa. Originally called Neue Haas Grotesk, Helvetica was created in 1957 by Basel-based Max Miedinger and Eduard Hoffmann.

Helvetica is synonymous with the clean, mathematically precise lines, functionality and elegant simplicity of what is known as Swiss Style (also called International Typographic Style) – a way of designing that has been one of the most influential of the last century.

40 Schaffhausen's
HEART

HISTORY | ARCHITECTURE | SCENERY

Sitting prettily on the Rhine, Schaffhausen is 50km north of Zürich and close to the German border. Ornate frescoes and oriel bay windows grace the medieval houses lining the pedestrian-only Altstadt while the circular Munot fortress lords it over a vineyard-streaked hill. Cycle out west of town to see more vineyards and sample wines in the scenic Klettgau region.

FEDOR SELIVANOV/SHUTTERSTOCK

🗺 How To

Getting here Trains from Zürich reach Schaffhausen in 36 minutes.

When to go Any time. The music fest Stars in Town (*starsintown.ch*) is held over two weeks from the end of July.

Pit stop The terrace of art nouveau–style tearoom **Café Vordergasse** is a prime spot to take in the comings and goings of the Altstadt.

Top tip At the helpful **tourist office** you can also taste wines.

TRABANTOS/SHUTTERSTOCK

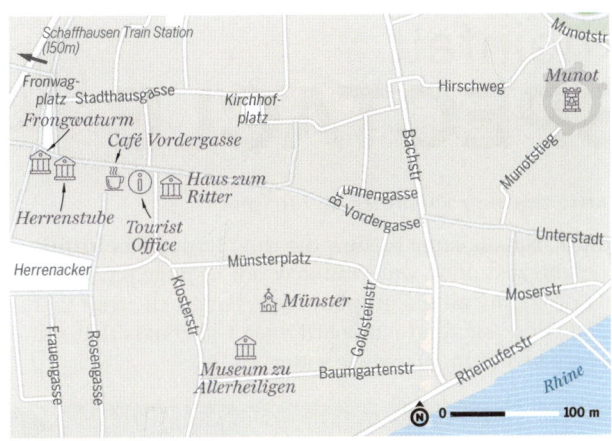

Top left Munot
Below left Münster

Altstadt Highlights

The square Fronwagplatz is overlooked by the large clock tower **Fronwagturm**, an ornate astrological timekeeper dating to 1564. Next door is **Herrenstube**, a 1748 society house with an ornate baroque facade.

The masterpiece among the Altstadt's frescoes are those covering **Haus zum Ritter**. What you see on the building today are 1943 re-creations by Carl Roesch of Tobias Stimmer's mid-16th century paintings. The originals were removed in 1935 to be conserved in the **Museum zu Allerheiligen** (allerheiligen. ch). A small portion of the original fresco is on display in the museum alongside a replica by Roesch. The museum also has top-class exhibitions on history and art. Room 105 displays an 18th-century guild-house interior with magnificent woodwork and a ceiling painting.

The museum adjoins the **Münster**. Dating to the early 12th century, this former Benedictine abbey is one of the few well-preserved Romanesque monastic complexes in Switzerland. Although the main cathedral was largely rebuilt in the 1950s, the tranquil cloister and adjoining herb garden are little changed since the Middle Ages.

Climb the Munot

East of the Altstadt, stone steps lead up through terraced vineyards to the **Munot** (munot.ch). This circular fortress was built in the 16th century and conceals an extraordinary vaulted casemate. Head up to the roof for spectacular views. For five minutes at 9pm each night a bell is rung by hand from the fortress' tower.

🚢 Rhine Cruises

April to October, cruises with **Untersee und Rhein** (urh.ch) from Schaffhausen to Kreuzlingen at the west end of Bodensee cover a beautiful stretch of the Rhine in just under five hours.

If you don't have time for that, take the two-hour cruise to enchanting **Stein am Rhein**, a town famous for its remarkably well-preserved Altstadt with painted facades and half-timbered houses. Stand in Rathausplatz, the square named after the town hall, to be surrounded by gorgeously decorated medieval houses. The stiff 40-minute hike to the 12th-century hilltop fortress **Burg Hohenklingen** (burghohenklingen.com) is worth it for the views.

41 Rheinfall
SPECTACLE

EXTREME NATURE | PANORAMIC DINING | AWESOME ADVENTURE

Goethe, Rousseau and Byron all came to view the thunderous **Rheinfall** and you should, too. Europe's biggest plain waterfall may not be huge but it is impressive, with viewpoints providing abundant photo ops. Follow the trail that wends down from medieval Schloss Laufen then board one of the boats that sail into its billowing plumes of spray and raging white water.

RICHARD CAVALLERI/SHUTTERSTOCK

🗺 How To

Getting here The Rheinfall is just 7 minutes by train from Schaffhausen. Either alight at Schloss Laufen am Rheinfall, south of the falls, or Neuhausen Rheinfall, to the north.

When to go From May to July the falls are at their most powerful. On 31 July a spectacular fireworks display attracts massive crowds.

Top tip Dine in style at **Schlössli Wörth** while admiring the Rheinfall through floor-to-ceiling windows.

OSCITY/SHUTTERSTOCK

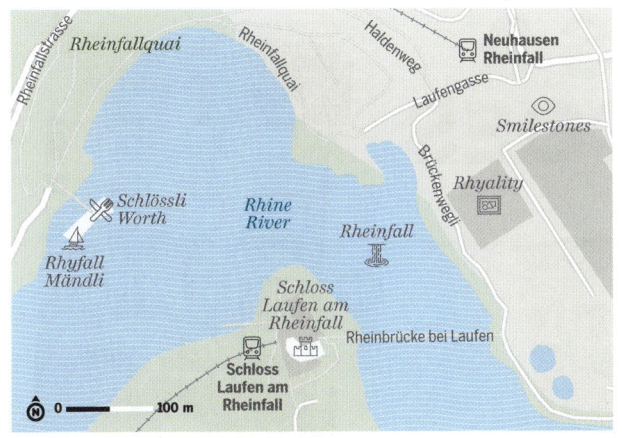

Top left Rheinfall
Bottom left Viewing platform at Schloss Laufen am Rheinfall

Schloss Laufen am Rheinfall

Standing guard over the falls is **Schloss Laufen am Rheinfall** (*schlosslaufen.ch*). There's been a castle here for over 1100 years and today the fortress houses a restaurant, function rooms and Historama, a small exhibition about the history of the falls. Trails lead down from the Schloss to several viewing platforms from where you can experience the cascades very close up amid a haze of spray.

Climb the Rock

April to October, **Rhyfall Mändli** (*rhyfall-maendli.ch*) boats flit in and out of the torrents of water at the bottom of the cascades. One of its short cruise options pauses at the tall rock in the middle of the falls, from where you can climb to the top and watch the water rush all around you. The main boarding point is next to the restaurant Schlössli Wörth on an islet off the west bank of the river. Longer cruises to the falls and along the river are offered by **Schiffmaendli** (*schiffmaendli.ch*). These include a half-day cruise to Rheinau power station every second Sunday from May to mid September.

Walks & Other Attractions

There are pleasant circular walks (one to two hours) along the Rheinfall Basin past the old watermill and over the railway bridge. At Neuhausen the old SIG Areal factory has been redeveloped. Here you'll find **Smilestones** (*smilestones.ch*), Switzerland's largest indoor miniature world, and the immersive art hall **Rhyality** (*rhyality.com*).

ⓘ **Rheinfall Facts**

Located on the border of Zürich and Schaffhausen cantons, Europe's most powerful waterfall was formed by tectonic shifts around 15,000 years ago. Erosion-resistant rocks narrow the riverbed here with the water dropping 23m in a series of swirling cascades across a width of 150m.

At their peak in summer, 600,000l per second flow through the Rheinfall. Unsurprisingly there have been several attempts down the centuries to harness the energy of this flow, first with a water mill in the 17th century and later with a proposed electric power station – a plan quashed by public outcry in the 1950s.

ORIELS & FRESCOES

Displays of Wealth

Elaborate frescoes and beautifully carved wood *Erker* (oriel or bay windows) were a way for Swiss homeowners of the past to show off how rich they were.

01 Haus zum Ritter

This 16th-century masterpiece among Shaffhausen's Altstadt frescoes is considered the most important facade painting of the Renaissance north of the Alps.

02 Zum Grossen Käfig

The Turkish sultan Bajazet being paraded in a cage by the triumphant Mongol leader Tamerlane features on this Shaffhausen Altstadt facade.

03 Weisse Adler

Dating from around 1520 this *pièce de résistance* of Stein am Rhein's many frescoes includes the story of an emperor testing his wife's fidelity.

04 Klostermuseum St Georgen

This 11th-century Benedictine monastery in Stein am Rhein has stunning murals and

other decoration in its restored Banquet Hall.

05 Kamelerker
The panel from this 1673 St Gallen oriel window featuring its namesake camel now hangs in Kulturmuseum St Gallen.

06 Kugelerker
On St Gallen's Kugelgasse, this polychromatic 1680 oriel window features some of the labours of Hercules.

07 Schwanenerker
Also on St Gallen's Kugelgasse, this *Erker* depicts the Greek myth

of the love of the deity Alpheus and the maiden Arethusa.

08 Pelikanerker
This 1708 St Gallen *Erker* depicts scenes from four continents and is topped with a gilded pelican feeding chicks with its own blood.

09 Greiferker
The adjacent wall fresco of a griffin provides the name for this St Gallen oriel window carved with Biblical scenes.

42 Admiring the Abbey OF ST GALL

HISTORY | ARCHITECTURE | ART

St Gallen's roots are intertwined with that of its UNESCO-listed **Abbey of St Gall**, a place of pilgrimage for over 1000 years. Centuries of textile production generated the wealth to create an exceedingly handsome city – striking architecture abounds, from the pretty half-timbered houses of the Altstadt to the belle époque grandeur of buildings such as the railway station and post office.

ZÜRICH & NORTHEASTERN SWITZERLAND EXPERIENCES

GERRY H./SHUTTERSTOCK

🗺 How To

Getting here St Gallen is an hour east of Zürich by train. The abbey and Altstadt are five to ten minutes' walk from the station.

When to go Year-round.

Pit stop Klosterbistro St Gallen in the abbey precincts is perfect for a refreshment break.

Top tip Drei Weieren (Three Ponds) is a prime vantage point over the city and a favourite spot with locals for swimming and sundowners.

MARTIN THURNHERR, CC BY-SA 4.0, VIA WIKIMEDIA COMMONS ®

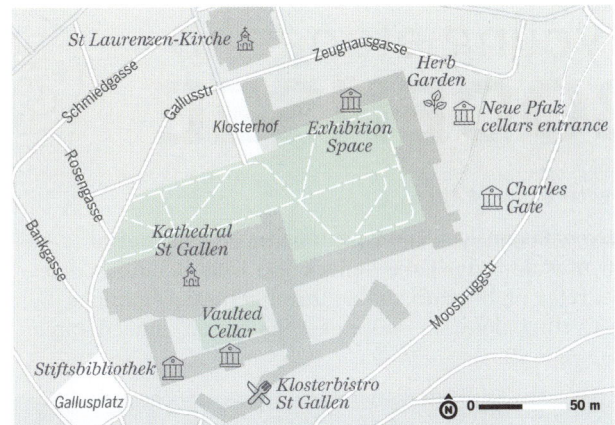

Klosterhof *Exhibition Space*
St Laurenzen-Kirche
Zeughausgasse *Herb Garden*
Schmiedgasse *Gallusstr* *Neue Pfalz cellars entrance*
Rosengasse *Charles Gate*
Bankgasse *Kathedral St Gallen* *Moosbruggstr*
Vaulted Cellar
Stiftsbibliothek *Klosterbistro St Gallen*
Gallusplatz N 0 ――― 50 m

Top left Abbey of St Gall
Bottom left Stiftsbibliothek

ZÜRICH & NORTHEASTERN SWITZERLAND EXPERIENCES

Abbey precincts Much of the current abbey dates from the 18th century when architects Peter Thumb and Johann Michael Beer built their late-baroque cathedral, library and abbot's palace. The interior of the twin-towered **Kathedral St Gallen** features dramatic frescoes and mint-green stucco embellishments.

The abbey's highlight is the **Stiftsbibliothek**, a library lavishly decorated with frescoes, stucco, cherubs and parquetry. Only a handful of its 170,000 books and precious manuscripts are on display in regularly changing exhibitions. Other curiosities include a magnificent 16th-century globe and an Egyptian mummy.

In the **Vaulted Cellar** is an exhibition on the abbey's history and pieces of sculpture from the former buildings on the site, dating back to the 8th century. In the **Exhibition Space** across the Klosterhof, view the Plan of St Gall, one of the most important architectural drawings of the Middle Ages.

Also check out the **Charles Gate** in the wall that once divided the abbey from the town, the monastic **herb garden** and the Santiago Calatrava–designed entrance to historic **Neue Pfalz cellars**.

In the Altstadt The Protestant neo-Gothic **St Laurenzen-Kirche** features a mosaic-tiled roof, delicate floral frescoes and a star-studded ceiling resembling the night sky. Climb the tower for views over the Altstadt. As you walk around St Gallen also look out for 111 *Erker* (oriel windows; p204).

📖 Abbey History

St Gallen's origin tale begins around 612 CE with the itinerant Irish monk Gallus and the legend of his tumble into a bush and a fortuitous encounter with a friendly bear. Gallus' hermitage in the Steinach valley led onto the creation of a convent named after him by Otmar, the first abbot, in 719. By 747 this had become a Benedictine abbey.

This Catholic stronghold thrived, surviving the turbulent years of the Reformation secure within its walls. The current Kathedral and library were completed in 1767. Dissolved in 1805, the abbey was designated a UNESCO World Heritage Site in 1983.

43 Cycling along the BODENSEE

SCENERY | OUTDOOR ACTIVITIES | ORCHARDS

Covering 536 sq metres, Bodensee – aka Lake Constance – is Central Europe's third-largest body of water after Lake Geneva and Lake Balaton. Come here to swim, sail or canoe, relax on beaches, amble through flowery gardens and picturesque Altstadts. Cycling along the shore past the region's famed apple orchards is the best way to see it all.

📍 Trip Notes

Getting here Places along the lake are easy to reach by train or bus. The flat and well-signposted Bodensee-Radweg cycle path runs for 269km around the lake through Germany, Austria and Switzerland.

When to go May to October is best for weather.

Top tip Donkey Republic bicycles (*donkey.bike/cities/kreuzlingen*) can be rented from near the entrance to Seeburgpark.

Don't forget Pack your togs and towel so you can hop in the lake for a cooling dip during this 45km ride along the Swiss shoreline.

☼ Three-Part Lake

Bodensee has three sections: the main upper lake (Obersee); the smaller lower lake (Untersee), and the connecting stretch called Lake Rhine (Seerhein). Along the lake's southern Swiss flank the main towns are, from west to east, Kreuzlingen, Romanshorn, Arbon and Rorschach.

0 ____ **5 km**
0 ____ **2.5 miles**

Markdorf

Meersburg

Bodensee

Immenstaad
am Bodensee

Konstanz

Friedrichshafen

Kreuzlingen

Landstrasse

Bodensee

02 **Seeburgpark** offers superb natural areas, enclosures for rare breeds of farm animals and alpine goats, an observation tower, a fab kids' playground and the small museum **Seemuseum Kreuzlingen** (pictured).

Uttwilerstrasse

01 Marking the line between Swiss Kreuzlingen and German Konstanz is the **Art Border**, 22 metal sculptures designed by Johannes Dörflinger and representing tarot symbols.

Romanshorn

Amriswil

03 In Romanshorn, **Hafenlounge** is a pleasant outdoor pit stop with deckchairs, sandpits, drinks and nibbles. For the kids there's **Robins Horn**, an imaginatively designed playground next to the lake.

Buch

04 Detour inland to **MoMö** (pictured; *moehl.ch*) a family-run distillery where you can taste locally made ciders and spirits, and take a tour of the interesting museum.

Seestrasse

MOMÖ

Rorschach

05 The gallery at **Würth Haus Rorschach** (town of Rorschach pictured opposite page) has free themed exhibitions curated from its 20,000-piece collection of modern and contemporary art. Around the building is a sculpture garden.

St. Gallen

44

From Appenzell
TO EBENALP

OLD TOWN | MOUNTAINS | LAKE

━━━ Wooden chalets in velvety green, buttercup-speckled meadows, the tinkling of cowbells and a dusting of snow on the lofty peaks in the distance – this dreamy vision of Switzerland is within easy day trip reach of St Gallen. Appenzell has one the country's most photogenic Altstadts and is watched over by Ebenalp and Säntis in the Alpstein, the region's high point.

ZÜRICH & NORTHEASTERN SWITZERLAND EXPERIENCES

STEFANO POLITI MARKOVINA/SHUTTERSTOCK

🏞 How To

Getting here Appenzell Bahnen trains connect St Gallen to Appenzell and Ebenalp. Buy an Ostwind day or multiday travel pass (valid after 9am).

When to go For hiking May to October is best.

Pit stop Aescher on Ebenalp has a stunning location and serves very good food.

Top tip In Appenzell **Drei König** is a traditional bakery famous for its Appenzeller cheese quiche and sweet treats.

STEFANO EMBER/SHUTTERSTOCK

Top left Hauptgasse
Bottom left Wildkirchli Caves

Hub of the Alpstein Appenzell, 16km south of St Gallen, is a visual delight. **Hauptgasse**, the Altstadt's main pedestrian thoroughfare, is lined with lavishly painted facades and shops selling everything from traditional costumes to local cheese and antique cowbells. Look up to see little details on the pitched roofs and intricate shop signs. **Landsgemeindeplatz** is the centrepiece square, on one side of which is the friendly and helpful **tourist office**.

Drop by the **Museum Appenzell** *(museum.ai.ch)* for the inside scoop on the region's rural life and folk traditions. On display are beautifully painted wooden furniture with pastoral scenes in local Bauernmalerei style, lacework, costumes, weapons, religious art, flags, banners and more.

Next door, **Pfarrkirche St Mauritius** is easily identified by its whopping great late-Gothic bell tower, embellished with a mural of the cantonal patron saint, St Maurice. The interior offers a dizzying display of frescoes, stained glass and gilding.

Mountain to lake Ride the **Ebenalpbahn** *(ebenalp.ch)* cable car from Wasserauen to reach **Ebenalp** (1640m). Walk for 10 minutes down from the upper cable-car station to the **Wildkirchli Caves** and a mountainside chapel.

A little further on is **Aescher** *(aescher.ch),* one of the oldest mountain guesthouses in Switzerland, dating to 1860. The knee-wobbling descent on foot from here to **Seealpsee** takes around one hour. This sublime, emerald-coloured lake is a gorgeous place to linger.

 Säntis

Säntis (2503m) is eastern Switzerland's highest peak. The **Säntisbahn** *(saentisbahn.ch)* cable car, which runs to the summit from Schwägalp, is closed until early 2027 for reconstruction. During this time the only way up is to hike, either from Schwägalp or Ebenalp, both tough climbs.

From the summit on clear days, you'll be able to see parts of Austria, France, Germany, Liechtenstein and Italy as well as Switzerland. Säntis' top station has two restaurants plus great exhibitions on geology, history and climate. Nestling just beneath the summit is the historic inn **Berggasthaus Alter Säntis**, open between mid-May and mid-October.

Listings

BEST OF THE REST

Classic Swiss Dining

Alpenrose   €€

Bags of old-world charm at this wood-panelled restaurant in Zürich's trendy Kreis 5. On the menu are traditional Swiss dishes and wines served in a sophisticated manner.

Weisser Wind   €€

Dine in a 1425 guild house in Zürich. Decorated in modern art, the restaurant offers a delicious contemporary spin on Swiss cuisine including plate-sized veal schnitzel and pork medallions.

Wirtschaft Zum Frieden   €€

In business since 1445, this historic restaurant is a Schaffhausen institution. Its award-winning cooking gives a modern twist to the Swiss culinary repetoire and the service is friendly.

Wirtschaft Zur Alten Post   €€

One of St Gallen's historic *Erststockbeizli* (1st-floor taverns), this cosy, wood-panelled place stands out for its delicious contemporary cooking as well as its fat veal sausages with rösti.

Family Fun

Zwerg-Bartli Erlebnisweg

In the car-free village of Braunwald in the Glarus Alps, follow this child-focused hiking trail inspired by the adventures of Bartli the dwarf. Along the way there's a water playground by the Brummbach waterfall.

FIFA Museum

This visually engaging and interactive Zürich museum is heaven for soccer fans. It includes a giant football 'pinball' machine where you can put your skills to the test.

Baumwipfelpfad Neckertal

This brilliantly designed treetop walkway and nature play site is an easy day trip from St Gallen. Meander along the wheelchair-accessible, 500m platform rising up to 45m above the forest floor.

Planetenweg

Hike 6km along the forested mountain ridge of Uetliberg, passing scale models of the sun and planets. Pause for splendid views over Zürich and Zürichsee.

A Taste of Switzerland

Lindt Home of Chocolate

With a 9m chocolate fountain as its centrepiece, this sleek Willy Wonka experience in Zürich is also an educational one. Learn how Switzerland perfected commercial chocolate production and taste the results.

Appenzeller Schaukäserei

This show dairy in Stein, 8km southwest of St Gallen, is a slickly run operation. Arrive before

Baumwipfelpfad Neckertal

3pm for a behind-the-scenes look at the mechanised cheesemaking process.

Brauquöll Appenzell

Sample a wide range of beer in the tasting room and shop for the Appenzeller Brewery. Also try its Säntis malt whiskies and vinegars, and grain chips made from brewing-process by-products.

 ## Art & Architecture

Kunst Museum Winterthur

Winterthur's world-class art collection is displayed in three venues and includes everything from early 16th-century portraits to post-impressionist and contemporary art by the likes of Van Gogh, Monet and Picasso.

Markthalle Altenrhein

In Staad am Bodensee, 3.5km east of Rorschach, this delightfully wonky, multicoloured building topped with a roof garden and golden onion domes is a whimsical design by Austrian Friedensreich Hundertwasser.

Militärkantine

This beautifully restored military canteen in St Gallen is an award-winning boutique hotel with a superb restaurant. It also has regular art exhibitions, music and other performances.

 ## Lake Cruising

ZSG Cruises

It's a pleasure cruising across the sparkling waters of Zürichsee. Between April and December ZSG runs a wide range of cruises as well as riverboats along the Limmat River.

Walensee

Sandwiched between the jagged Churfirsten range and Flumserberg, this stunning, 9km-long lake is like a fjord. Schiffsbetrieb Walensee runs boat services across the lake from the end of March to mid-December.

Markthalle Altenrhein

 ## Mountains & Waterfalls

Chäserrugg

At the east end of the saw-toothed Churfirsten range is this 2262m peak. Herzog & de Meuron's architecture here makes it a contemporary design highlight as well as a scenery and sports destination.

Seerenbachfälle

Hike from the Walensee village of Betlis to these three colossal waterfalls, thundering 585m from top to bottom. The middle waterfall, a 305m single drop, ranks as Switzerland's highest.

 ## Romantic Castles

Schloss Rapperswil

This 12th-century fortress overlooks Rapperswil's charming Altstadt and Zürichsee. A contemporary architectural intervention marries a concrete design inspired by a glacier with the castle's stone walls and timber beams.

Schloss Kyburg

This fairy-tale medieval fortress sits high above the Töss River south of Winterthur. Inside, try on a suit of armour, climb up towers, and inspect the iron maiden and other torture instruments.

GRAUBÜNDEN

ALPS | WILDERNESS | ROAD TRIPS
RESEARCHED BY KERRY WALKER

GRAUBÜNDEN
Trip Builder

The Swiss Alps rise sheer and rugged where they shoulder up to Austria and Italy in the country's southeast. From the ritzy slopes of St Moritz and Davos, to epic road trips and rail journeys like the Bernina Express, Graubünden delivers big wilderness around every bend.

FROM LEFT: ADRIAN MICHAEL, CC BY 3.0, VIA WIKIMEDIA COMMONS ©; OCTAVIAN LAZAR/SHUTTERSTOCK. PREVIOUS SPREAD: SIMON DANNHAUER/SHUTTERSTOCK

Walenstadt

✪ **Vaduz**

AUSTRIA

Live the Swiss dream of childhood fantasies at **Heididorf** (pictured; p221)
🚗 *20min from Chur*

Bad Ragaz

Landquart

SWITZERLAND

Marvel at the mountains from every heart-pumping bend driving the **Flüela Pass** (p232)
🚗 *20min from Davos*

Chur

Klosters

Selfranga

Experience off-the-charts alpine beauty in the nature-gone-wild **Swiss National Park** (pictured; p228)
🚗🚆 *40min from St Moritz*

Unplug and tune in to the great wilderness of **Parc Ela** (p218)
🚗 *35min from Chur*

Flims

Domat/Ems

Davos

Valbella

Lenzerheide

Zernez

Swiss National Park

Thusis

Lenz

Tiefencastel

Bergün

Savognin

Parc Ela

La Punt

Carve the slopes and strike a pose with snow yoga at **Corviglia** (p222) in St Moritz
🚗🚆 *1½-2hr from Chur*

Samedan

St Moritz

ITALY

0 — 10 km
0 — 5 miles

Practicalities

ARRIVING

Chur is the transport hub, well connected by rail to the rest of Switzerland. It's a 1½-hour train ride from the nearest international airport in Zürich.

MONEY

If you plan on exploring a lot by train and bus, invest in the money-saving Graubünden Pass.

FIND YOUR WAY

Local tourist offices can help out with planning routes and city/hiking maps. Visit sbb.ch for public transport timetables and tickets.

WHERE TO STAY

Town /Village	Pro/Con
Chur	Historic heights, the Alps on the doorstep and great rail journeys.
St Moritz	Ritzy slopes, sparkling lakes, glacier skiing. Excellent public transport.
Zernez	Gateway to charismatic, Romansch-speaking villages.
Davos and Klosters	These twin resorts entice with epic slopes, culture and sustainable credentials.

EATING & DRINKING

Graubünden specialities include: *Bündnerfleisch* (dried beef, smoked and thinly sliced), *Bündner Nusstorte* (pictured top left; delicious caramelised pastry tart with a sweet walnut filling), *Capuns* (pictured below left; chard dumplings simmered in cream) and *Gerstensuppe* (barley soup flavoured with stock and vegetables).

Best cheese and ham tasting platter with alpine views
Anitas Alpstübli

Must-try rösti and raclette
Alpina Hütte

GETTING AROUND

Train Graubünden towns and villages are connected by rail. Chur is the hub, with trains from Zürich.

Bus Where trains stop, bright yellow PostBus services take over. Many routes begin in Chur.

Car The best way to explore Graubünden's remotest corners and hair-raising mountain passes.

APR-JUN
Quieter days for low-level hikes, cycling and paddling.

JUL-AUG
High-level, hut-to-hut hiking, swimming in alpine lakes and a flurry of folk festivals.

SEP-NOV
Leaf peeping in golden larch forests, wine festivals, wildlife spotting.

DEC-MAR
Graubünden's slopes buzz with skiers from mid-December to Easter.

45 Nature's Call: PARC ELA

MOUNTAINS | NATURE | VILLAGES

Wave bye-bye to civilisation and tiptoe into the wilds of **Parc Ela**. Never heard of it? That's because folk whisper quietly about Switzerland's biggest nature park. Spanning 600 sq km, the park is a treasured glimpse of the Alps before the dawn of tourism. Here nature runs riot, with snow-frosted peaks whooshing above cottongrass-stippled moors, flowery pastures and stunning turquoise lakes.

How To

Getting here Trains run at least hourly from Chur to gateways like Savognin (one hour) and Bergün (1¼ hours).

When to go Spring brings the eruption of wildflowers. Summer is ideal for hut-to-hut hikes. Come in autumn for colour-changing foliage and quiet days.

Top tip Reached on foot from Savognin, **Anitas Alpstübli** is an enchanting spot for a sharing-platter lunch and seductive mountain views.

Village gateways Base yourself in one of the pin-drop-peaceful villages rimming the park, such as **Alvaschein**, **Tiefencastel** or **Filisur**, where you'll be blown away by the 65m-high curves of the gravity-defying **Landwasser Viaduct**, the showstopper of the UNESCO-listed Albula railway line. Fairest of the lot, however, is **Bergün**, with its cobbled alleys, Romanesque church and historic houses embellished with sgraffito, frescoes and oriel windows. Punching high above, the dagger-shaped peak of Piz Ela (3339m) looks loveliest in the rosy glow of sundown.

Escape to Alp Flix Heading further south, you reach **Savognin**, famous for its sheep-shearing festival in October. It's a charismatic base for striking out to nearby **Alp Flix**, a spectacularly biodiverse wonderland of high moors, stone pine forests, flower meadows, peaks and jewel-like lakes.

VIACHESLAV LOPATIN/SHUTTERSTOCK

～～ Landwasser Viaduct

You'll never forget the moment you first clap eyes on the **Landwasser Viaduct** – the park's architectural showstopper. Making a spectacular leap between sheer-sided, forest-flanked mountains, this marvel of engineering forms part of the UNESCO-listed Albula/Bernina Railway. If the six-arch, 65m-high viaduct wows today, you can only imagine what folk thought when it was unveiled in 1901. You can admire it fleetingly by train, but for a closer look make for Filisur, where a 2km, 50-minute hike follows the railway line and dips into forest, emerging at a lookout platform with tremendous views of the viaduct.

The plateau is best explored on the 5.5km **circular trail** (keep an eye out for resident marmots, chamois, ibex and bearded vultures).

Hike Parc Ela You can swoon over the views on mood-lifting road trips over alpine passes (Albula, Julier and Septimer), but to properly immerse yourself in the wilderness, swap the wheel for boots. Beginning in Preda above Bergün and ending in Savognin, the 22km, three-pass, nine-hour **Trans Parc Ela** reveals the park from its most flattering angles. The trail keeps you constantly on a high. Download the app from parc-ela.ch for more details.

Above Landwasser Viaduct

46 Heidi's Intoxicating HEARTLAND

HEIDI | ALPS | WINE

If you've ever harboured a desire to skip Heidi-style down the slopes, head to Maienfeld. With cute timber chalets, bell-rattling cows and wildflower-freckled pastures, this village makes you want to yodel out loud. Apparently, these landscapes fired the imagination of Swiss author Johanna Spyri (1827–1901), who penned *Heidi* in 1881. Linger for wine tastings and barrel sleeps among the vines.

VOLKERPREUSSER/ALAMY

🗺 How To

Getting here S-Bahn trains breeze from Chur to Maienfeld (11 minutes) and Bad Ragaz (14 minutes).

When to go Dodge peak summer for fewer crowds. Come in spring for meadows in brilliant bloom and autumn for wine harvests and festivals.

Wine backpack How clever: cowshed turned wine bar **Stall 247** in Maienfeld offers a wine backpack, combining an audio-guided hike of the vines with a trio of regional wines. Snacks, water, glasses and napkins are included.

KECKO/FLICKR/CC BY 2.0 ®

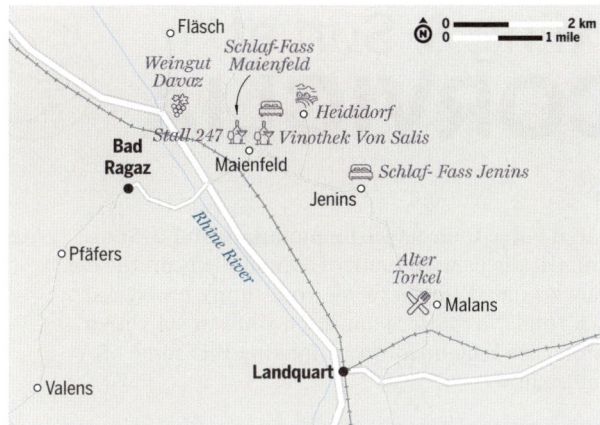

Hiking to Heididorf The village of Maienfeld fits the Swiss childhood fantasy bill neatly and has been declared Heidi's own. The 2.4km, 1½-hour **Heidiweg** loop trail trots through valleys, forests, mountain meadows and vineyards to **Heididorf** (heididorf.ch), where you'll find the rustic **Heidihaus** where, of course, she never lived because she never existed. The scenery is glorious, however. And the shop sells Heidi-everything: dirndls, dolls, chocolate, wine, you name it.

Bündner Herrschaft Heidi isn't Maienfeld's only claim to fame. Unfolding east of the Rhine, Bündner Herrschaft is wine country and its Fünf Dörfer (Five Villages) – Fläsch, Maienfeld, Jenins, Malans and Zizers – produce cracking Pinot noir, Riesling and Sylvaner wines. Each year the villages take turns to celebrate **Herbstfest**. This autumnal wine celebration brings much drinking, eating and merrymaking to these normally quiet streets.

Tastings and tours After swanning around the vines, pop into **Von Salis** (vonsalis-wein.ch) wine bar in Maienfeld for tastings of plummy reds and peachy sparkling whites. Perched above the vines, wine cellar **Alter Torkel** (alter-torkel.ch) in Jenins puts creative riffs on regional dishes, which are expertly matched with wines. Go for lunch on the terrace or a 30-minute, four-wine tasting. For more insight into grape-growing and winemaking, hook onto a guided tour at **Weingut Davaz** (davaz-wein.ch), a cork pop away from Maienfeld, or simply roll by for a tasting.

Top left Alter Torkel
Bottom left Heidihaus

 Roll out the Barrel

More wine-related fun, you say? At **Schlaf-Fass Maienfeld** (schlaf-fass. ch) you can roll out the barrel by spending a romantic night snuggled up in a cutely converted Fass (wine barrel) just big enough for two. Toast your arrival with a glass of Riesling, Pinot noir or Silvaner wine. **Schlaf-Fass Jenins** offers a similarly novel experience. Here dinner and breakfast are sorted in the form of a basket brimming with local goodies such as alpine cheese, fresh bread and Bündner Nusstorte (walnut tart).

Skiing & Sun at
CORVIGLIA

YOGA | SKIING | MOUNTAINS

Ask St Moritz locals to divulge their favourite mountain and 2486m Corviglia is bound to feature. On the eastern flank of 3056m Piz Nair, the ski area's 155km of immaculately groomed slopes swing from sunny, cruisy red runs to knee-trembling black runs. No matter your level, you can ski with a clean conscience here: cannons use reclaimed water, making this some of Switzerland's most sustainable snow.

IMAGO/FLEIG/EIBNER-PRESSEFOTO/ALAMY

🗺️ How To

Getting here The **Chantarella-Corviglia** (*engadin.ch*) funicular runs between 7.50am and 5pm from mid-November to late April.

When to go When the flakes fall in winter, from December to early April. The season is longer at Diavolezza, running from late October to early May.

Hut heaven Going strong since 1903, the **Alpina Hütte** has knockout mountain views. Refuel over specialities like *Gerstensuppe* (barley soup) and *Bündnerteller* (a sharing platter of cheese and air-dried beef).

SERGII KOVAL/SHUTTERSTOCK

JAHVI PROCA/SHUTTERSTOCK

Top left Corviglia
Bottom left Gerstensuppe
Left Diavolezza

Morning sun As the first light illuminates the jagged summits of the Albula Alps, the Engadine Valley below lies in shadow. It's early morning and the snow is as crisp and white as a fresh sheet on a newly made bed. If ever a backdrop was going to inspire you to embrace the moment and stretch, Paradiso piste on **Corviglia** mountain is it.

Snow yoga Cue the world's first snow yoga piste, a red run with four peaceful, tremendously scenic stops, where you can practise *asanas* (poses) while gliding effortlessly downhill. Each stop has a Sanskrit-named theme such as *om* (essence of the universe), *prana* (life force) and *vinyasa* (movement and breath). Giving new meaning to *tadasana* (mountain pose), snow yoga brings meditative breathwork, mantras and mindfulness of movement to the slopes.

Ski technique From muscle-strengthening extended triangle poses to balance-improving tree poses, the theory goes that yoga can be seamlessly combined with skiing to hone your technique – boosting confidence, channelling strength and stability, helping to negotiate tricky turns and, above all, forging a deep connection with the mountains.

Get a guide You can go it alone on the marked piste, practising *asanas* at your leisure, but for more insight consider signing up to a half- or full-day course with the pro ski instructors and yoga teachers at **Suvretta Sports** (*suvretta-sports.ch*).

 Glacier Skiing at Diavolezza

Things take a turn for the wilder at **Diavolezza** (*corvatsch-diavolezza.ch*), just south of St Moritz, at 2978m. Here you'll swoon over stupendous views of Piz Bernina (4049m), the highest peak in the Eastern Alps. In winter, there's a mix of red and black ski runs, ski touring and free-riding. The big one is Switzerland's longest glacier run, a 10km ride over marked but ungroomed terrain taking you over the Pers and Morteratsch Glaciers. Time your visit right for a pinch of magic at Glüna Plaina, when you can ski by the shimmering light of full moon on a silent winter night.

MARKUS MAINKA/SHUTTERSTOCK

On the Green Run

SUSTAINABILITY ON THE SLOPES IN GRAUBÜNDEN.

Every year in Switzerland the snow level creeps higher up the mountains, glaciers shrink, winters get warmer and eco snow is the hot topic. Climate change is inevitable, meaning that the future of winter sports has to be sustainable. Graubünden is blazing ahead with green transport, renewable energy and a flurry of low-impact activities.

Left Swiss Railways
Centre Artificial snow machine
Right Valsana hotel

Sustainable Transport

Arriving is a big deal, with trains generating just a tiny percentage of the carbon emissions of flights. Graubünden is well connected by rail, with Eurostar services to Paris linking up to high-speed trains to Chur in around 5½ hours. And when you get there, the fabulous train rides continue, whisking you deeper into the Alps on the Glacier and Bernina Express. Even better: since January 2025, Swiss Railways (SBB) trains have run 100% on electricity generated from renewable sources. And beyond town and city, an increasing number of funiculars and cable cars are run on green energy, too.

Future Is Green

There are many issues Graubünden's ski resorts need to confront: how they make snow; the need for clean, green, free public transport; addressing the financial implications of shorter seasons and diversifying to emphasise low-impact sports like snowshoeing, winter hiking, cross-country skiing and sledging. These encourage visitors to go slow and venture beyond the pistes, drawing attention away from traditional downhill skiing, which causes erosion. On-the-ball resorts are also implementing conservation schemes involving replanting and rewilding over the summer months to enhance habitats and attract wildlife.

Eco Trailblazers

Right at the forefront of the sustainable winter-sports movement is St Moritz, whose Clean Energy project has made waves over the past two decades. At Piz Nair, reached by solar-panelled gondola, the Clean Energy Tour combines

sublime mountain scenery with a spotlight on energy derived from the sun, wind, water and biomass. On Corviglia, the Nair Pitschen reservoir gathers recycled meltwater to create snow on the mountain. At glacier-capped Diavolezza, snow is harvested at season's end, stockpiled and kept for the next season. Luxury hotels are in on the eco act in this ritzy resort, too – take Badrutt's Palace, for instance, which is reducing its impact on the environment by using geothermal energy from the lake.

But St Moritz is just one example, with many towns, villages and resorts in Graubünden swiftly following suit. Aiming for energy self-sufficiency by 2036, Davos-Klosters is another pioneer, with sustainable snowmaking using hydropower, solar panels at Jakobshorn and moorland regeneration projects to boost biodiversity and attract wildlife. The twin resort also branches away from downhill skiing with gentler pursuits like snowshoeing, cross-country skiing, sledging and ice skating by night.

> At glacier-capped Diavolezza, snow is harvested at season's end, stockpiled and kept for the next season.

Over-the-mountain Arosa-Lenzerheide has ramped up its sustainability with solar-powered lifts, free buses zipping around the largely car-free resort, e-vehicle charging points, waste-heat recovery systems and green hotels such as Arlenwald and Valsana. Downhill skiing here is complemented by winter hiking, tobogganing, cross-country, ice bathing, curling and horse-drawn sleigh rides, reminding visitors that the beauty of snow goes way beyond the speed of the slopes.

Greenstyle: Flims-Laax

West of Chur, Flims-Laax is a shining star of sustainability, with carbon neutrality in its sights by 2030 and the Greenstyle Foundation propping up an eco-conscious winter-sports model to protect the environment. Tree planting, lake clean-ups and wildlife sanctuary zones are all in the mix. Here all lifts run on hydro and solar panels (some even on demand to save energy) and e-shuttles buzz around the resort. Cannons run on hydropower and recycled meltwater is gathered so snowmaking is CO_2 neutral. Symbolic of its ethos is the Last Day Pass, a project designed to protect the Vorab Glacier. It is estimated that 8 April 2056 will be the last day the glacier will be skiable. Each pass purchased is expected to slow the process by 10 minutes and offset 1000kg of CO_2.

48 Riding the Bernina **EXPRESS**

EPIC RAILWAYS | ALPS | VIEWS

Skipping from snow-capped peak to palm trees, the **Bernina Express** (pictured) is right up there with the world's most sensational train rides. Climbing high into the glaciated realms of the Alps and traversing 55 tunnels and 196 bridges on the four-hour journey from Chur to Tirano, the journey has views so riveting you'll be glued to the window throughout.

COLOMBO NICOLA/SHUTTERSTOCK

🗺 Trip Notes

Getting there The Bernina Express runs daily year round, departing Chur at 8.17am and arriving in Tirano at 12.49pm. From mid-May to late October, there is an extra service at 1.28pm.

When to go Choosing between summer sun or the white magic of winter snow is a tough one – this train ride is gorgeous whenever you go.

Top tip Seat reservations are required (the sooner you book these for the panoramic carriages, the better).

🍴 Buongiorno, Italia!

Board the morning train in Chur and you can reach Tirano in time for an alfresco *pranzo* (lunch) or gelato. With its pretty piazzas, pastel-painted buildings and Renaissance basilica, the town is a tantalising taste of Italy. Try the local *bresaola* (air-dried beef) and *pizzoccheri* (buckwheat pasta with potatoes, chard, cheese, butter and garlic).

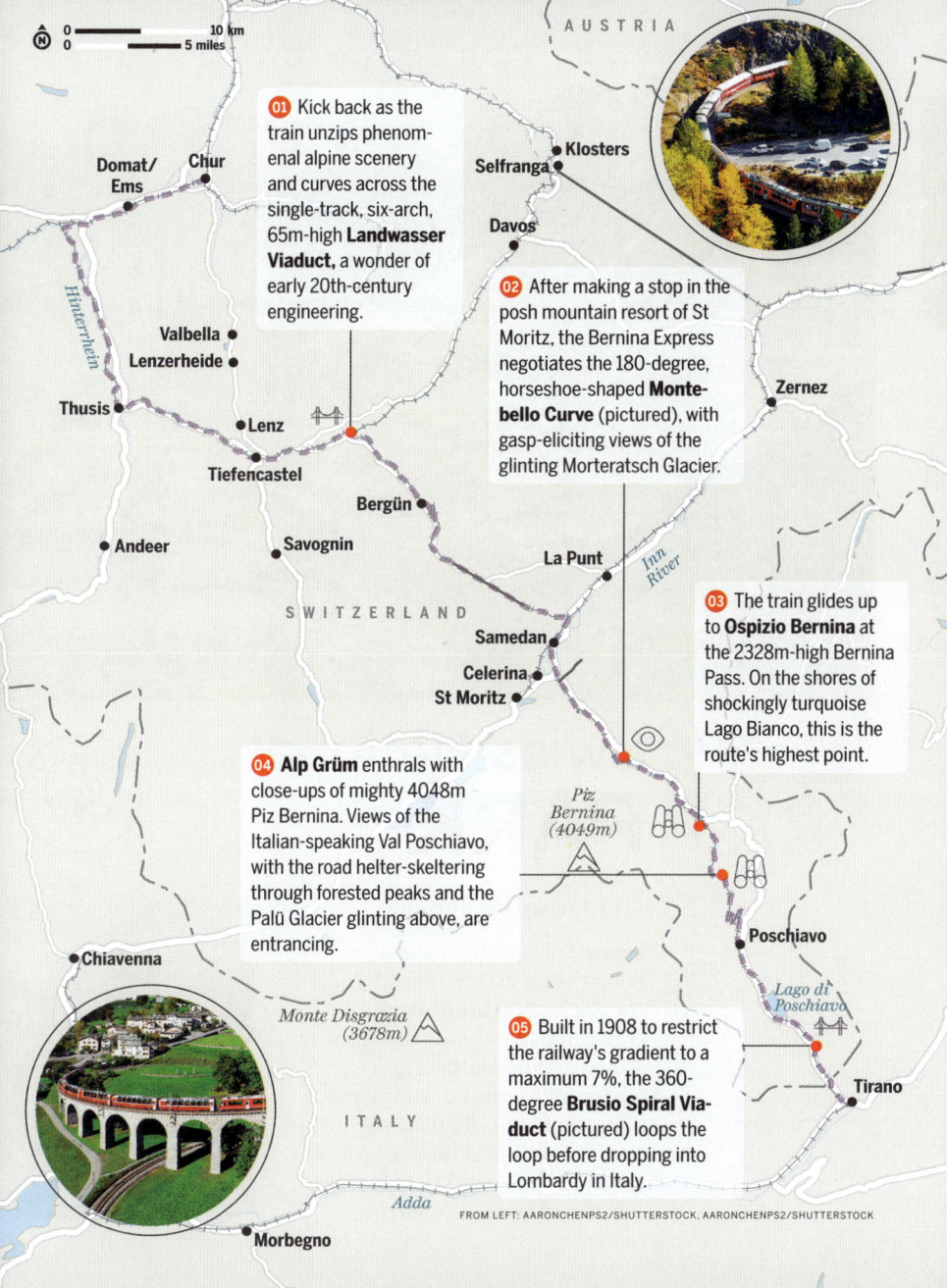

AUSTRIA

01 Kick back as the train unzips phenomenal alpine scenery and curves across the single-track, six-arch, 65m-high **Landwasser Viaduct,** a wonder of early 20th-century engineering.

02 After making a stop in the posh mountain resort of St Moritz, the Bernina Express negotiates the 180-degree, horseshoe-shaped **Montebello Curve** (pictured), with gasp-eliciting views of the glinting Morteratsch Glacier.

03 The train glides up to **Ospizio Bernina** at the 2328m-high Bernina Pass. On the shores of shockingly turquoise Lago Bianco, this is the route's highest point.

04 **Alp Grüm** enthrals with close-ups of mighty 4048m Piz Bernina. Views of the Italian-speaking Val Poschiavo, with the road helter-skeltering through forested peaks and the Palü Glacier glinting above, are entrancing.

05 Built in 1908 to restrict the railway's gradient to a maximum 7%, the 360-degree **Brusio Spiral Viaduct** (pictured) loops the loop before dropping into Lombardy in Italy.

0   10 km
0   5 miles

Domat/Ems
Chur
Selfranga
Klosters
Davos
Valbella
Lenzerheide
Zernez
Thusis
Lenz
Tiefencastel
Bergün
Andeer
Savognin
La Punt
Inn River
SWITZERLAND
Samedan
Celerina
St Moritz
Piz Bernina (4049m)
Poschiavo
Chiavenna
Lago di Poschiavo
Monte Disgrazia (3678m)
Tirano
ITALY
Adda
Morbegno
Hinterrhein

49 Swiss National PARK

ALPS | WILDLIFE | HIKING

 For a taste of the Alps before the tourists rocked up, the **Swiss National Park** in Graubünden's Lower Engadine Valley is unbeatable. Here – where high, rugged, snowcapped mountains muscle their way into Italy – you'll find the backcountry dream in a 172-sq-km wilderness unscathed by development.

 ## How To

Getting here Frequent trains run from St Moritz to Zernez (42 minutes), the gateway to the national park. From here, buses run to Il Fuorn in the heart of the park.

When to go Come in summer for high-level hiking and wildlife watching, and autumn for leaf peeping and deer rutting.

Maps and apps Pick up a 1:50,000 map covering 21 walks in the park at the visitor centre in Zernez, or get the digital hiking guide app at nationalpark.ch.

GRAUBÜNDEN EXPERIENCES

Great Hikes

Time for just one walk? Make it the **Lakes of Macun**. Starting in Zernez, this corker of a 21-km, eight-hour hike treks up through flower-freckled meadows to a 2600m-high alpine plateau bejewelled with 23 lakes shimmering turquoise, topaz and sapphire. Take picnic goodies and ample water.

Brushed with golden larches in autumn and crowned by ragged peaks, the wildly wooded **Val Trupchun** is accessed by a 14km, four-hour circular hike from **S-chanf**. Listen out for rutting stags in September and October.

Switzerland's last native bear was shot in the remote **Val Mingèr** in 1904. The 5.5km, two-hour uphill hike from Pradatsch takes in weirdly eroded rock formations, and you might spot chamois and deer.

 ## Guided Ranger Hikes

You can go it alone, but for more insight, join one of the half-or full-day guided hikes run by the **National Park Centre** in Zernez from late June to mid-October, including Val Trupchun, the Ofen Pass and Lakes of Macun. Most are in German, but guides usually speak some English.

Top left Lakes of Macun
Left Val Trupchun
Above S-chanf

You'll also find secluded beauty on the 12.7-km, 4½-hour hike from **Buffalora** via **Munt la Schera** through a one-of-a-kind steppe landscape, granting views into Italy's Stelvio National Park.

Wildlife Spotting

Visually, the park is a feast: streams rush through larch and pine forests, lakes sparkle on high moors, wildflowers carpet slopes and glaciers frost fin-shaped peaks. True to its founding principles in 1914, nature is left totally to its own devices: no trees are felled, no meadows are cut and no animals hunted. With a little luck and a decent pair of binoculars, you can sight some fantastic alpine wildlife. Hotspots include **Alp Stabelchod** at 1958m, where you might glimpse red deer and chamois, and almost certainly marmots. Bearded vultures can often be seen from the nature trail near **Il Fuorn**, ibex around the **Lakes of Macun**.

A Night in the Park

Slip back to nature by overnighting in the

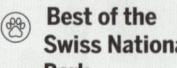

Best of the Swiss National Park

Val Trupchun

A wildlife hotspot, with chances to see deer, chamois, ibex, marmots and, with luck, bearded vultures and golden eagles.

Munt la Schera

At 2586m, it offers fantastic park views. The contrast between the dry, steppe-like south and the mountainous, forested north couldn't be greater. Up here, you can see ptarmigans, snow hares and chamois.

Autumn

During the late September red-deer rut, and the roaring of stags resounds through the forest. October is also beautiful, with crisp light and larch forests in their mantle of gold.

■ *Recommended by Hans Lozza, Swiss National Park head of communications.*

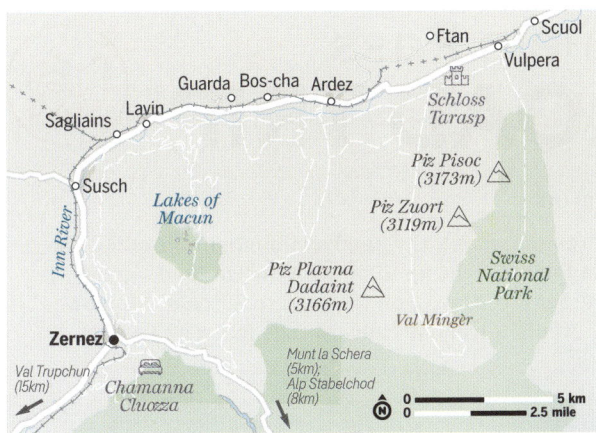

FROM LEFT: GOLDZITFOTOGRAFIE/SHUTTERSTOCK, VUESTOCK/SHUTTERSTOCK

Left Deer, Swiss National Park
Below Schloss Tarasp

park's thickly forested heart. Built in 1910, **Chamanna Cluozza** (*nationalpark.ch*) is a rustic hut open from mid-June to mid-October, reached by a moderately challenging 3½-hour uphill hike from Zernez. Bring your own sleeping bag liner. Climb the saddle in the early morning to see chamois grazing. Lunch packs can be ordered if you're off hiking – as most folk here are.

Engadine Villages

All along the train line, the quaint Engadine villages of Lavin, Scuol, Zuoz, Zernez and S-chanf merit a closer look before you chuck on hiking boots and stride into the park's trail-laced heart.

Zernez is an attractive cluster of stone chalets outlined by the profile of a baroque church and the stout medieval tower of its castle. Framed by rippling peaks and topped off by 1000-year-old turreted castle **Schloss Tarasp**, **Scuol** is a joy to stroll, with Hobbit-like, sgraffito-decorated houses, cobbled lanes, geranium-filled window boxes and fountains spouting pure spring water. It is rivalled only in looks by lovely **Guarda**, just down the valley, with its twisting lanes, frescoed houses and Piz Buin views.

Hungry? Dig into local specialities like *Pizokel* (stubby wheat-and egg-noodles with parsley, speck, cheese and onions), *Bündnerfleisch* (air-dried beef) and *Nusstorte* (caramelised walnut tart).

50

Flüela Pass
ROAD TRIP

EPIC DRIVE | VIEWS | MOUNTAINS

Twisting deep into a remote, silent, thrillingly wild mountain valley, the road over the 2384m **Flüela Pass** is right up there with Switzerland's greatest drives. The pass is 14km southeast of Davos, on the road to Susch in the Lower Engadine, which passes waterfalls, silvery streams, spruce forest and snow-encrusted mountains.

TALJAT DAVID/SHUTTERSTOCK

🔖 Trip Notes

Getting here The Flüela Pass is best explored with your own wheels, but bus 331 plies the route several times daily in summer, with a journey time of one hour.

When to go The pass goes with the snow and generally opens from late May to October. Check conditions at alpen-paesse.ch before heading out.

Top tip For a blast of nostalgia, book a carriage ride on the historic, horse-drawn Flüela post coach, which heads every Tuesday from Davos to the pass, returning by bus.

📖 Bronze Age Roots

Spear tips unearthed here show that the road was used as far back as the Bronze Age. It was particularly well trodden during medieval times, when farmers from Valais went with pack mules over the pass to trade goods as far north as Tyrol in Austria, returning with precious salt in exchange.

02 Take a break from the wheel at **Wägerhus**, where you can hike the 11km, 4½-hour **Jöriseen circuit trail** (pictured), climbing uphill over pastures and scree to a sprinkling of startlingly turquoise lakes.

03 At the **Flüela Pass** (pictured opposite page) itself, pause to stroll along the shores of **Lai da la Scotta** and **Lai Nair**. The lakes are ensnared by rugged peaks that reflect brilliantly in their mill-pond-calm waters in the morning.

01 Kicking off in **Davos**, the drive packs in scenic drama, with the road snaking around hairpins high above the valley and the jagged, oft-snow-capped Silvretta Alps flinging up 3000m either side.

04 Go for lunch at **Flüela Hospiz** (pictured; *flueela-hospiz. ch)*, a pine-clad hut on the shores of the lake. The restaurant prides itself on game specialities, from Prättigauer venison sausage to wild boar ham.

AUSTRIA

Silvrettahorn (3244m)

Davos

Flüelapassstrasse

Dischmastrasse

Lai Nair

Lai da la Scotta

Pass dal Flüela

Susch

SWITZERLAND

HOTEL FLÜELA HOSPIZ

CAFÉ

En (Inn) River

N

0   5 km

0   2.5 miles

Listings

BEST OF THE REST

History & Heritage

Chur Altstadt

Strolling the cat's cradle of alleys is like time travel, with cobbles, frescoed facades, fountains, hidden courtyards and the medieval remains of the defensive walls and towers.

Rätisches Museum

Housed in a baroque patrician residence, this museum spells out the canton's history in artefacts, with Bronze Age jewellery, Roman statuettes and more.

Kloster Disentis

Rising like a vision, this Benedictine monastery wows with its lavishly stuccoed baroque church. A monastery has stood here since the 8th century.

Art & Literature

Thomas Mann Trail

Thomas Mann found romance in the Silvretta Alps above Davos, which inspired his seminal novel, *The Magic Mountain* (1924). Walk in his footsteps on this 2.8km, one-hour trail from Davos' Waldhotel to Schatzalp.

Bündner Kunstmuseum

Chur's beautifully domed Villa Planta is a dazzling celebration of the artistic legacy of Augusto Giacometti (1877–1947), forefather of Swiss abstract art, as well as his cousin Giovanni and expressionist nephew, Alberto.

Kirchner Museum

In a striking cubic building in Davos, this showcases German expressionist Ernst Ludwig Kirchner's work in the place where he created much of it.

Nietzsche-Haus

Feel the rumble of existential philosophy in the chalet where Friedrich Nietzsche summered from 1881 to 1888 in the enchantingly time-lost Val Fex.

Natural Wonders

Caumasee

Ringed by thick woods, this exquisitely turquoise lake, just south of Flims Waldhaus, is an attractive spot for a cool summer swim.

Ruinaulta

Limestone cliffs have been eroded into a forest of pinnacles and columns at glacier-gouged, 400m-deep Ruinaulta, hailed the 'Swiss Grand Canyon'. Beginning in Trin, a dramatic 3½-hour trek leads through the gorge, shadowing the Vorderrhein River.

High-Altitude Hikes

Lai da Tuma

Stride from the rugged Oberalp Pass to the sparkling blue-green Lai da Tuma (Tomasee), the source of the Rhine, on this high-level, 8.5km circular route.

Tamina Therme

Fünf Seen Wanderung

Kicking off at 2227m-high Pizolhütte above Bad Ragaz, this 11.5-km, five-hour walk takes in a crest of limestone peaks, glaciers and five jewel-coloured lakes.

 ## Rail & Road Trips

Oberalp Pass

Buckle up for a dreamy alpine drive on the snaking, 32km mountain road from Disentis to Andermatt via the starkly wild, wind-beaten Oberalp Pass at 2044m.

Bernina Pass

Alpine views wow on this road that clambers into the glacier-tipped mountains and lonely realms of the 2328m Bernina Pass from Pontresina to Italy.

 ## Spa Time

Tamina Therme

Bad Ragaz' miracle-working, 36.5°C thermal waters bubble to the surface at this ultra-sleek spa, with thermal pools for hot-cold dunking, jets, whirlpools and saunas.

7132 Therme

Basel-born architect Peter Zumthor has tapped into the brilliance of Vals' thermal waters, waving a magic wand to transform thermal baths into a temple of cutting-edge cool.

 ## Regional Flavours

Veltliner Weinstuben zum Stern   €€

Dine by candlelight in this wood-panelled parlour, serving regional, seasonal cooking from freshest asparagus in spring to game in autumn.

Rätisches Museum

Fidazerhof   €€

At this dark-wood chalet with expansive alpine views, the menu bigs up regional slow-food in dishes like *Capuns* (egg dumplings) and *Gerstensuppe* (barley soup).

Burestübli   €€

On a crisp winter's night, haul a sledge up to a peak above Arosa to bump down through twinkling forests on a floodlit toboggan run, before fondue at this gorgeously rustic chalet.

Outdoor Thrills

Swissraft

The turbulent 17km stretch of the Vorderrhein between Ilanz and Reichenau is white-water-rafting heaven. Swissraft gets you out on the water rafting, canoeing and hydrospeeding.

Olympic Bob Run

For a buzz, nothing beats careering headfirst across glass-smooth ice at speeds of up to 135km/h on the world's oldest bobsleigh run. Book a hair-raising 75-second guest ride.

Swiss Kitesurf

Every day at 11am sharp, the Maloja wind rips down from the mountains, ruffling the turquoise, glacially cold waters of Lake Silvaplana, perfect for kitesurfing and wing foiling.

Practicalities

ARRIVING

238

GETTING AROUND

240

SAFE TRAVEL

244

MONEY

245

RESPONSIBLE TRAVEL

246

ACCOMMODATION

248

ESSENTIALS

250

LANGUAGE

252

Right Pilatusbahn (p166)

EASY STEPS FROM THE AIRPORT TO THE CITY CENTRE

Bordering France, Germany, Austria, Liechtenstein and Italy, Switzerland is at the heart of Europe and easily accessible by train and road. The most important international airports are in Zürich (pictured), Geneva, Basel and Bern. In addition to Swiss, the national airline, there are many budget or smaller airlines with connections to the country.

AT THE AIRPORT

MICHAEL DERRER FUCHS/SHUTTERSTOCK

SIM CARDS

It's cheapest, quicker and less hassle to buy an eSIM online prior to arrival. To buy a card immediately on arrival, get a local Swisscom or Salt SIM at the duty-free shop or at Travelex in Arrivals. Both Swiss providers have outlets in the airport shopping centre.

WI-FI

Select the 'Zurich Airport' wi-fi network on your device to access four hours of free wi-fi; register by SMS or your boarding pass. There's also the option to purchase additional hours (Chf6.90/ 9.90/14.90 per hour/4hrs/24hrs).

ATMS

ATMs are located throughout terminals. They accept foreign cards and have multiple language options.

MONEY

International currency exchange bureaux are located in the Arrivals areas, though you'll get better rates at banks in town.

MORE INFORMATION

Head to the Welcome Desk in the Arrivals hall, or see the airport website at flughafen-zuerich.ch.

CUSTOMS

Regulations Visitors may import 250 cigarettes or cigars, or 250g of pipe tobacco. The allowance for alcoholic beverages is 1l for beverages containing more than 18% alcohol by volume, and 5l for beverages containing up to 18%. Gifts up to the value of Chf150 may also be imported, as well as food provisions for one day.

GETTING TO ZÜRICH CITY CENTRE

TAXI & CAR
Count Chf50 to Chf70 and up to 20 minutes to the centre, 9km south. The A3 approaches Zürich from the south along the southern shore of Zürichsee. The A1 is the fastest route from Bern and Basel. It proceeds northeast to Winterthur.

TRAIN
Regular services run from Zürich Airport station to the downtown Hauptbahnhof (12 minutes, Chf7) from around 5am until midnight. The airport station appears on timetables as Zürich Flughafen; the downtown station is Zürich HB.

TRAM
Ride tramline 10 from the airport to Bahnhofplatz in the centre (35 minutes, Chf7). Tickets are valid one hour and children aged four to 15 are charged half-fare.

HOW MUCH FOR A...

Taxi
Chf50 to Chf70
20 mins

Train
Chf7
12 mins

Tram
Chf7
35 min

PUBLIC TRANSPORT TICKETS
Download the ZVV app (zvv.ch) to purchase tram tickets, consult timetables and check traffic. Bikes require a separate ticket.

TRAIN TICKETS
Download the SBB app (sbb.ch) before arrival to plan train trips, buy digital tickets and save time queueing.

ZÜRICH CARD
Unlimited public transport for 24/72 hours (Chf29/56) is included in this city card along with admission to many city museums and sights. Buy online at zu-erich.com. The Zürich Card Bike version (24/72 hours Chf34/65) additionally includes use of a PubliBike public-sharing bike to freewheel around the city and lighten your carbon footprint.

SWITZERLAND ARRIVING

OTHER POINTS OF ENTRY

Geneva Airport SBB trains (Chf3) run at least every 10 minutes to Gare de Cornavin in the city centre; taxis charge Chf50 to Chf60 for the 30-minute drive. In winter coaches run to Verbier, Crans-Montana and ski resorts in neighbouring France.

EuroAirport Basel-Mulhouse-Freiburg This airport serves Basel (as well as Mulhouse, France and Freiburg, Germany) with flights from many European cities. It's located 5km north of the Swiss city. Take the Swiss exit, then hop on bus line 50 (Chf6.60, 20 minutes) to Basel SBB train station.

Boat Switzerland may be landlocked, but you can sail to the country aboard passenger paddle steamers and commuter boats year-round on Lake Geneva (CGN boats link the French towns of Évian-les-Bains and Thonon-les-Bains with Lausanne, Yvoire with Nyon, and St Gingolph with Montreux and Lausanne) and from April to October on Bodensee (cruises operated by Switzerland's Bodensee Schifffahrt, Austria's Vorarlberg Lines and Germany's BSB).

Train Zürich is Switzerland's busiest international terminus, with trains to Munich and Vienna, from where there are extensive onward connections to cities in eastern Europe.

TRANSPORT TIPS TO HELP YOU GET AROUND

So scenic are many journeys in Switzerland, that getting from A to B becomes an adventure in its own right. The country's interconnected network of trains, boats, cable cars and buses is justifiably famous – public transport really does run on time and like clockwork, meaning your own wheels are by no means the only way to get around.

SPEED LIMITS Be aware of speed limits: 30km/h in major urban areas, 80km/h on main roads outside towns, 100km/h on single-lane main roads, rising to 120km/h on motorways. Speed cameras are prolific and fines hefty.

BUSES Bright-yellow PostBuses supplement the rail network and link less accessible towns and villages. Departures are synchronised with train arrivals, with PostBus stops conveniently located by train stations. Travel is one class only and fares are comparable to the train.

CYCLING & E-BIKING

Well-signposted, highly scenic cycling routes spaghetti across the country; find cycling and mountain-biking pages on schweizmobil. ch. With SBB Rent-a-Bike (*rentabike. ch*), bikes can be collected at one train station and returned to another. Most stations have e-bikes, tandems and trailers.

ROAD CONDITIONS

Roads are well maintained. Road signs for motorways are green (unlike in neighbouring France where they're blue). Higher alpine passes are snow-blocked and shut in winter; signs on lower approach roads will clearly indicate if a pass is open or closed.

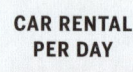

CAR RENTAL PER DAY

Car rental per day Chf65

Unleaded petrol Approx Chf1.72/l

Motorway tolls Chf40 per calendar year

DRIVING ESSENTIALS

Drive on the right.

Headlights must be turned on at all times, day and night.

November to March, winter tyres are an essential.

.05 The blood alcohol limit is 0.05%.

To use motorways, pay an annual toll (Chf40) online at *vignette-schweiz.com*.

CAR HIRE & SHARING Major car-rental companies have offices at airports, and in major cities and towns. Book well in advance during ski season, December to April; rental cars are usually equipped with winter tyres. Flying into Geneva Airport, you have the choice of renting on the Swiss or French side – France is cheaper. Cars can be hired for as little time as an hour with car-sharing scheme Mobility (*mobility.ch*).

TIMETABLES Transport timetables often refer to Werktags (workdays), which means Monday to Saturday, unless there is the qualification 'ausser Samstag' ('except Saturday'). At train stations, look for poster-sized printed timetables on walls in underpasses and on platforms: departures are printed on yellow boards and arrivals on white. Printed timetables are generally written in German, French, Italian and English.

LAKE STEAMERS Switzerland's larger lakes are serviced by steamers operated by either SBB or allied private companies for which national SBB travel passes are valid. These include Lakes Geneva, Constance (Bodensee), Lucerne, Lugano, Neuchâtel, Biel, Murten, Thun, Brienz and Zug. It does not include Lago Maggiore.

SUPERSAVER FARES When buying train tickets on the SBB app, look for suggested train departures marked with a % symbol. This means a super-saver fare is available on that train – providing an easy way to instantly save a few francs.

KNOW YOUR CARBON FOOTPRINT A road trip by car from Geneva to Lauterbrunnen would emit around 60kg of carbon dioxide. A bus would emit 30kg for the same distance, per passenger. A train would emit about 2kg. There are a number of carbon calculators online. We used *almightytree.ch/co2calculator-individuals*.

ROAD DISTANCE CHART (KM)

	Geneva	Sion	Zürich	Basel	Bern	Bellinzona	Lugano	Lucerne	Neuchâtel
Sion	160								
Zürich	278	275							
Basel	254	262	87						
Bern	159	157	121	99					
Bellinzona	404	160	177	239	251				
Lugano	432	179	205	267	279	30			
Lucerne	265	262	52	100	112	140	169		
Neuchâtel	123	163	154	132	56	281	310	143	
Interlaken	216	106	175	152	56	199	286	68	112

TRAIN TRAVEL

Eco-friendly Switzerland makes rail travel a joy. In keeping with the country's love for precision and timekeeping, its trains typically run like clockwork and are a true pleasure to travel around the country on. Fares are not cheap – study the numerous discount travel cards and tickets on offer to ensure you get the best deal.

HOW MUCH FOR A...

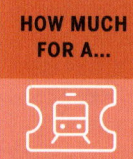

Glacier Express 2nd class
Chf208

Left-luggage locker
Chf5-13 per 12hrs

Three-day Swiss Travel Pass
Chf244

MELISSAMN/SHUTTERSTOCK

CLASSES, FARES & RESERVATIONS

Second-class compartments are comfortable and fill fast; 1st-class carriages are spacious. Both have power points. Standard 2nd-class fares are roughly Chf40 per 100km; 1st-class fares average 75% more. Book tickets in advance to bag discounts.

Tickets purchased the day of travel are the most expensive. Seat reservations (Chf5) are recommended for longer journeys, particularly in July and August. Bikes require a ticket. For longer journeys, a bike Day Pass (Chf15) will be cheaper. March to October, reserve a place for your bike on board InterCity trains.

SBB APP

Download the SBB app *(sbb. ch)* to plan rail routes, consult schedules and buy tickets for **Swiss Federal Railways**, abbreviated to SBB in German, CFF in French and FFS in Italian. You can also store any rail passes you have on the app. Return fares are only cheaper than two singles for longer trips.

SWISS TRAVEL SYSTEM

The Swiss Travel System is an interconnected web of trains, boats, cable cars and buses that puts almost the entire country within easy car-free reach. You can consult integrated routes and available passes (national and region rail passes exist), calculate the right ticket and make purchases on *swissrailways. com* and *travelswitzerland.com*.

MICHAEL DERRER FUCHS/SHUTTERSTOCK

PANORAMIC TRAINS & ROUTES

Glacier Express (p130; *glacier express.ch*) Famous train journey between Zermatt and St Moritz, aboard cherry-red panoramic coaches with extended-height windows meaning HUGE views. The Brig–Zermatt Alpine leg makes for powerful viewing, as does the area between Disentis/Mustér and Brig.

Bernina Express (p226; *tickets. rhb.ch*) Travels 156km through the Engadine one-way from Chur to Tirano in four hours, again in panoramic coaches. Between May and October, you can continue from Tirano to Lugano by bus. The train is operated by the Rhaetian Railway.

GoldenPass Express (pictured; *gpx.swiss*) Variable-gauge bogies mean the journey between the mountain resort of Interlaken and Montreux on Lake Geneva can be done in a single 3½-hour journey. Prestige Class offers comfy, heated seats that are raised higher for improved views from the panorama windows.

Centovalli Railway (p151; *vigezzinacentovalli.com*) An under-appreciated gem of a line that snakes along fantastic river gorges from Locarno to Domodossola in neighbouring Italy in 1¾ hours. Trains run through the day and it's easy to connect to Brig and beyond from Domodossola.

Gotthard Panorama Express (*gotthard-panorama-express.ch*) April to October, this five-hour journey starts with a 2½-hour paddle-steamer cruise across Lake Lucerne to Flüelen, from where a train winds its way through ravines and past the mighty St Gotthard mountain range to Bellinzona/Lugano.

RAIL PASSES & RESERVATIONS

Saver Day Pass One-day pass *(Chf119)* covering unlimited travel on SBB trains, lake boats and some cable cars. Book at least a month in advance to bag its exceptional-value, lowest rate of Chf52.

Swiss Travel Pass The best value for train buffs wishing to widely explore the country, this pass covers unlimited travel by train, bus and boat all over Switzerland for 3, 4, 6, 8 or 15 consecutive days. Under-16s travel free with parents, making it a great family deal.

Swiss Travel Pass Flex More expensive, non-consecutive version of the standard pass.

Half-Fare Card Valid for a month or a year, this gets you 50% discount on all fares, including panoramic rail routes, cable cars and mountain railways.

Eurail and Interrail passes are valid on Swiss national railways, but not on buses, city transport, cable cars or mountain railways.

LUGGAGE SERVICE

Within Switzerland, travellers can drop their luggage off at one train station and collect it two days later at another. It costs Chf12 per item of luggage (maximum weight 23kg) and Chf20/30 for a bicycle/e-bike.

SAFE TRAVEL

Switzerland is a very safe country and street crime is uncommon. Streets are well lit, and petty theft and scams are hardly rampant. As weather becomes increasingly fickle and extreme, and rockfalls/landslides more frequent, a warming climate poses the greatest threat.

ALPINE HAZARDS
Mountain risks include snow storms, avalanches, landslides, flooding and thunderstorms. Keep up-to-date with natural-hazards.ch.

WEATHER CHECK
Before heading into the mountains, check weather forecasts on meteoswiss.admin.ch. Subscribe to alerts for your specific location.

DRINKING WATER
Tap water is safe to drink. Bring a water bottle to fill for free at fountains in towns and villages.

TICKS Check carefully for tick bites after a hike. Ticks are found up to altitudes of 1200m, and typically live in underbrush at the forest edge or beside trails. Some carry tick-borne encephalitis (TBE) or Lyme disease.

FEDOR SELIVANOV/SHUTTERSTOCK

ART OF THE SMALL/SHUTTERSTOCK

LIFT PASSES Summer or winter, when you buy your lift pass online or in situ, resorts offer an optional insurance (usually Chf3 per day) covering emergency rescue off the mountain and medical care.

INSURANCE
If you're skiing, snowboarding or trekking, ensure your policy covers helicopter rescue and emergency repatriation. Most standard policies don't cover many outdoor activities; you'll need to pay a premium for winter-sports cover and further premiums for adventure sports like bungee jumping and skydiving.

ALERTSWISS
Download the app or consult its website *(alert.swiss)* to receive national alerts, notifications, extreme weather warnings and information about a variety of hazards. The national service also issues relevant safety instructions.

QUICK TIPS TO HELP YOU MANAGE YOUR MONEY

CONTACTLESS PAYMENT Almost every hotel, shop, restaurant, cafe, bar and business supports contactless payments – there is no minimum payment amount. You will undoubtably hear mention of TWINT – Switzerland's mobile-payment system was introduced way back in 2017 and is used by almost every Swiss. It's only available to those with a Swiss telephone number and bank account.

CARDS & ATMS
Credit cards are widely accepted; EuroCard/ MasterCard and Visa are the most popular. ATMs are widespread.

EUROS
Businesses throughout Switzerland will accept payment in euros. Change will be given in Swiss francs at the rate of exchange calculated on the day.

CURRENCY

Swiss francs

HOW MUCH FOR A...

Staffed toilet at a train station Chf2

Cheese fondue for two people Chf150-250

A night in a hotel CHF 150 to CHF 500

TIPPING Tipping is generally not necessary; hotels, restaurants, bars and even some taxis are legally required to include a 15% service charge in bills. In restaurants, round up the bill after a meal for good service.

CASH Swiss francs (CHF) are divided into 100 centimes (Rappen in German-speaking Switzerland). Many shops and small businesses don't accept larger-denomination notes (100, 200 and 1000 franc notes can be challenging to actually spend!).

CHANGING MONEY
Change money at banks, airports and nearly every train station until late into the evening. Banks tend to charge about 5% commission; some money-exchange bureaux don't charge commission at all.

DISCOUNTS & SAVINGS
Swiss Travel Pass This offers unlimited travel throughout Switzerland for a set number of days; variants are available, but all include free admission to over 500 museums countrywide.

Guest Card When checking into a hotel, ask for a Guest Card allowing you travel for free on public transport.

ISIC Students get some discounts with an International Student Identity Card.

Free admission days Check with local tourist offices about free admission days for museums.

TAXES & REFUNDS

Standard value-added tax (VAT) is 8.1% in Switzerland and applies to most goods and services. There's a reduced rate for hotels (3.8%), and food and drink (2.6%). Non-Swiss nationals may claim a refund of the taxes they paid on goods of more than Chf300. For details, see *estv.admin.ch*.

RESPONSIBLE TRAVEL

Calculate your carbon There are a number of online calculators. Try almightytree.ch/co2calculator-individuals.

Sort your rubbish Find separate bins for plastic, paper, organic waste and non-recyclables at train stations, in hotel rooms and numerous public spaces.

Use food-waste apps Too Good to Go *(toogoodtogo.com)* and GoNina *(gonina.com)* to search by location for supermarkets, bakeries and restaurants selling produce, food and full meals that would otherwise go to waste. Enjoy huge discounts.

Ski sustainably Favour ski resorts with commendable sustainable policies. Verbier Green *(verbiergreen.com)* is working to ensure all types of waste are recycled in Verbier.

Go car-free Favour a car-free mountain resort, with sledges or dinky electric taxis to transport luggage, such as Bettmeralp or Zermatt in the Valais.

Visit nature reserves and parks working hard to conserve wildlife and biodiversity. Find a list at parks.swiss.

GIVE BACK

Eat out for a good cause Check 1francpourleclimat.ch for a list of 'eco-restaurants', mainly based in French-speaking Switzerland, that donate Chf1 to planting trees with every meal they serve.

Support social enterprises Seek out businesses giving back to their community. In Sion (p112), grab a coffee at L'Entre 2 or Café de Valère – two community cafes by the nearby châteaux created to teach new skills to the unemployed.

Clean up lakes and rivers Join volunteers in Geneva picking up plastic, litter and other debris from the city's eponymous lake and two rivers. Check *globalshapersgeneva.org*.

Go forest bathing and help plant trees Find upcoming events and volunteering ops in the Zürich area at *wandelwege.ch* and *reforestationworld.org*.

DOS & DON'TS

Punctuality is considered a great virtue. Being late is rude.

Be mindful of polite/informal vous/tu rules In French-speaking parts, tu is for family and close friends. Use *Comment allez-vous?* (How are you?) with people you don't know well.

Know the house rules Swiss apartment living imposes some stringent demands on residents: no vacuum cleaners, washing machines, musical instruments or other noise before 8am or after 9pm.

LEAVE A SMALL FOOTPRINT

Leave no trace Take your rubbish home with you when hiking in the mountains.

Be wild Make the most of the wondrous Swiss National Park and Parc Ela, and of multiday hikes, campsites and mountain huts.

Bring your own water bottle Resist German-speaking Switzerland's unhealthy penchant for bottled sparkling mineral water.

Look beyond high season (winter ski season, plus July and August) Most Swiss say autumn (empty hiking and mountain-biking trails, grape harvests, seductive light…) is best.

SUPPORT LOCAL

Eat locally Buy fresh produce at open-air markets and farms. Pick your own pumpkin, fresh from the field, in autumn.

Use honesty boxes in vineyards and on roadsides to pay for wine, cheese and other local producer goodies.

Buy gifts and souvenirs directly from artisans, local distillers (Faceplant gin, bought at the source in Guttannen, is a personal favourite) and independent boutiques.

CLIMATE CHANGE & TRAVEL

Lonely Planet urges all travellers to engage with their travel carbon footprint, which will mainly come from air travel. While there often isn't an alternative, travellers can look to minimise the number of flights they take, opt for newer aircraft and use cleaner ground transport, such as trains. One proposed solution – purchasing carbon offsets – unfortunately does not cancel out the impact of individual flights. While most destinations will depend on air travel for the foreseeable future, for now, pursuing ground-based travel where possible is the best course of action.

The UN Carbon Offset Calculator shows how flying impacts a household's emissions:

The ICAO's carbon emissions calculator allows visitors to analyse the CO_2 generated by point-to-point journeys:

RESOURCES

pronatura.ch
bafu.admin.ch
myclimate.org
swisstainable.ch

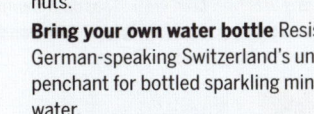

ACCOMMODATION

A good night's sleep typically accounts for a sizeable chunk of your daily budget anywhere in the world. Thankfully pricey Switzerland offers well-maintained accommodation in every price range, invariably with a priceless dusting of twinkling night stars or glittering lake view. Seasonal campgrounds often seduce with a beautiful green setting, and family-run B&Bs and old-school pensions ooze an authentic, wonderfully low-key charm.

HOW MUCH FOR A...

Half-board in a mountain hut Chf90

Double in a three-star Zermatt hotel Chf150-250

A night's sleep on straw Chf20-30

PANORAMASUISSE, CC BY-SA 3.0, VIA WIKIMEDIA COMMONS ©

HOTELS

Swiss hotels range from small village inns to palatial belle époque monuments, luxury alpine retreats with hot tub and urban 'grand dame' hotels with all the five-star facilities and amenities. Breakfast is usually included in room rates. An increasing number of hotels are green-thinking and eco-responsible: plastic-free, with seasonal and/or organic breakfast produce, biodegradable soap and lake water heating.

HOSTELS

Not to be ruled out, Swiss hostels can be a real bargain. Covering the gamut of accommodation styles, they range from older, institutional affairs to dorms in historic castles and palaces, or twin-bed 'dorms' in a renovated 1920s mountain hut with five-star mountain panoramas (such as Verbier's Cabane du Mont Fort). A handful dazzle with designer interiors, pool and spa. Around 50 are managed by Swiss Youth Hostels (*youthhostel.ch*). Run on sustainable principles, they often offer cheap dining and organised outdoor activities.

MARCEL GROSS/ALAMY

MILLION STARS HOTELS

Ranging from transparent igloos and converted feed silos to 'floating' tree tents and even, simply, a very comfortable bed alfresco in a field with bucolic view, Million Stars Hotel locations take camping and glamping to the next level. The common feature of the country's scattered 'rooms' are their unobstructed view of night skies. See myswitzerland.com for details.

SLEEPING ON STRAW

No other European country does it: encourage travellers to bunk up with the cows in haylofts, that is. A fabulous way to experience life on a Swiss farm close up, Switzerland's Agrotourismus Schweiz (*myfarm.ch*) is the ultimate adventure in the straw.

When the cows are out to pasture in summer, Swiss farmers charge travellers a modest fee (usually half-price for children under 15) to sleep on straw in their barns or lofts (invariably with earthy odour and the distant jangle of cowbells as a melodic soundtrack!). Farmers provide cotton undersheets (to avoid straw pricks) and woolly blankets for extra warmth, but guests need their own sleeping bags and – strongly advisable – a head torch. Nightly rates include a farmhouse breakfast and a morning shower. Evening meals can often be cooked up for an additional fee, with an advance reservation. Peruse the complete collection of Agrotourismus Schweiz–affiliated farms online, and book.

Should you prefer a traditional room in a farmhouse, converted barn or outbuilding, try Swiss Holiday Farms (*bauernhof-ferien.ch*), an association of about 200 farms nationwide that open their doors to both overnight B&B guests and self-caterers keen to rent a farmhouse cottage for a week or longer.

PLANNING & BOOKING

For a complete lowdown on what's available, the accommodation pages of Switzerland Tourism (*myswitzerland.com*) are a one-stop planning tool. Searchable themes include Bees and Friends (countryside hotels with bees!), family hotels, bike-friendly hotels, spa escapes and wellness retreats.

Advance reservations are essential – in high season and any time of year if you want to bag the best-value beds. Tourist offices have listings; some make reservations.

BnB (*bnb.ch*) Listing of B&Bs nationwide, rare in towns and cities, plentiful in the countryside.

Camping in der Schweiz (*camping.ch*) Camping directory with 350 detailed listings, plus practical info, tips and news on camping and caravanning in Switzerland.

Swiss Camping and Caravanning Federation (*sccv.ch*) Search online for the perfect pitch for tent or van.

Interhome (*interhome.ch*) All types of self-catering homes, searchable by theme (dog-friendly, ski resort, secluded retreat, for families, etc).

My Switzerland (*myswitzerland.com*) Click on the Accommodation tab to search for hotels all over the country recommended by the Swiss Tourist Board.

Swiss Heritage Society (*ferienimbaudenkmal.ch*) Self-catering rental accommodation in historic or culturally significant properties, often in remote, rural regions.

RENTAL ACCOMMODATION

Self-catering chalets and apartments require advance booking. In ski resorts and other alpine destinations, reserve six to 12 months ahead during peak periods (winter ski season, plus July and August).

ESSENTIAL NUTS AND BOLTS

CANTONAL DIFFERENCES

Minor legal variations do exist between Switzerland's 26 cantons: street busking is allowed in some, but not in others. If in doubt, ask.

TOASTS

Look your toasting partner in the eye when clinking glasses and say *Prost* or *Santé* (cheers). No eye contact is said to bring bad luck!

SMOKING & VAPING

Both are illegal in enclosed indoor public spaces, including restaurants, pubs, offices and public transport.

FAST FACTS

Time Zone GMT+1

Country code +41

Electricity 230V/50Hz

GOOD TO KNOW

Visas are generally not required for stays of up to 90 days. From the end of 2026, non-EU citizens will need an ETIAS pass. Get updates at schengenvisainfo.com and sem.admin.ch.

Bargaining is not the done thing – no one does it, so don't try.

The legal drinking age for beer and wine is 16 years and 18 for spirits.

Call places by their local name, not the anglicised version.

To call the police dial 117 and ambulance 144. Swiss Mountain Rescue is 1414.

ACCESSIBLE TRAVEL

Switzerland is refreshingly navigable for travellers with physical disabilities.

Airports Switzerland's main airports (Zürich, Geneva, Basel, Bern) offer assistance to travellers with a variety of different needs. For help, contact the airports at least 48 hours in advance.

Train stations Most have a mobile lift for boarding trains, city buses are equipped with ramps, and many hotels have accessible access.

Assistance If in need of assistance getting on or off a train, call SBB on 0800 007 102 at least one hour beforehand.

Accommodation Many Swiss youth hostels offer barrier-free rooms. The Claire & George Foundation (*claireundgeorge.ch*) lists accessible accommodation options.

Mountain access Wonderful Swiss landscapes can be accessed without hiking or mountain climbing via scenic train and boat rides. Funiculars, cable cars and gondolas provide easy access to the peaks.

Resources SwitzerlandMobility (*schweizmobil.ch*) details accessible trails across the country. Active Motion (*activemotion.ch*) in Interlaken specialises in snow sports for people with special needs.

TOILETS

Public toilets are clean and in reasonable supply. There may be a small charge for use.

WEIGHTS & MEASURES

The metric system is used. Decimals are indicated with commas, thousands with full stops.

POLICE

Swiss police have wide-ranging powers of detention. If asked, you must show your passport – always carry it.

FAMILY TRAVEL

Facilities such as nappy-changing areas, cots in accommodation, highchairs and children's menus are widespread.

Bike-rental shops have wheels, seats and trailers for all ages.

Admission to sights is often free for under-18s. Many have audioguides and activity booklets for children.

Under-6s travel free on SBB trains; 6-15 years get free unlimited rail travel with an annual Junior Travelcard (Chf30).

Swiss playgrounds, often all wood, are five-star. On mountains, seek out giant marble runs, playful rafts on lakes and barefoot 'tickle' trails.

GREETINGS Shake hands when meeting for the first time and when saying goodbye. Handshakes are firm with eye contact. Friends kiss three times on the cheek – right, left, then right again. Say *Bonjour*, *Grüezi* or *Buongiorno* (hello) to sales assistants when entering a shop.

WHAT TO WEAR In cities dress is smart casual, except in formal situations such as a night at the theatre when the Swiss dress up. In summer expect to see city slickers switching suit for bathers for a quick lunchtime dip in a lake or river.

LGBTQI+ TRAVELLERS

Switzerland is a tolerant country and reasonably progressive on LGBTQI+ rights.

Same-sex marriage, same-sex adoption and IVF access for queer couples have only been allowed since 2022.

Zürich has Switzerland's liveliest LGBTIQ+ scene; see kweer. io for queer dance parties and events.

Geneva, Lausanne, Bern and Lucerne also have active LGBTQI+ scenes.

Pride kicks off on the snow in Verbier in April. Other hot Pride dates: Geneva and Zürich (June), Martigny (July), Bern and Lucerne (August).

Resources *gay.ch, 360.ch, pinkcross.ch, queertravel.ch*

LANGUAGE

Switzerland's most common language is German, spoken by about 60% of the population, followed by French (about 23%) and Italian (about 8%), with Romansh being spoken by less than 1%.

BASIC FRENCH

Hello.	*Bonjour.*	bon·zhoor
Goodbye.	*Au revoir.*	o·rer·vwa
Yes./No.	*Oui./Non.*	wee/non
Please.	*S'il vous plaît.*	seel voo play
Thank you.	*Merci.*	mair·see
Excuse me.	*Excusez-moi.*	ek·skew·zay·mwa
Sorry.	*Pardon.*	par·don

What's your name?
Comment vous appelez-vous? ko·mon voo·za·play voo

My name is ...
Je m'appelle ... zher ma·pel ...

Do you speak English?
Parlez-vous anglais? par·lay·voo ong·glay

I don't understand.
Je ne comprends pas. zher ner kom·pron pa

BASIC ITALIAN

Hello.	*Buongiorno.*	bwon·jor·no
Goodbye.	*Arrivederci.*	a·ree·ve·der·chee
Yes.	*Sì.*	see
No.	*No.*	no
Please.	*Per favore.*	per fa·vo·re
Thank you.	*Grazie.*	gra·tsye
Excuse me.	*Mi scusi.(pol)/Scusami.* (inf)	mee skoo·zee/ skoo·za·mee

BASIC GERMAN

Hello.	*Guten Tag.*	goo·ten tahk
Goodbye.	*Auf Wiedersehen.*	owf vee·der·zay·en
Yes.	*Ja.*	yah
No.	*Nein.*	nain
Please.	*Bitte.*	bi·te
Thank you.	*Danke.*	dang·ke
Excuse me.	*Entschuldigung.*	ent·shul·di·gung
Sorry.	*Entschuldigung.*	ent·shul·di·gung

What's your name?
Wie ist Ihr Name? (pol) vee ist eer nah·me
Wie heißt du? (inf) vee haist doo

My name is...
Mein Name ist... (pol) main nah·me ist...
Ich heiße... (inf) ikh hai·se...

Do you speak English?
Sprechen Sie Englisch? (pol) shpre·khen zee eng·lish

Sorry. *Mi dispiace.* mee dees·pya·che

What's your name? *Come si chiama?* ko·me see kya·ma

My name is ... *Mi chiamo...* mee kya·mo...

Do you speak English? *Parla/parli inglese?(pol/inf).* par·la/par·lee een·gle·ze

I don't understand. *Non capisco.* non ka·pee·sko

Index

DESTINATION SWITZERLAND

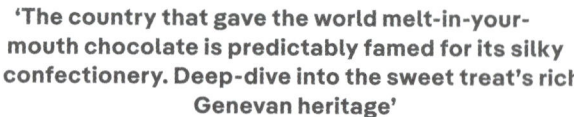

'The country that gave the world melt-in-your-mouth chocolate is predictably famed for its silky confectionery. Deep-dive into the sweet treat's rich Genevan heritage'

NICOLA WILLIAMS

'From the forested hills of the Jura mountains to the velvety pastures of the Fribourg Pre-Alps, with three serene lakes in between, this geographically varied region is steeped in history and tradition'

CAROLINE BISHOP

'Beyond the medieval charm and modern art of Bern, dive into some of the most exhilarating landscapes in the Alps.'

KERRY WALKER

'The Italian-speaking canton of Ticino in Switzerland's far south is like a breathe of warm, Mediterranean air.'

MARC DI DUCA

'They call these the craziest three days of the year – Basel's Fasnacht begins in the early hours of the morn on the first Monday after Ash Wednesday. '

ANTHONY HAYWOOD

THIS BOOK

This 1st edition of Lonely Planet's Experience Switzerland guidebook was researched and written by Caroline Bishop, Marc Di Duca, Anthony Haywood, Simon Richmond, Kerry Walker and Nicola Williams.

Destination Editor
Sandie Kestell

Production Editor
Graham O'Neill

Cartographer
Vojtech Bartos

Image Researcher
Fabrice Robin

Coordinating Editor
Bridget Blair

Assisting Editors
Sofie Andersen, Michelle Bennett, Peterjon Cresswell, Melanie Dankel

Cover Researcher
Sam Ubinas

Thanks Gwen Cotter, Alison Killilea, Darren O'Connell

EVANNOVOSTRO/SHUTTERSTOCK, BURBEN/SHUTTERSTOCK